BLACK SEA

58

SAMOTHRACE

LEMNOS

HELLESPONT

Troy (Hissarlik)

MT. IDA

BALI DAGH (BOURNABASHI)

TROAD

(PLAIN OF TROY)

LESBOS

CHIOS

ASIA MINOR

AEGEAN

SAMOS

CYCLADES

SEA

RHODES

Knossos

CRETE

Wong

# THE
# DREAM
# OF
# TROY

Heinrich Schliemann. Courtesy of William Henry Smith Memorial Library, Indiana Historical Society

ARNOLD C. BRACKMAN

# THE
# DREAM
# OF
# TROY

Mason & Lipscomb PUBLISHERS    NEW YORK

Library of Congress Cataloging in Publication Data

Brackman, Arnold C
  The dream of Troy.

  Bibliography: p.
  1. Schliemann, Heinrich, 1822–1890. I. Title.
DF212.S4B67    913′.031′0924 [B]    74–7078
ISBN 0–88405–081–5

*For the five S's*

# Contents

# List of Illustrations

# Preface

THIS BOOK had its genesis a decade ago when the author was reading *Troy and the Trojans* by Carl W. Blegen, dean of American archaeologists, who complained that biographers had misread Heinrich Schliemann. Blegen sounded the call for a new biography of Schliemann to set the record straight. That was in 1963.

"It seems to me," Blegen wrote, "that his [Schliemann's] ruling motives have been misinterpreted or at least distorted by some writers who think his driving force was a passion for gold, and they have laid undue emphasis on this—imagined—overpowering desire for gold and its effect on the course of his life."

In the late twenties, the German writer, Emil Ludwig, published the first biography of Schliemann and it set the pattern for later biographies. Schliemann is invariably portrayed as a man who lusted for gold. In Ludwig's caricature, he is viewed as unearthing Troy largely to reclaim the gold hidden beneath it by the dust of ages.

This is nonsense.

On the contrary, as the record shows, Schliemann turned his back on the acquisition of gold for its own sake. In his forties, a self-made multimillionaire, he abandoned the counting house and embarked in search of mythical Troy. Since then, as Blegen's comment testifies, Schliemann's stature has grown steadily among modern archaeologists as a giant while his public image has remained largely that of a gold-seeker.

I was astonished at the vast amount of material available here and abroad—diaries, notebooks, papers, correspondence, and the like—indeed, so much paper that it is understandable how a study of limbs obscures the tree.

Schliemann had a passion for detail. For example, on his voyage to Central America he did not simply note in his diary, "at sea," or "en route to Panama." Instead, a typical entry (for Tuesday, 18 March 1850) reads: "Lat. N. 10° 22'; Long. 87° 30' W." This is not a diary; it is a ship's log.

And some twenty-odd years later, as he was stomping around Asia Minor, he was entertained by the Turkish *caimacam,* or mayor, of the small village of Iné. The mayor made him comfortable in the coolest room in the house and then rushed off to arrange for lunch. He had no sooner left the room than his guest extracted his ever-present thermometer from his waistcoat and recorded in his equally omnipresent notebook as follows: "It is the height of summer; my thermometer marks 34°C = 93.4°F in the coolest room of the mayor's house."

In any event, a reappraisal of Schliemann's work is overdue. Gold was not Schliemann's passion. Homer was. And while the academics and press of his day laughed, Schliemann sacrificed his personal fortune to prove that fabled Troy did exist at the dawn of Western civilization, even as Homer had written.

And with that discovery, modern archaeology was born.

*Arnold C. Brackman*

*Brookfield Center, Connecticut*
*March, 1974*

# I

⊓⊔⊓⊔⊓⊔⊓⊔

⊓⊔⊓⊔⊓⊔⊓⊔

# Shadow or Substance?

*And which of the gods was it that
set them on to quarrel?*

The Iliad, BOOK I

IN THE WINTER of 1868, with a 39,000 word manuscript in hand, a wealthy, forty-six-year-old German merchant-turned-amateur-archaeologist descended on Leipzig, the book-publishing capital of Europe. As he walked briskly through the narrow streets lined with publishing houses, book dealers, printing plants, and binding shops, the lean, bespectacled figure with deep, brown eyes stood out in the crowd. For he was attired in a long, black coat of Russian cut, richly trimmed with fur.

The manuscript, about his travels around the Aegean Sea, was hardly the kind to attract a publisher; the academic title, *Ithaca, the Peloponnesus and Troy,* was even less likely to attract a reader. Worse, the shelves in many European bookstalls were already thick with travel books in anticipation of a boom in tourism following the remarkable strides in the development of steam-driven ships and the opening, within a few months, of the Suez Canal.

A self-created multimillionaire, the merchant could well afford to bear the financial burden of bringing out the volume.

1

Characteristically, however, Heinrich Schliemann did not seek out a "vanity" house. His vanity would not approve of that. Instead, he selected the reputable firm of Giesecke & Derrient and offered to meet the cost of publishing the initial 750 copies of the manuscript on condition he receive half the profits of every copy sold. Of profits, he was certain. For the publisher, the risk was minimal. For Schliemann, the arrangement smacked of a commercial venture and appealed strongly to his stern and rugged nature, his sense of independence, and his spirit of individual enterprise.

The manuscript was, surprisingly, in two languages—English and Greek. But the house of Giesecke & Derrient dealt with a surprising individual. Self-taught, Schliemann had mastered a dozen languages and he wrote (and spoke) in whichever language caught his mood. His publishers also discovered they were dealing with a hotheaded, impatient author who fancied himself an archaeologist, however putative. Schliemann, accustomed to action on demand, given his enormous wealth, expected Giesecke & Derrient to abandon everything, wave a wand, and publish his book, figuratively anyway, overnight. The correspondence between author and publisher filled several folders before copies of the book were delivered to his two residences—one in Paris, where he arranged to bring out a French edition, and another in St. Petersburg, Russia. Clearly, Schliemann was no ordinary man.

In bringing out the book, Schliemann enlisted the aid of an old teacher, Carl Anders, as translator and editor. At the age of ten, for a year, a young Heinrich had "the good fortune," as he later described it, to study under Anders. Now the librarian of the modest Neu Strelitz Library and keeper of the equally modest Neu Strelitz Museum of Antiquities. Anders was steeped in the mythological Heroic Age of ancient Greece, or Hellas, as the Greeks, who consider themsèlves Hellenes, call their country in their native tongue. In the classroom, Anders had kindled Schliemann's imagination with the earliest legends and traditions of Western man, especially as depicted in the Western world's first book, *The Iliad,* in which the poet Homer recounted fifty-one days in the tenth and last year of the monumental Trojan War.

Anders read the manuscript first with curiosity, then surprise, and finally wry amusement. He enthusiastically approved of his former pupil's effort and gladly offered to lend an editorial hand. "You realize," Andres said, "that you will be subject to criticism."

"Heavy and adverse criticism," Schliemann corrected him.

Little did Schliemann realize that the criticism would continue unabated for the remainder of his life—twenty years—and that when death closed his eyes, a solemn conclave of scholars would be in session to put an end once and for all to the idiotic theories he first put forth in the book and then, spade in hand, proved.

For in Schliemann's day, the dawn of Western civilization as portrayed by Homer was almost universally considered a product of poetic imagination. Poetry was not history, obviously. As an Oxford scholar observed, it was absurd to expect a poet to write a chronicle. The Trojan War was known only in Homer. There was not an iota of proof that the Trojan War was ever fought, indeed that Troy ever existed. From Paris, a French scholar put it succinctly. *The Iliad,* he said, is "imaginary from first to last." In the same year that Schliemann published his book, the French view prevailed on both rims of the Atlantic, in America as well as in Europe.

However, 1869 would mark a watershed year in the study of the Heroic Age. With the publication of Schliemann's slim book, the scholarship of the period came crashing down and was never put back together again. Thereafter, it became increasingly difficult, and finally impossible, to deny the existence of Troy and the Homeric Age.

Although Schliemann himself later freely admitted that his first book on Troy was studded with wild generalizations, the book's central theme was not only confirmed later but gained luster with each succeeding generation since his death —as mounting evidence conclusively proved that Schliemann, for all his hyperbole, was right and all his critics wrong. Heinrich Schliemann shook the foundations of the Western world, forced the rewriting of the origins of Western civilization, provided reams of lurid copy for Sunday supplements, and founded a new science—archaeology.

Schliemann's theme was straightforward and emphatic. With "complete certainty," he boldly asserted, Troy existed at the daybreak of Western civilization. Furthermore, he was "completely convinced" that he had found the site of the lost city on the Aegean coast of Asia Minor, in Turkey, beneath a desolate, barren hill at uninhabited Hissarlik. From atop this hill, Schliemann gazed out across the Plain of Troy and, in his mind's eye, the siege of Priam's citadel was reborn as shield pressed on shield, spear against spear, helm on helm, man on man. From atop this hillock, too, Schliemann gazed out across the Aegean Sea and watched spellbound as the vessels of the invading armada, more than a thousand in number—drawn from Argos, Mycenae, Pylos, and other points along the western reaches of the Aegean—disgorged fifty thousand troops and sent them swarming onto the Trojan Plain as the ground rang like brass under their armor.

As he forewarned Anders, the book was greeted by heavy and adverse criticism. The catcalls were loud and clear. The Heroic or Homeric Age at the beginning of the Western enterprise was shadow, not substance. Schliemann was a fool. What some people will do to promote tourism. Why did he pursue a will-o'-the-wisp in far-off Turkey when he might just as well have claimed to have recovered the fabled hoard of gold guarded by the mythical Nibelungs at the bottom of the Rhine?

In Berlin, the distinguished Professor Rudolph Hercher flatly and openly declared, "Troy never existed." In Paris, an academician confirmed that "everyone was taken by surprise." As Professor Victor Berard later expressed it, the academic community "thought it useless, childish even, to attempt to look for underlying truth, for any grain of reality [in Homer]."

What troubled some scholars was not simply the possiblity of discovering an underlying truth but the grisly, chilling notion that if the lost city had been found, then Homer's heroes had lived and "it should be possible to find traces, their remains, perhaps even bones."

This was too much to bear, even for Greeks. M. G. Nikolaides, a leading editor in Athens, attacked the merchant-turned-explorer with an argument which would have perplexed Aristotle, who invented the system of logic. "The site of

Troy cannot be discovered by means of excavation or other proofs," he said, "but solely from Homer's *Iliad*." On the one hand, he argued that the site of Troy could never be found; on the other hand, he argued that *The Iliad* offered proof that it once had existed. As a Greek, he could not betray Homer directly but did so indirectly. Schliemann, who rarely restrained himself when clawing critics, blunted Nikolaides' attack (perhaps out of deference to his Hellenic ancestry) with the mild admonition that if he believed Troy once existed, then his assertion "appears most strange." In private, given his arrogance and combustible temperament, Schliemann raged, "Idiot! Idiot!"

The scholars, however, were even more critical. Arrogantly, they believed that they alone possessed a monopoly on truth. Schliemann was contemptuous of them. A businessman, he had no vested redoubt to defend. He was an amateur and, like many amateurs who were to achieve so much in the nineteenth century, had an uncluttered vision.

In antiquity, Schliemann observed, the Greeks considered the Trojan War of *their* antiquity historical fact. For that matter, so did the Persians, the Egyptians, and the Romans in their clay tablets, papyri scrolls, and Latin parchments. Then, reasoned Schliemann, why shouldn't Troy have existed?

Admittedly, he conceded, during the aptly named Dark Ages, Troy vanished. Every physical trace of Priam's acropolis, or citadel, named Pergamus, disappeared. Troy evaporated. There simply was no hard evidence that the city had existed. The Trojan War, immortalized by Homer, was labeled invention. So was Troy.

Yet, Schliemann repeatedly asked himself, how was it possible for Troy not to to have existed when the most warlike commanders, remarkable for exploits and skillful strategies, as Plutarch described them—Xerxes, Alexander the Great, Julius Caesar—made pilgrimages to Troy, offered hecatombs there for the slain and prayed at the fane of the Trojans' patron, Athena, or Minerva, as the Romans later called her, incongruously, the goddess of wisdom and war.

Herodotus, writing in 400 B.C., for example, wrote eloquently about the Trojan War and reported that the Asians thought the direct cause of the war patently ridiculous. The Asians could understand the war as a basically East-West struggle, not dissimilar to the East-West struggles since then, including the presently thawing Cold War. But what troubled the Asians, he said, was that the war was fought in the name of a woman, the lovely Helen of Troy—wife of Menelaus, son of Agamemnon—the most beautiful creature of her day, who was kidnapped by Paris, son of the ruler of Troy, Priam.

Abducting a woman was wrong, the Asians told Herodotus, "but to make a stir about such as are carried off, argues a man a fool . . . since it is plain that without their consent they would never be forced away." When a Westerner ran off with an Asian woman, they continued, "we never troubled ourselves about the matter," but the Westerners, "for the sake of a single Lacedaemonian girl, collected a vast armament, invaded Asia, and destroyed the kingdom of Priam."*

Whatever the merits of the Asian viewpoint, thereafter, as the armies of Asia and Europe clashed regularly around the Aegean, the warring sides always halted in their passage across the Plain of Troy to pay homage to those who died in the Trojan War.

The Romans, who believed they sprang from the loins of Aeneas, the sole known survivor of the holocaust at Troy and, therefore, the seed of hope in the future for the survival of mankind in the nuclear age, accorded special honors to Troy. As their legions marched through Asia Minor and extended the Roman Empire in ever-widening circles over the known world, Julius Caesar visited Troy and openly wept on the site "so moved was he by the extent of its terrible destruction." Indeed, for a time, first Julius and then Augustus Caesar entertained the thought of transferring their capital from Rome to Troy.

Troy lived into the Christian era. Constantine the Great actually began to build the capital of his empire, Constantinopole, on the Plain of Troy before he shifted it to its present site at the northern end of the Hellespont, present-day Istanbul.

Even in the Dark Ages, when Troy was lost from view and

---

*The debate over Troy and the Trojan War continues unrelentingly today. See "Author's Note."

dissolved into pure mythology, the Crusaders who crossed the Hellespont to invade Asia and liberate the Holy Land from the "infidel," carried in their New Testaments a seed linking Jesus of Nazareth and Troy. The apostles St. Luke and St. Paul rendezvoused at Troy—Troas, in the Holy Bible—before embarking on their journey into the Western world to spread the message of the Christ.

Against this rich history, Schliemann, tough-minded, practical, a man who had fought his way to the summit of the commercial world, found it impossible to understand why so many people now refused to believe in Homer, in Troy, and the Trojan War. How could a city, a world vanish without a trace? "Why," he asked, "do so many eminent scholars regard Troy as a myth?" Why? Schliemann was puzzled, for the evidence strongly favored the existence of Troy at the sunrise of recorded history.

"For my part," he later wrote, "I have always firmly believed in the Trojan War. My full faith in Homer and in this tradition will never be shaken by modern criticism."

Intuitively, Schliemann knew he was right. Everyone was out of step but him; well, almost everyone.

# II

Crossing the Aegean

*All was uproar and confusion.*

The Iliad, BOOK XII

FOR CENTURIES, the controversy over Troy, into which Schliemann openly plunged in 1869, raged inconclusively. Like fierce ravening wolves fighting over a wounded stag, the scholars scrapped interminably about Homer. In addition to its intrinsic artistic value as the first literary work in the history of Western civilization, the question of the true identity of Homer and the problem of whether his writing was based upon historical and geographic truth stirred uproar and confusion.

One school of prominent academicians firmly believed that Troy never existed. "The siege of Troy is a myth," Professor Jacob Bryant, an eighteenth-century British authority, emphatically declared. His statement was echoed in Berlin and Paris. A second school—led by the Frenchman M. Lechevalier —confronted by the references to Troy in Persian, Greek, and Roman chronicles and the geographic clarity and general air of verisimilitude which lends a sense of historic reality to *The Iliad,* contended just as heatedly that Troy once existed. In fact, this group singled out the exact spot as Bounarbashi, a small Turkish village nestling at the foot of the hill of Bali Dagh.

When Schliemann's book appeared, the Bryant school coolly rejected his case out of hand and considered his contribution to the debate unscholarly and unworthy of serious attention. Who ever heard of Schliemann? Worse, he was a businessman, a common merchant—albeit not so common, a millionaire, but still tainted by commercialism—a pseudo-scholar who sought treatment as an equal. Clearly, Schliemann was an upstart.

By contrast, the Lechevalier school was furious. Schliemann had selected a desolate hill at Hissarlik as the site of the lost city, assuming the city once existed, of course. Only a fool would fail to recognize Bounarbashi as the site of Homer's Troy.

Thus, Schliemann's modest literary and archaeological effort fueled the debate instead of extinguishing it.

As Schliemann himself conceded, the question of Troy's location "slept during the Middle Ages" and, when the West emerged from this slumber, Troy was vaguely remembered as a dream. Surprisingly, or perhaps not, few took the trouble to visit the Aegean to explore the basis for the dream. Those who visited Asia Minor, Schliemann noted, "limited their research to superficial inspection of the Plain of Troy or only of its coast."

Unlike Bryant and most of his colleagues, Lechevalier, shortly before the French Revolution, embarked on a "romantic pilgrimage" in search of the lost city. On the basis of his sojourn in the region, especially the discovery of hot and cold springs, as described in Homer, the Frenchman concluded that Bounarbashi was the site of Troy, "intuitively, without even touching the ground with the spade, and as if by divine inspiration." Schliemann's sarcasm, however, was flecked with envy. "Since there were no archaeologists," he observed, "there was no archaeological criticism."

Lechevalier had no sooner drawn his conclusion than the French Ambassador at Constantinople, Count Choiseul Gouflier, rushed to the spot, enthusiastically endorsed the claim, and embellished it by declaring that he, himself, had found "ancient ruins" there—a claim that not even Lechevalier had made. Thereafter, infrequent travelers to Asia Minor re-

stated the French scholar's claim, while the armchair archaeologists, confined to their debating halls in London, Paris, and
Berlin, supported the Bounarbashi theory, that is, if they even
believed that Troy had once existed. In their defense, it should
be said that these scholars, by supporting Lechevalier, defended Homer and vindicated his account of the Trojan War.
If Bounarbashi was the site then, a priori, Troy once lived.

Scholars and occasional tourists were not the only ones
who supported the Bounarbashi argument. So did the military,
among them, Field Marshal Count von Moltke, the greatest
strategist in Europe since Napoleon and the man whose armies
paved the way for Bismarck's unification of Germany in
Schliemann's lifetime. In 1838, von Moltke served as a military
adviser to the already tottering Turkish Empire. In this role, he
frequently traveled across Asia Minor, the seat of Ottoman
power, including the Plain of Troy. Fascinated by Homer's detailed account of the Trojan War, as are all military men, he
visited Bounarbashi and promptly endorsed Lechevalier's theory. "We who are not scholars," he intoned with a pompous air,
"suffer ourselves to be guided simply by a military instinct to
the spot, which, in old times as well as now, would be colonized,
if an inaccessible citadel were to be founded."

The generals were not the only ones at sea. So were the
admirals.

Among the latter was Admiral T. A. B. Spratt, who, as a
young lieutenant in the Royal Navy, charted the coastline of
Asia Minor and identified among the coastal features the
heights of Bali Dagh as the site of ancient Troy—or Ilium or
Ilios, as it was called in Roman times. Later, Spratt and
Schliemann became fast friends, and Spratt encouraged the
German merchant's untiring effort to recover Troy from the
make-believe world of myths and legends.

Perhaps the most enterprising figure among those supporting the Bounarbashi theory was the Austrian, J. G. von Hahn,
who did a rare thing in the pre-Schliemannesque era: He dirt-
ied his hands. Putting theory aside, and accompanied by
Professor Hans Schmidt, an astronomer in residence in Athens,
von Hahn set out for Bounarbashi to excavate the site. For von
Hahn, this was an especially courageous act. He belonged to the

Bryant school. Frankly, he said, he was convinced Troy never has existed, that *The Iliad* was a fable. Beautiful, magnificent poetry, yes; history, no.

In May 1864, von Hahn arrived at Bounarbashi as spring flooded the Trojan Plain. A work party organized, he selected a shovel and started to dig. After a foot and a half of digging, he struck virgin soil. Elsewhere, the same thing happened. He expected to find nothing, and he found nothing. Homer, he concluded, had obviously adapted his poem to fit the topography of Bounarbashi. Von Hahn published his findings at Leipzig that same year, five years before Schliemann set forth on a similar quest in search of the phantom city.

The confusion surrounding Bounarbashi, like the misty vale which enveloped Homer's heroes and heroines whenever they were swept up by the gods, was deepened by still other claims as to the genuine site of Troy. A number of academicians insisted, for example, that if Troy existed, then the site was at Chiblak, also in Turkey.

But at least those few who believed in the existence of Troy agreed that the lost city must be located in Asia Minor close upon the imperishable Aegean Sea.

Although the spotlight of history shines brightly on Schliemann, he was neither alone nor the first to identify the site of Homer's Troy.

In 1822, the year of Schliemann's birth, a Scottish geographer published a thin book at Edinburgh which identified "Issarlik" as the lost site. Charles Maclaren wrote:

> By an extraordinary chain of consequences, attempts to ascertain the site of the city have led many to doubt its existence altogether; and not a few are now ready to pronounce researches on this subject to be equally idle and hopeless with those which exercised the sagacity of the learned two centuries ago, respecting the position of the Gardèn of Eden.

Two hundred and fifty-seven pages later, Maclaren unequivocally stated: *"I conclude that the Trojan war was a real event and not a poetical fiction."*

He based his conclusion, he said, on the internal evidence

afforded by Homer's poems, on a diligent comparison of Homer's local details with Asia Minor's topography, on the testimony of such Greek and Roman writers as Hesiod, Herodotus, Thucydides, and others, and "on the great variety of traditions relating to the event, found not only in Greece and Asia Minor, but even in Egypt and Persia." (In truth, Maclaren never visited the Aegean. His conclusion was a case of brilliant deduction.)

Maclaren's work drew little attention, as he himself feared. "The author's hopes with regard to the sale of this book are not very sanguine," he wrote.

But reflecting a strong sense of justice, Schliemann, in his first book on Troy and in later books and private papers, lavished heavy praise on Maclaren as "the first" to recognize the site of ghostly Troy. "He showed by the most convincing arguments that Troy could never have been on the heights of Bounarbashi," Schliemann wrote admiringly, "and that, if it ever existed, Hissarlik must mark its site."

Yet Maclaren receded into history and rarely receives more than a token footnote in the rediscovery of Troy. Why? Didn't Schliemann first get his idea from Maclaren?

Schliemann may have gotten his idea from Maclaren; we shall never know. But not necessarily. More likely, Schliemann used Maclaren to support his theory rather than derive the theory from Maclaren for, as we shall observe, Schliemann's infatuation with Troy began at the age of eight, and it is highly improbable that he had access to Maclaren's dissertation at that time, or that he could read and understand it if he did, or, for that matter, was even aware that it existed.

The point is this: It was left to Schliemann to dirty his hands to prove the theory. While the scholars and other indoor experts wrestled interminably with the problem of Homer and Troy, Schliemann bestirred himself, abandoned the lecture hall, and sallied forth to bring Priam's Pergamus back into the light of day.

Schliemann was restless. Now forty-six, he had amassed a fortune, but he had no interest in a life devoted solely to the acquisition of gold. He scorned the pursuit of gold for gold's sake. In the autumn of his life, when the lust for gold should have swept him deeper into the vortex of the commercial and financial world, Schliemann turned his back on commerce and embarked on an adventure which brought him a millionfold greater riches than all his gold. It gave Schliemann immortality. For the rest of recorded time, the names of Troy and Schliemann will be inextricably interwoven.

In the summer of 1868, alone, with scanty baggage and a thoroughly worn and annotated copy of Homer in his hands, Schliemann retraced von Hahn's footsteps, driven by what now amounted to a passion. That August he sailed from Piraeus, the fishing port of Athens on the edge of the Aegean. Schliemann's destination was the Hellespont.

It was Schliemann's first venture across the Aegean of antiquity and he trembled with anticipation. At the Hellespont (now called the Dardanelles), he proceeded by horse-drawn carriage directly for the shabby, impoverished village of Bounarbashi. On the journey, he gazed out on the Plain of Troy and wondered who was right: Lechevalier? Von Hahn? On his arrival at the village, he was astounded. Bounarbashi's topography bore no resemblance whatever to Homer. None whatever.

In Homer, for example, Achilles and Hector engaged in an epic single combat under the eyes of the Achaean host assembled on the plain with the Trojans and their allies peering from the walls of their citadel. The combatants flew along the base of the wall "till they came to two fair springs which fed the river Scamandar." Homer described the springs in detail, one so warm that steam rose from it as smoke from a burning fire, and the other even in summer as cold as hail or snow.

At Bounarbashi, Schliemann quickly spied the famous springs. To his horror, however, there were not two springs but forty or more. Indeed, the villagers, he later learned, called the springs *kirk-gios*, or "forty eyes." Even so, Schliemann was prepared. With Teutonic thoroughness, Schliemann put his right hand into his vest pocket and withdrew a thermometer. He plunged the instrument into the first spring—62.6° F (17° C. on his German-made instrument). He recorded the figure in a notebook. The Turkish villagers, meanwhile, looked on incredulously. Schliemann's odd behavior only confirmed the conviction of peasants the world over: Foreigners are crazy.

Schliemann wiped the thermometer dry and plunged it into the next spring. Again the instrument registered 62.6°. Systematically, with precision, the German tested each spring. "I found in all the springs a uniform temperature," he recorded. Until that moment, the principal argument in favor of Bounarbashi was that there were two springs at the site, one hot and one cold.

"This argument now falls to the ground," Schliemann penned in his notebook.

The ageless academic debate over Bounarbashi was ridiculous. "How could so many scholars make such fools of themselves?" he asked in wonderment.

When he completed his preliminary research, the first visitor to Bounarbashi to employ so common a dollar-and-dime instrument as a thermometer, Schliemann climbed the heights of Bali Dagh and surveyed the plains around the village and the Aegean coastline in the distance. Again he was shocked.

"The distance of Bounarbashi from the Hellespont is, in a straight line, eight miles, while all the indications of *The Iliad* seem to prove that the distance between Ilium and Hellespont was but very short, hardly exceeding three miles," Schliemann observed.

Leafing through his heavily marked copy of the celebrated German translation of Homer by B. J. H. Voss, he reenacted, pocket watch in hand, like a field grade officer of the German general staff, the initial battle between the warring confederations. He estimated that the battle had ebbed and flowed "from ten in the morning to seven in the evening" and that the battlefield had been transversed at least six times in that space of time. "It is therefore evident," he concluded, "that the distance between the two camps was assumed to be very short, less than three miles."

Since Bounarbashi was at least eight miles from the coast, where the invaders beached their vessels, it was physically impossible for the two armies to battle to and fro over a space of about fifty miles in a mere nine hours. Moreover, as Schliemann and others had established, Homer was invariably accurate in estimating time, speed, and distance problems; for example, when he said the Achaean fleet could sail a distance of two hundred miles in three days or three hundred miles in four days, he spoke of a passage by sail, which is common to this very day.

Schliemann applied still another test to Bounarbashi. In their single combat, according to Homer, Hector cried out to Achilles, "Three times have I fled round the mighty city of Priam, without daring to withstand you, but now, let me either slay or be slain." But, Schliemann bitingly noted, this was "utterly impossible" at Bounarbashi because the hill above the village fell off sharply on three sides, particularly the southern slope.

With the broiling sun now overhead, and with an ever larger crowd of villagers following him as if he were the Pied Piper of Hamelin, the crazy foreigner engaged in a mock combat on the spot. He attempted to run around the height "by myself" but barely made it the first time around.

As he approached the southern slope, which sheered off at a 25° angle, he recorded, "I was forced to crawl on all fours."

"No mortal being," he complained, "not even a goat, has ever been able to run swiftly down a slope which descends at an angle of twenty-five degrees."

The scene was extraordinary, beyond the ken of a Hollywood script writer. Here was an impeccably attired multimillionaire, alone, crawling around a forlorn hill on all fours as the sun sizzled overhead and a gallery of stupefied peasants looked on. What was more extraordinary, perhaps, was that Schliemann never once regarded himself as eccentric. He simply did what came naturally to him. He was so consumed by the desire to find Troy that he would have walked on his hands if necessary, and would have felt his behavior quite explicable.

Descending the hill, Schliemann was more convinced than ever that Bounarbashi was not the site of Homer's Troy. Unlike von Hahn, however, Schliemann did not attribute the impossibility of the situation to poetic license. His faith in Homer remained unshaken.

"Homer never intended us to believe that Hector and Achilles, in making their circuit of the city, could have run down this impossible descent," he said with finality. Homer was not wrong. The scholars who touted Bounarbashi were wrong.

Although he was convinced that Homer's Troy could not

possibly have been located at Bounarbashi, he wrote, "I wished to investigate so important a matter by actual excavation."

"Actual excavation"—so simple a phrase, and out of it emerged a new science.

In a pattern that he would develop into an art form in the years ahead, Schliemann hired a few of the now thoroughly bemused onlookers to "sink pits in hundreds of different places." At this stage, the villagers were completely convinced that he was mad. But the opportunity to earn a few piasters was worth the effort, however silly the whole project.

"Dig there," Schliemann ordered, pointing to the springs. "And there. Dig everywhere."

And everywhere, they dug.

And everywhere, they struck rock within two or three feet.

"Everywhere," Schliemann recorded in his diary, "I found only pure virgin soil."

Schliemann's contempt for the scholars of his day mounted with every spadeful of earth. The overwhelming body of evidence, tangible and intangible, was, if Troy existed, it must have existed elsewhere. Unlike von Hahn, who, on the basis of his own improvised dig, concluded that Troy was a product of Homer's flight of fancy, Schliemann clung stubbornly to a childish belief that Troy lay hidden somewhere in Asia Minor, in Turkey, on the "Plain of Troy." The very name of the plain was suggestive. But where?

Tired, covered from hat to shoes with a film of dust and grime, he returned to his carriage. His immaculately tailored Bond Street suit—Schliemann always wore expensive, custom-tailored apparel from London—was soiled; his shirt missed a button; his hands were discolored, and perspiration trickled down his face, forming rivulets along the base of his short, expertly trimmed and brushed moustache. Repeatedly, he wiped his gold-rimmed spectacles dry.

Leaving impoverished Bounarbashi after several days, he ordered his driver to take the next fork to the right. Surveying the scene from the bumpy carriage—the road was clotted with boulders and pot holes—nothing resembled Homer's topography. Not even remotely. Schliemann then ordered his driver to return to the fork and turn left. Once again, he studied the landscape and coastal area, particularly the occasional heights which rose from the grassy plain. Again, nothing.

"I carefully examined all the heights to the right and left of the Trojan Plain," he wrote in exasperation. "My researches bore no fruit."

Then, suddenly, Schliemann later said, "my particular attention was attracted to the hill called Hissarlik." Situated "only three miles from the Hellespont," he instantly realized that the hill, and the river and plain around it, "answered perfectly to the requirements of *The Iliad*." His spirits soared, he trembled uncontrollably with excitement.

Intuitively, without even touching the ground with the spade, as if by divine inspiration, in the fashion of Lechavalier, whom he had consigned contemptuously to the dustbin of history, Schliemann then and there decided that this desolate, uninhabited, barren, empty hill on which occasional herds of goats and sheep grazed, rising 162 feet above sea level, marked the site of the lost city. Storied Troy was encased in that hillock.

Overcome with excitement, Schliemann wept for joy. "Troy lives!" he shouted for all the world to hear. "I have found Troy!"

Then and there, unlike Lechevalier or the geographer Maclaren, the man of action came into play. He decided to return in force and "commence excavations here." Formally, he announced his decision with the publication of *Ithaca, the Peloponnesus and Troy* the following year.

At this stage in his life, Schliemann recognized that the currents which had buffeted him through a lonely, unhappy, and tremendously successful business career had pushed him inexorably toward the discovery of Troy. For four thousand, nay, almost five thousand years, Troy had been waiting for delivery. Unearthing the phantom city, restoring her glory, this was the mission of his life, his destiny. The decision was not his; it was the work of the gods. Troy had pursued him since his youth, since a cold December morning in 1829 when, at the age of eight, his imagination was set afire—a fire which, on the slopes of Hissarlik, consumed him body and soul.

# III

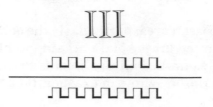

# A Gift Becomes a Dream

*Let him suffer whatever fate may have
spun for him when he was begotten
and his mother bore him.*

The Iliad, BOOK XX

FITTINGLY, Christmas was a day of peace in the Schliemann household, which is more than could be said for it during the rest of the year. And Christmas, 1829, proved doubly memorable. It marked the last time the family gathered at the table to celebrate the Feast of the Nativity—Frau Luise Schliemann, exhausted by an unhappy marriage, was dead within a year at the age of forty. It also marked young Heinrich's receipt of a gift from his father, Pastor Ernest Schliemann, which lit his imagination and put him on the road to Troy.

Married at sixteen, almost half her husband's age, Frau Luise thought often of a separation. But a sense of pride, loyalty, and devotion to her children, doggedness and determination—qualities Heinrich inherited from his mother—kept her at the Pastor's side. Sensitive and compassionate, she took refuge in martyrdom, which only worsened matters.

Her difficult marriage lasted twenty-four years, and she bore seven children. Shortly before her death in 1830, a few weeks after the delivery of her third and last son, Paul, she wrote a pathetic letter to her eighteen-year-old daughter, Elsie, which gave rein to her sorrow. The oldest of the Schliemann offspring, sufficiently mature to appreciate her mother's plight, Elsie was the only one of their children who never married. "If I die in childbirth," the mother wrote, "rejoice in the knowledge that God has liberated me from a terrible trial." During her pregnancy, the tension within the household attained unbearable heights; she was aware that her husband was carrying on another affair, this time with the housemaid.

Pastor Schliemann, a Protestant clergyman like his father and his father's father before him, was ambitious, egotistical, vindictive, a martinet who flew into periodic rages and relished an occasional bout with schnapps as well as with a different woman. His behavior made a mockery of his protestations against sin from the pulpit each Sunday morning.

Poverty aggravated the Schliemanns' thorny relationship. The pastor's income was barely sufficient to meet expenses, and the family frequently found itself in serious financial difficulty. The housemaid was little more than an indentured servant. And yet, despite the ugly situation, the Schliemanns were considerate parents. Both were educated, a rarity in those days, and within their limited means, they sought to instill a spirit of learning in their children. They took notice of their children's interests, encouraged reading habits, and whetted intellectual curiosity.

Against this background, the Christmas truce unfolded that year. In this setting, the Pastor presented young Heinrich, who would observe his eighth birthday on Epiphany, a copy of George Ludwig Jerrer's *Universal History*. The boy's dark eyes glowed appreciably as he thumbed the pages, and a light snow fell outside while the Yule log crackled in the fireplace. Midway, he halted abruptly and stared, transfixed at an engraving of Troy aflame, its huge walls collapsing, the famed Scaean gate buckling, and a youthful Aeneas fleeing the holocaust.

The selection of the book was hardly surprising. "My father," Schliemann later observed, "was neither a scholar nor an archaeologist, but he had a passion for ancient history."

Ordained at twenty-six, the Pastor immediately displayed a scholarly penchant. Within five years, he mastered Hebrew and recited the New Testament so expertly in its original tongue that he won a testimonial from church superiors. The Pastor was also well versed in Latin and, as Schliemann recalled, "availed himself of every spare moment to teach me." With enthusiasm, the father often retold the story of the tragic fate of Pompeii, where superficial excavations were then in progress, and told the boy that if he had the money and leisure, he would rush off to Italy and consider himself "the luckiest of men" to witness firsthand the resurrection of a dead world.

With the boy kneeling at his side, the pastor frequently related the spectacular deeds of the Homeric Age and the events of the Trojan War, always finding in Heinrich a warm defender of the Trojan cause. "With great grief I heard from him," Schliemann wrote later, "that Troy had been so completely destroyed that it had disappeared without leaving a trace of its existence."

Fascinated, the boy could hardly put aside the illustration of burning Troy—the crumbling walls and the column of smoke rising above Priam's Pergamus. He asked his father— like most fathers at that age a depository of all knowledge— about Troy's destruction. With juvenile simplicity, the boy reasoned that Jerrer must have seen Troy; otherwise, he could not have drawn the picture. The father brushed aside the query with a laugh.

"My son," he said, "that is merely an illustration—a fancy of the artist's imagination."

But the boy persisted. "Did Troy really have such walls or was that fanciful, too?"

The father pondered a moment and confirmed the walls' thickness. They were called Cyclopean walls, he explained, since only a giant Cyclops had had the strength to build such walls—or, at least, so it was said in Homer's days. Naturally, Homer was myth and legend.

"But Father," Heinrich insisted, "if such walls once existed, they cannot possibly have been completely destroyed."

With uncomplicated, childish logic, the boy argued that "vast ruins must still remain" and that, if nobody had found them, it was because they were hidden beneath the dust of ages. This the father seriously doubted. But the boy was adamant. In the manner of most debates between parent and child, the dialogue ended on an inconclusive note. At last, Schliemann recalled triumphantly in an autobiographical sketch published in 1880, "We both agreed that I should one day excavate Troy."

Clearly, Homer's epic poem about the Trojan War exercised a hypnotic spell over Heinrich, as it has among young boys before and since. Almost a hundred years later, for example, another incurable romantic—the creator of the prefabricated adventure—Richard Halliburton, recalled after his first visit to Troy "how many a night, as a very small boy, I was rocked to sleep in my father's lap to the romantic tales of this romantic city."

And, in a Schliemannesque manner, Halliburton remembered:

> A hundred times and more I heard the story of the wooden horse, until, if my father failed to recite every smallest word in the telling, I would know it and solemnly correct him. And a hundred times my eyes filled with tears [when] my heroic, unconquerable Troy fell before the miserable treachery of a wooden horse. How vividly I saw it all from the high battlements of my father's lap . . . I never grew tired of Troy. . . . The years passed, but not my ardor for Troy.*

From the day of his birth, Troy seemed inextricably bound up with Heinrich Schliemann's destiny. When he entered the Schliemann household on January 6, 1822, in the town of Neu Buckow in the Grand Duchy of Mecklenburg-Schwerin, on a cold, blustery Sunday, a world away, along the rim of the Aegean Sea, *The Iliad* was being reenacted in nineteenth century dress. The Achaean and Trojan hosts, of course, had faded into mythology, if not history. Their place was taken by the Greeks on the western shore of the Aegean and the Turks on the eastern shore of that selfsame "wine-dark sea," as Homer described it.

During that first week of the New Year, Mahmud II, the Sublime Porte or reigning sultan of the Ottoman Empire, issued a *firman* or decree which called on the peoples of Asia Minor to take up arms in defense of their land, pledged victory,

---

*Richard Halliburton, *Book of Marvels*. Indianapolis: Bobbs-Merrill, 1937.

and offered them prizes which recalled the Homeric Age. "You will overflow with gold, riches and women," the Sultan promised, "and you shall erase from the earth that perifidious and imperious nation, the Greeks, who are an abomination."*

Schliemann's birth also coincided with the first glimmer of European interest in "antiquities." Archaeology was not a discipline, although the Sorbonne and Oxford, among others, offered courses in "classical antiquity." Some excavations had been undertaken, but haphazardly. No thought was given to a systematic study of the ruins of the past which showed above the ground, much less those hidden from view. The sciences of archaeology—stratigraphy, for example, which Schliemann pioneered—were unheard of at the time of his birth.

Even so, superficial excavations were carried out at Herculaneum in Italy in the middle of the eighteenth century by Johann Wunckelmann and, in the early 1800s, cursory excavations at Pompeii created a sensation in Europe. In 1809, thirteen years before Schliemann's birth, Thomas Burgon unearthed fragments of Mycenaean pottery, identified them as belonging to the "Heroic and Homeric Age," and published a paper on his finds in 1847. Eight years later, Giovanni Battista Belzoni, a circus strongman turned explorer, discovered the tomb of the Egyptian Pharaoh Seti I. But these activities were considered "exotic adventures," and so-called antiquarians were usually dilettantes at best and, more often than not, simply itinerant travelers. But curiosity about the past burgeoned at the time of Schliemann's birth. The weekend he was born, for example, *The Times* carried a front-page advertisement inviting London's "amateurs of antiquities," for a shilling apiece, to inspect the Egyptian Tomb—a composite model of a Pharaoh's tomb, temples, and pyramid—and a collection of manuscripts and mummies. The advertisement did not make clear whether the manuscripts and mummies were genuine.

Neu Buckow, however, was focusing on a more exciting

---

*The struggle for power in the Aegean basin has continued into the present. In the aftermath of World War II, in part as a result of Russian pressure on the Hellespont and Aegean, the Greeks and Turks buried their long rivalry and, in 1949, joined the North Atlantic Treaty Organization. NATO thus became the first confederation to embrace voluntarily both shores of the Aegean basin.

development, the end of serfdom as feudalism receded in the duchy and the Industrial Revolution reshaped the lives of Mecklenburgers. A new spirit of freedom walked the countryside. It was, of course, too early to feel the full effects of the Grand Duke's action in abolishing serfdom only three years earlier, an institution which the Romans reported flourishing in the German states in the time of Tacitus, before the birth of Christ. The nobility and landed gentry still controlled the countryside. Pastor Schliemann and his peasant flock were far removed from the Establishment, and they had no hope of breaking into it, even if they wanted to do so. But the end of serfdom was a harbinger of social and economic change. It foreshadowed the rise of a new class, a class based on the acquisition of capital, and Heinrich Schliemann, the rugged individualist who would bend the free enterprise system to his own end, was destined to epitomize the emergence of that class.

Now situated behind the rusting Iron Curtain, the former duchy, in Schliemann's day, was exclusively agricultural—rye, wheat, hay, and potatoes; an occasional sheep pasture; a woolspinning mill. The duchy's inhabitants were largely impoverished farmers. Freed from serfdom, they had yet to free themselves from poverty. The Pastor and his family, however, were at least a rung up the social ladder from "the lower classes," as Schliemann called his parishioners. As a clergyman's family, the Schliemanns were educated and members of the second estate. For all that, they were as poverty-stricken, in the material sense, as their flock.

In earlier days, Mecklenburg was a favorite battleground between Teutonic and Slavic tribes—Poland lay only 150 miles to the east—and later both Charlemagne and Napoleon extended their empires across its pasturelands. In Heinrich Schliemann's lifetime, the duchy was drawn into Bismarck's creation of the First Reich and, like her sister states, Mecklenburg-Schwerin provided cannon fodder for Germany's expansionists in 1870, 1914, and 1939.

A year after Heinrich's birth, Ernest was elected pastor at Ankershagen, and the family moved into the village parsonage. Here Heinrich developed his first roots.

Among the villagers, the young boy, slim and of medium

height, was known as a lad with an insatiable curiosity and incurable imagination. For such a youngster, Ankershagen was ideally suited. His interest in "the mysterious and marvelous," as he termed it, was stimulated by the tales handed down for generations among his father's parishioners. For one thing, the Schliemann garden was said to be haunted by a ghost. For another, just behind the garden was a pond out of which a maiden rose each midnight, holding a silver bowl. Vast treasures were buried close by in the ruins of a stone tower. Also there was a medieval castle "with secret passages in its walls." The castle, naturally, was haunted by fearful specters, and contained buried treasure. So genuine was Heinrich's faith in these tales that "whenever I heard my father complain of his poverty, I always expressed my astonishment that he did not dig up the treasures and become rich," he recalled.

But the most terrifying legend of all dealt with a notorious errant knight, Henning von Holstein, a plunderer and sadist who fried a man alive in a large iron pan and gave him, when he was dying, a final kick with his left foot. A long line of flat stones in his father's churchyard was said to mark the malefactor's grave, from which, for centuries, his left leg grew out, covered with a black silk stocking. Pastor Schliemann's sexton and sacristan swore to the boy that when they were young, they cut off the leg and used its bone to knock down pears from neighbor's trees but that, alas, in the beginning of the eighteenth century, the leg suddenly stopped growing out of the tomb.

"In my childish simplicity," Schliemann confessed in the autumn of his life, "I, of course, believed all this."

In this atmosphere, Troy, with its Cyclopean walls and its hoard of gold—"Priam's Treasure," Homer called it—fermented in the boy's mind like the casks of freshly pressed grapes in the cellars of the Grand Duke. Indeed, Jerrer's drawing of burning Troy had such an effect on the boy that, he said, "I talked of nothing else to my playfellows. And I was continually laughed at by everyone."

Everyone, that is, except two young girls, Louise and Minna Meincke, the daughters of a prosperous farmer. Louise was six years older than Heinrich; Minna was his age. When Heinrich drafted schemes to find the lost city and excavate it, they did not laugh. They listened attentively and rapturously. "Especially Minna," Schliemann said, "who showed me the greatest sympathy and entered into all my vast plans for the future."

He promptly fell in love with Minna and in "our childish simplicity"—a favorite Schliemann phrase—"we exchanged vows of eternal love."

In the winter of 1829–1830, the happiest season of Heinrich's childhood, the romance flourished. The two children took dancing lessons together in their respective homes and when a lesson ended, they slipped off to visit the parish cemetery to see whether Henning's foot had reemerged from his grave. Or, they visited the haunted castle with its reputed secret passages and walled-up treasure.

In the village, the eight-year-olds were also a familiar couple. Among their favorite meeting places was the shop of the village tailor, Peter Woller, who had lost an eye and a foot in an accident. Hopping Peter, as he was cheerfully called by the children, was illiterate. But he impressed young Heinrich with an extraordinary memory and easily repeated each of his father's weekly sermons word for word. He also regaled them with tales of far-off places, and told them of the great seaport of Hamburg whose ships sailed the seven seas in search of gold and strange lands.

Through Hopping Peter, the illiterate, and through his pastor father, who lacked money and leisure to pursue his scholarly interest in the worlds of the past, Heinrich, at an early age, drew a number of conclusions which subconsciously shaped his adulthood. People could not be judged solely on the basis of their social, economic, or educational background. In school, Heinrich discovered that many of his well-educated teachers were dull, unimaginative, and petty. In an illiterate, he found an exciting, imaginative individual eager to share his ideas with others. Yet an education was indispensable. "If only Hopping Peter could read and write," he told Minna. "If only he had an opportunity. He might possibly become a great scholar." Poverty was Peter's problem. Similarly, although his father was educated, he lacked the time to pursue his studies. Again, poverty. An "independent position" was necessary in both cases

and could be achieved by acquiring wealth. Fame and fortune
was a familiar couplet, but the order was inverted. Money
spelled titles and degrees, and, above all, leisure. Leisure
spelled time, time to pursue true interests and win acclaim. All
his experiences in childhood confirmed this strategic assessment of life.

Like most boys his age, Heinrich considered the dancing
lessons a bore. But they provided him with the opportunity to
see Minna, and to hold her hand. With a copy of the *Universal
History* before them, they spent hours planning their future.
When they grew up, of course, they would marry. Then they
would set about to excavate the buried treasures of Ankershagen. Certainly, the treasure must be worth a hundred reichthalers or more. With the acquisition of an independent position,
hand in hand, they would set out in search of Troy.

"We could imagine nothing pleasanter than to spend all
our lives in digging for the relics of the past," Schliemann
wrote in his memoirs.

It was not to be. The little world of Minna and Heinrich
collapsed with the death of Frau Schliemann. His mother's
death was, in Schliemann's words, "an irreparable misfortune." The family came asunder. With her death, the Pastor felt
free to carry on openly his affair with the housemaid. The
children and villagers were shocked.

Demands were raised that he be defrocked and, as a pretext, official charges were brought against him for the misap-
propriation of parish funds. The Pastor turned on his critics
with ferocity, as his son would do a generation later. The senior
Schliemann won his court case but the affair served its purpose
—he resigned from the church. Undaunted, he tired of the
housemaid, cast her aside, and took up with another woman,
whom he subsequently married. His second marriage was
stormier than the first. Schliemann again outlived his wife
(he died in 1871 at the age of ninety) and fathered two more
children, one when he reached the age of sixty-seven.

In his various published writings, quite understandably,
Schliemann kept these skeletons stacked in the family closet.
"My mother's death," he said in a typical commentary, "coin-
cided with another misfortune which resulted in all our ac-

quaintances suddenly turning their backs upon us and refusing to have any further intercourse with us."

Ankershagen's townspeople, of course, were visibly shaken by their pastor's behavior, and they milled as many rumors about him as potatoes in their stills that summer. The scandal crushed Heinrich. The dancing lessons stopped abruptly, and the boy was no longer welcome at the Meincke farmhouse, although it is difficult to appreciate how the Meinckes could hold an eight-year-old boy accountable for his father's behavior. "To see the family of Meincke no more," he confessed, "to separate altogether from Minna, never to behold her again, this was a thousand times more painful to me than my mother's death, which I soon forgot under my overwhelming grief for Minna's loss." Not a pleasant summary of his emotions but typically forthright, a measure of Schliemann's character.

A final straw. "Even Troy itself lost its interest for a time," he said.

Sullen, dejected, the boy moped around the house while his father found it increasingly difficult to pursue his affair with six children underfoot and a baby in the crib. The Pastor solved his problem by packing the children off to relatives; young Heinrich was dispatched to Kalhorst to live with Uncle Friedrich, also a village pastor. The uncle, embarrassed by the situation, arranged for him to enter the Gymnasium and there Heinrich Schliemann came under the wand of candidate Carl Anders, the teacher who edited his first book on Troy thirty-eight years later.

As a "candidate," Anders was on probation. He had yet to acquire his scholarly credentials and teaching tenure. Like many teachers of the period, Anders possessed a good command of Latin, but unlike many of his colleagues, he also possessed a fascination for Roman and Greek antiquities. He read everything available on the subject, sometimes at the expense of work in the classroom. Little is known about Anders other than that he later abandoned teaching and turned to his real interests, books and antiquity. He became a librarian and then keeper of the Museum of Antiquities at Neu Strelitz, which contained a rather pathetic collection of odd bits and pieces from the past.

Under Anders, young Heinrich's interest in Troy revived; he made such rapid progress in classical studies that, as a Christmas gift in 1832, at the age of ten, he presented his father with a badly written essay in Latin. The subject? Drawn from Homer, of course. The essay centered on the Trojan War and the adventures of Ulysses and Agamemnon.

With a glowing commendation from Anders, the father arranged for Heinrich to attend the Gymnasium at Neu Strelitz, which was known for its Latin and Greek studies. But "another misfortune," as Schliemann quaintly expressed it, overtook the boy. Now the father was embroiled in the parish's court action, and the family's slim savings dissolved to meet legal expenses. Unable to meet the Neu Strelitz tuition, Heinrich withdrew and entered a *Realschul,* with its emphasis on a practical, pedestrian, non-classical education.

Again, the boy did well. In 1835, at the age of thirteen, he advanced to the first grade. The following year, he graduated but, with the situation at home still roiled, Heinrich was compelled to fend for himself. He secured an apprenticeship in a grocery in the small town of Furstenberg in Mecklenburg-Strelitz, a neighboring duchy. His formal academic career had ended. Yet within a few years, he would match wits with the financial giants and classical scholars of the Western world. In these encounters, he would emerge on top.

Shortly before his departure for Furstenberg, on a Good Friday, his spirits were raised. By chance, he encountered Minna, whom he had not seen for five years. The fourteen-year-olds looked at each other, burst into tears, and fell speechless in one another's arms. Several times, they attempted to speak but were overcome by emotion. She was attired in a black frock, and Schliemann found her beauty "fascinating." When Minna's parents arrived on the scene, the teenagers separated. "It took me a long time to recover my emotion," he recalled. "But I was sure that Minna still loved me."

The chance encounter stimulated his ambition. He was more determined than ever to conquer the world and win her hand in the process. That night, the Pastor's son "implored God to grant that she might not marry before I had attained an independent position."

After a few days on the job, Heinrich was plunged into despair. The "independent position" appeared beyond reach. The grocery shop barely grossed three thousand reichthalers ($2,250) a year and a ten-dollar sale constituted "a big day." His duties were routine: sweep the shop; grind potatoes for the still —Mecklenburg was noted for potato whisky—and serve customers in the owner's absence. Most of the trade turned on the sale of basic commodities: herring, butter, potato whisky, milk, salt, coffee, sugar, oil, and candles. He worked five and a half years "at this most miserable business." The hours were intolerably long: from five in the morning until eleven at night.

Each night, exhausted, he slipped into deep slumber, only to rise six hours later. He had no time for reading and, worse, he complained that he began to forget what little he had learned. Yet, he clung desperately to his father's inheritance, a love of learning. "Indeed," he wrote toward the close of his life, "I never lost it."

Heinrich, approaching manhood, dreamed of Minna, of course, and of Troy. But as the years lengthened, he panicked. He would never escape the ghetto; he would never achieve an independent position.

"There seems no hope of escape," he wrote depressingly. "None."

One day in 1837, Hermann Neidhoeffer, like himself the son of a clergyman, who had almost completed his studies at the Gymnasium before his expulsion for disorderly conduct, stumbled into the shop. Half-intoxicated, known as the village drunk, he bought a round of potato whisky and, in his stupor, began to recite *The Iliad,* observing the rhythmic cadence of the verses. The rolling, lilting, and melodic outpouring of words enchanted the boy, although Schliemann did not understand a syllable. What was that?

"Homer," Neidhoeffer said, slurring over the name.

"The words," Schliemann later said, "made a deep impression on me." So deep that he took out the few pfennigs he had saved, "my whole fortune," and bought Neidhoeffer another round as compensation for repeating those "divine verses." Then he purchased for him a second and third shot of schnapps, filling the glass liberally, and conscientiously depositing the money in the receipt drawer. By now, Heinrich's fortune was exhausted and so was Neidhoeffer's ability to stand upright. "Never," Schliemann said, "as long as I live shall I forget that night."

When the grocer's apprentice fell into bed that night, he again prayed to God, not for Minna's hand this time but "that by His grace I might yet have the happiness of learning Greek." Then he was overcome by bitterness. He wept. He was suffocating in his environment.

"As if by a miracle," he later recounted, an escape materialized. The "miracle" was a broken blood vessel in the lung. Lifting a cask of chicory, he coughed and, to his astonishment, spat blood. "My patron," he wrote in his diary, "seeing my broken health, turned me out."

Schliemann drifted back to Ankershagen and found the domestic situation more deplorable than ever. "Disgraceful," he wrote his sister. "Scandalous." Now he began to think, for the first time, of an escape route broad and long enough to take him away from Mecklenburg and Europe altogether.

Hessians, returning from service as British mercenaries in the American Revolution, told wondrous tales about the former colonies across the Atlantic. First as a trickle, and then as a torrent by the nineteenth century, increasing numbers of Germans set their sights on a new life and new opportunity in a new world: *Amerika!* In this situation, Heinrich appealed to his father to advance him money for the passage to New York, arguing that the sea voyage would also cure his lung condition. His father adamantly refused but agreed to advance him 88 reichthalers to study bookkeeping at Rostock, the duchy's intellectual center. Money invested in education, he admonished his son, was money well spent.

Heinrich made the most of the opportunity and left for Rostock to learn bookkeeping by double entry, the then-current Schwanbeck system which normally took from twelve to eighteen months. Schliemann, however, applied himself with an intensity, impatience, zealousness, and determination later mirrored in his climb to the summit of the mercantile world and in his quest for Troy.

"I worked from early morning until late at night," he

remembered. Within four months, to the amazement of teachers and students alike, he mastered the system. Returning to Ankershagen, he found the household in new tumult. Remarried, his father quarreled throughout the day with Heinrich's new stepmother and made love to her throughout the night. Their behavior, he wrote his sister, "was disgusting." Then and there, he decided to turn his back on his native village and set out for illustrious Hamburg, the bustling seaport of which he had heard so much—first from Hopping Peter, and then from fellow students at Rostock. His possessions were meager—a few old clothes and the equivalent in reichthalers of thirty-seven dollars. His health was deteriorating; he still coughed and still spat blood.

"I was," he wrote in a diary, "half-desperate."

Prideful, he took the coach from Ankershagen and, outside the village, alighted and walked the rest of the way, covering the distance in ten days.

As September drew to a close, with the crisp smell of autumn in the air, Heinrich Schliemann arrived in Hamburg, "the town which stood supreme above all others in the world of commerce." The impressionable country bumpkin was awestruck by the huge, squat stone buildings, the five towers hovering over the city, the crowded wharves, and the forest of matchsticks rising from the harbor mouth as square riggers, barques, brigs, and brigantines nestled along the quays or lined the Elbe's banks.

The throngs, the noise, and the color invigorated him as much as the chill creeping into the autumn afternoon. "I was seized with wonder and amazement and I thought Hamburg to be the largest city in the world," he wrote in his diary. "When on entering the gate, I saw the bustle and life in the streets, I did not cease, full of enthusiasm, to cry Oh! Hamburg! Hamburg!

"The sight of Hamburg," he said, "turned me into a dreamer."

Obtaining a small room near the fish market, he stood transfixed for an hour before the window, paralyzed by the wonderful sights below when, as he wrote his sister in high humor, he suddenly realized that he was standing completely naked. Clearly, he would never return to Ankershagen—and he never did. There was a world out there to win—and he would win it.

Hamburg was in the midst of a boom, and Heinrich encountered little difficulty in landing a job at the fish market. But the job was short-lived. His chest was still weak and he was unable to wrestle with boxes of cod, barrels of herring, blocks of ice, and bags of salt. The necessity to skirt heavy duty cost him the job. At this juncture, his mother interceded on his behalf from beyond the grave. He ran into a "very kindhearted shipbroker," W. F. Wendt, who recognized the Schliemann name. Wendt had been raised with Heinrich's mother. The shipbroker took a liking to the boy and advised him of a "brilliant opening" in La Guaira.

"La Guaira?" inquired the nineteen-year-old boy.

"Colombia, my boy," Wendt replied. "South America."

North or South, it mattered little; the word America possessed magic. Heinrich seized the chance, and the shipbroker promptly arranged for him to work his passage as a cabin boy aboard the brig *Dorothea.* Advised that sailors carried their own bedding, on the docks the boy bartered his only coat for a blanket. He was down to ten dollars.

Boarding the *Dorothea,* Heinrich was aware of a strange sensation common to landsmen: For the first time he felt a deck under his feet and an almost imperceptible motion as the vessel, like a chained spirit, bound to the land, sought to free herself. Bunking in the forepeak, he discovered from an itinerant seaman that La Guaira was not in Colombia. "Then where?" he asked, astonished. "Venezuela," the sailor said. Colombia, Venezuela, what difference did it make? The sea air would cure his lungs, and opportunity was to be found everywhere in the Americas. He was leaving an Old World in search of fortune in a New World and with that fortune he would set out to find a Lost World.

He would never reach Venezuela. Nor Colombia. He would never marry Minna. He would never unearth the treasures of Ankershagen. Fate, that hidden current, would disgorge him on a friendly Dutch coast, deposit him in Czarist Russia, and finally carry him across the Atlantic to America. Only then, after he established an independent position, with a firm hand on the tiller, would he sail for the Aegean and realize beyond his most daring dreams the supreme goal of his life, Troy's rebirth. He would journey back in time, as if a transfixed passenger in a Jules Verne fantasy. He would make of Homer and *The Iliad,* and later, *The Odyssey*, "but a thing of yesterday."

As the *Dorothea* ran up her Blue Peter, a white square on a blue field, signaling all in Hamburg that she was putting to sea, the date was November 28, 1841.

# IV

⊓⊔⊓⊔⊓⊔⊓⊔

⊓⊔⊓⊔⊓⊔⊓⊔

# The Merchant Prince

*Zeus had made him captain over the wind,
and he could stir or still each of them
according to his own pleasure.*

The Odyssey, BOOK X

THE WIND WAS fair as the *Dorothea* gathered seaway and the nineteen-year-old lad, perched on the cabin top, absorbed the sights, sounds, and smells of a vessel putting to sea. But as she nosed down the gray Elbe, the winds turned, the ship lacked sea room, and she luffed. For three days, a common experience in the great age of sail, the ship rode at anchor on the Elbe, near Blankenese, waiting for the return of a fair wind. On December 1, 1841, the wind shifted and the *Dorothea* resumed headway and entered the North Sea. The high seas beckoned, and Schliemann's spirits rose as the New World glistened over the horizon.

But the horizon quickly disappeared and the vessel was caught up in a tempest.

Schliemann took to his bunk, seasick. In the middle of the night, he awoke to a "horrible cracking sound" and shouts of, "We are lost! Save yourself!" Trembling with fear, he leaped from the berth into a cabin already half-filled with water. Almost naked, he rushed on deck and narrowly escaped being swept overboard. "The waves went continually over me," he wrote later in his diary. "All was confusion and horror."

Some crewmen cried, others prayed, still others blasphemed, and some looked for courage in schnapps. With the roll of the tormented ship, the ship's bell rang continually and "its doleful sound seemed to proclaim a watery grave," he said. Suddenly, the mainmast cracked, and the vessel foundered. Schliemann was flung into the icy sea and then was "dragged into a small stern boat by the second mate." Captain, crew, and passengers, fourteen in all—two sailors had drowned—huddled in the lifeboat. "It was a wonder, indeed," Schliemann later said, "that we did not sink."

The boat was oarless, and for seven hours Schliemann and his companions rode the spume-flecked sea. By chance, the boat was thrown by the waves upon a bank close to the shore of Texel, along the north Dutch coast, the jumping-off place for vessels from the prim little towns around the Zuider Zee. Schliemann lay exhausted on the sand, and in Homer's words, he could hear "the surf thundering up against the rocks, for the swell continued to break against them with a terrific roar and everything was enveloped in spray."

"I felt on that bank," Schliemann later said, "as if a voice whispered to me that the tide in my earthly affairs had come, and that I had to take it at its flood."

Dramatic? Assuredly, but completely in character. To Schliemann, life was a stage play in which he played the protagonist. Reality was a dream; dreams (and myths), reality. His luck often had a touch of unreality.

As he raised himself up, he realized that the inhabitants were busily engaged in the ageless and honorable islander profession of salvaging ("stealing" Schliemann wrote in his diary) cargo washed ashore. The Dutch "thieves," however, proved hospitable. They gathered up the survivors and "treated us with coffee and black bread." They also provided the half-naked Schliemann with wooden shoes and whatever clothes they could spare. The following day, a fisherman picked up Schliemann's chest, filled with a few shirts and letters of introduction. He was the only survivor who recovered personal effects. Jestingly, the beached skipper christened him "Jonah."

After three days on the island, the captain arranged for the crew's return to Hamburg. Schliemann balked. "I declined to return to Germany," he said, "where I had been so overwhelmingly unfortunate." Inwardly, he felt that the Muses had protected him during the storm and that his destiny was in Holland.

He remained at Texel, recovered his limited strength, and wrote Wendt about the shipwreck. Wearing layers of old clothing—he possessed no coat—and with a few florins which the impoverished Dutch islanders collected for him, he set out for Amsterdam. "I suffered cruelly from the cold," he said. The parallel with Ulysses when he landed on Ithaca is striking. "The cold will be the death of me," Ulysses complained, "for I have no coat; some god fooled me into embarking on the voyage with nothing but my shirt."

In Amsterdam, half-frozen and destitute, Schliemann sought to enlist in the Dutch army, then recruiting troops for the sultry East Indies, the diadem of the Dutch Empire. But his cough betrayed him. His fortunes reached a spring ebb. Desperate, he feigned serious illness and was admitted to the Amsterdam general hospital where he was assigned, jotting down in his diary in his orderly, detailed manner, "bed No. 66."

Fortuitously, his letter to Wendt reached the shipbroker while he was dining with friends in Hamburg. Amid steins of beer and platters of sausage, the diners were so moved by Heinrich's account of the shipwreck that they took up a subscription for him and raised ninety-seven dollars. Wendt also advised the young man to contact the Prussian consul general, an old friend. The official promptly landed him a job as office boy in a trading company. The job lacked physical and mental pressure: He stamped bills of exchange; cashed them in the financial district; made regular trips to the post office. He held the job two years and, during that time, the complaint in his chest disappeared.

Heinrich Schliemann had no intention of remaining at the base of the commercial pyramid and was not inclined to live on handouts. He exploited his free time to launch a program of self-education. "My mechanical occupation suited me," he explained, "for it left me time to think of my neglected education." He threw himself into it with the enthusiasm, doggedness, and self-discipline that characterized his later endeavors.

First, he enrolled in a course in calligraphy—the first practical typewriter would not be invented for another twenty years —and "took pains to learn to write legibly." Next, he applied himself to the study of English which, through the expansion of the British Empire, had already developed into the world's *lingua franca* (a phrase, interestingly, which cannot be rendered into English). In the process, he developed a method of language study which has a familiar echo in our era. He freely explained:

> This method consists of reading a great deal aloud without making a translation, taking a lesson every day, constantly writing essays upon subjects of interest, correcting these under the supervision of a teacher, learning them by heart, and repeating [aloud] at the next lesson what was corrected on the previous day.

He could not afford to subscribe to a paper from across the Channel, and he knew no Englishmen. Yet he felt it imperative to listen to the spoken language. His world, of course, was devoid of radios, television, tape recorders, motion pictures, record players—and Berlitz schools. Ingeniously, he resolved the problem. He attended Mass each Sunday at the *Engelsche kerk,* not once but twice, and repeated to himself in a low voice every word of the clergyman's sermon. People attend church for many reasons; few for language training.

As a consequence, Schliemann developed a prodigous memory. "I committed to memory the whole of Goldsmith's *Vicar of Wakefield* and Sir Walter Scott's *Ivanhoe,*" he said. In six months, he mastered English.

Then he turned to French and repeated the process. He memorized François Fénélon's *Les Aventures de Telemaque,* which Voltaire enthusiastically called "a Greek poem in French." A political novel, it was based on the adventures of Telemachus' search for his father, Ulysses, both of whom are prominent figures in *The Iliad* and *The Odessy.* For good measure, he memorized Gernardin de Pierre's *Paul et Virginia.*

As for Dutch, he picked that up rather effortlessly, as did

most Germans living in Holland. He then broadened his knowledge of the Romance languages by adding Spanish, Portuguese, and Italian to his repertoire and learning to speak and write fluently in each in "no more than six weeks"—an extraordinary accomplishment.

As office boy, Heinrich Schliemann earned $160 annually, half of which he invested in his studies. "On the other half," he said, "I lived—miserably enough, to be sure." Even later, when his bank account exceeded seven figures, he lived frugally and practiced thrift, so searing were the experiences of his impoverished childhood and adolescence.

In his early Amsterdam days, he rented a garret without a fire at $1.60 a month. "I shivered with cold in winter," he recalled, "and was scorched with heat in summer." His food bill averaged about $1.75 a week. His diet was invariably the same: rye-meal porridge for breakfast; bread and butter and tea with sugar for lunch and dinner; and in the evening, the luxury of a jigger of Dutch gin—a mixture of juniper berries and aromatics with a mash of barley malt and other grains, fermented and distilled—a bitter, acrid liquor bearing no resemblance to the London-style gin of the contemporary Martini circuit. In these days, too, he developed a stoic philosophy. "Nothing," he philosophized, "spurs one on to study more than misery and the certain prospect of being able to release oneself from it by unremitting work." Later, in the counting house and in the excavation of Troy, he was a hard taskmaster; hard on others, hardest of all on himself.

Two years' steady employment emboldened him to ask for a promotion to a better job. The request was denied. He was too valuable as an office boy and as F. C. Quien, his employer, doubtlessly remarked to friends at lunch that day, "It's hard to get good office boys these days." Rebuffed, Schliemann reacted in and out of character. In the spirit of free enterprise, he shopped for a better job, and he neglected his office duties.

His opportunity came when he filled an opening for bookkeeper at $240 a year at the office of B. H. Schroder & Co., to this day one of Europe's great trading houses. The investment in the Rostock business school paid its first dividend.

Schliemann worked with his customary zeal and enthusiasm and so impressed Herr Schroder that his salary was raised $160 a year by way of encouragement. Even when Schliemann achieved his elusive independent position, he retained close personal relations with the house of Schroder; they, for their part, never lost confidence in their young bookkeeper and later contributed a shipment of English wheelbarrows for his expedition to Troy.

Squirrel-eyed, Schliemann observed that despite the firm's burgeoning indigo trade with Russia, nobody in the office knew Russian. In those days, as in the days of Homer, indigo, obtained from a plant cultivated in India, was a primary source of dyestuffs, comparable to spices in Columbus' era (in the course of Schliemann's lifetime, the Germans labored to find a substitute—and did; it became the basis of their munitions industry).

With a blend of audacity and boastfulness based on a knowledge of his capabilities, Schliemann announced to his co-workers one day, "I shall learn Russian." Even a Schliemann, however, encountered enormous obstacles, not so much with his self-imposed assignment as in acquiring the tools. He could not find a teacher because "there was no one in Amsterdam who understood a word of the language" and the Czar's consular representative in the Dutch capital refused to be bothered. Schliemann browsed through the bookshops lining Kalverstraat and discovered only an old Russian grammar, a lexicon, and a bad Russian translation of his familiar counselor, Fénélon's *Les Aventures de Telemaque*. Still, it reminded him of his ultimate goal, Troy.

Schliemann's failure to find Russian books was understandable. In the middle of the nineteenth century, Russia was still on the other side of the moon, a light-year away from the West. Russia was still in the Dark Ages—"a crude and barbarous land," as his brother, Paul, called it in a letter to Heinrich —more Oriental than Occidental. Unlike Mecklenburg, for example, in Russia serfdom continued to flourish, the press was still shackled, the secret police overly efficient, and St. Petersburg, the ancient seat of the Czars, a nest of court intrigue. Russia? Why would anyone want to study Russian?

With the help of the grammar, and with his usual perseverance, Schliemann spent the evenings teaching himself the Cyrillic alphabet and its pronunciation. Following his old method, he began to write short stories and to learn them by heart. Of course, nobody corrected his work and he conceded that his effort was "no doubt, extremely bad." Impatient, Schliemann also considered his progress too slow, although he conceded that he "found this most beautiful language the most difficult tongue of all." He needed someone to listen to him recite aloud in Russian, but nobody in Amsterdam (except that uncooperative Russian consular official) could help him. As at Troy later, Schliemann ignored the impossibility of the situation and hired a poor Jew from the Amsterdam ghetto to hear him at eighty cents per week, the same ghetto from which Rembrandt, shortly before his death two hundred years earlier, recruited models for his most moving religious painting, "The Return of the Prodigal Son." The poor Jew visited Schliemann's quarters nightly for two hours and listened to his Russian readings without understanding a syllable, often falling asleep at the table.

Since the ceilings of the rooming houses in Holland were thin (the frugal Dutch put their stoutest timber into sidings), and although Schliemann's garret was on the third floor, the tenants were annoyed by his nightly ranting in Russian. The consensus was that Schliemann was stark, raving mad. The tenants complained to the landlord, and the landlord complained to him. While studying Russian, Schliemann dryly observed, he was compelled twice to change his lodgings. But in the pursuit of an objective, he was oblivious to inconvenience.

The house of Schroder was impressed and delighted when its young bookkeeper offered to write the Russians in Russian. "Try your hand, young man," Henry Schroder, the founder's son, told him.

As a measure of his phenomenal linguistic capabilities, within two months of launching his Cyrillic adventure, Schliemann drafted his first letter in Russian and addressed it to Vasili Poltnikov, the agent for Moscow's biggest indigo importer. The agent was as impressed and delighted as Schliemann's superiors, and shortly afterward, two Russian merchants descended on Amsterdam to attend the indigo auctions and to do business with *Mijnheer* Schliemann, the young marvel who could converse fluently with them in their native tongue. When Schliemann told them of the difficulty of obtaining books in Russian, they presented him with a copy of poems by Pushkin, who had died five years earlier and whose work was deeply influenced by Lord Byron. Like Byron, Schliemann was destined to become one of Greece's national heroes.

In January 1846, two years after joining the Schroder firm (in the same year, Dostoevsky published his first novel and was soon exiled to the penal colony at Omsk where, he said, he lived like a "person buried underground)," Schroder dispatched Schliemann to St. Petersburg as their business agent with the understanding that he would earn a one and one-half percent commission on new business. Since the posting of an agent in Russia was a novelty, Schliemann shrewdly arranged, with the firm's permission, to act as a free lance for a host of other firms —Dutch, German, French, Italian, Brazilian, and, significantly, Turkish. Whenever he transacted business for his Turkish customers, his thoughts wandered to Asia Minor, Homer, and mythical Troy.

Schliemann arrived in St. Petersburg in the middle of the winter. This was the capital of Nicholas I, a confused figure who, with one hand, codified the laws of the Russian Empire, limited serfdom, and instituted financial reforms, and, with the other hand, reorganized and toughened the secret police, exiled anyone with independent political opinions, and ruthlessly suppressed civil liberties. He died in the midst of the Crimean War; some whispered that he poisoned himself.

As Schliemann sauntered along the Nevsky Prospekt, Gorkhovaya, and Prospekt Vozensensky, he viewed with awe the grand palace of the Czars, the famed statue of Peter the Great astride a horse, the Gate of Triumph, and other imposing landmarks. He stood in wonder before the immense Cathedral of St. Isaac, then being built under Nicholas' personal direction. In St. Petersburg, the cost of the church was a conversation piece. The Czar, it was said, was spending the unheard sum of $12 million on the edifice.

The repressive atmosphere in Russia notwithstanding, the seat of the czars was a gay city made up largely of members of the aristocracy, army officers, and officials; indeed, most of the population lived on independent incomes as absentee landlords. The men outnumbered the women by as much as 150 to one. The number of illegitimate births was said to be ten times higher than in the rest of Russia (about 250 per 1,000 births), and the Russians boasted to Schliemann that this figure was on a par with that of Paris.

In the mating game, however, Schliemann possessed an advantage. There were few foreign residents in the Russian capital and almost none of them spoke Russian. Of medium stature, slim, impeccably dressed in the latest Western fashion, starry-eyed, youthful, friendly, a bit bombastic, perhaps, Schliemann was an object of curiosity among the ladies as well as the men. Not only was his command of the Russian language a marked advantage, but he was absolutely apolitical, a factor which impressed the "Third Divison," as Nicholas' secret political police was called.

Nor did he permit the snow to melt underfoot after he settled in. In those days, it was frequently said that St. Petersburg was the head of Russia and Moscow its heart. Beyond palace cabals, St. Petersburg possessed little to attract writers, artists, and intellectuals. These groups preferred Moscow, and young Schliemann lost little time in introducing himself to this "other Russia." No sooner had he satisfied his curiosity about St. Petersburg than he climbed aboard his first open sleigh and made the arduous forty-six hour, 400-mile journey to Moscow "with the wind and frost beating into my face." He reported to his superiors, with a sense of awe, that as he neared Moscow "the mercury in the thermometer at the relay station was frozen." As usual, Schliemann indulged in a bit of poetic exaggeration; mercury freezes at $-38.9°$ C, and it was not *that* cold. But he made his point.

The young German was an immediate social and business success. In Holland he had acquired the knack of adapting himself to foreign surroundings. Now a seasoned traveler, in Russia, known in the West as a dark and brooding country—100 years later, Russia was still described as a riddle wrapped in a mystery inside an enigma—Schliemann met, matched, and mastered the Russians in their own formidable geographical and psychological interior.

To his utter amazement, within a short time, "far exceeding the most sanguine expectations of my employers and myself," he wrote, he developed a flourishing business and found himself in "practically an independent position," the *sine qua non* before he and Minna married and set out in search of Troy.

Now twenty-five, he hastened to write a friend of the Meincke family to "beg for Minna at once for me in marriage." Eleven years of toil and hardship had elapsed since their last chance embrace. They would compensate for the lost years by sharing their future together. Schliemann was in a mood of ecstasy. Minna and the lost citadel were near at hand.

The reply from Mecklenburg shattered him. "The greatest disaster which could have befallen me," he said. Minna had given up hope of hearing from him and had just wed a Mecklenburg farmer and settled down at Friedland. Schliemann, in his own word, was "horrified." Suddenly and painfully, he realized that his pursuit of Minna had a phantomlike quality. "It often happens to us in our sleep," he said. "We dream we are pursuing an object and we never catch it because as often as we reach out it escapes us again."

Was this also true of Troy? Was Troy another will-o'-the-wisp? Would it, too, forever elude his outstretched grasp?

Schliemann plunged into despair, a despondency which lasted outwardly for months and, he confided in a letter to his elder sister, inwardly for years.

Schliemann sought release from his misery as he did in Amsterdam, "by unremitting work." For good measure, partly in revenge against his betrayal and partly in the hope of erasing Minna from his thoughts, he played the St. Petersburg field. He attended a seemingly endless array of receptions, dinner parties, and balls; boasted to his father of his conquests, was briefly engaged to "an adorable creature"; consumed the finest caviar—imported by the Russians from the Hudson River across the far Atlantic—and drank the strongest vodka. He became one of the most sought-after bachelors in the Czar's domain. Yet despite the social whirl, the inner Schliemann remained as he had always been, a man searching for an ideal mate with whom to share his dream of Troy.

While his love affair with Minna foundered, his commercial transactions flourished, as he conceded, "to an astonishing degree." Only a few years earlier, Schliemann did not possess a kopeck; yet, in his first year in Russia, as an opener, his savings grew to forty thousand dollars. Thereafter, he became Russia's leading indigo dealer and his profits came, in Homer's phrase, "as thick as leaves and blooms in summer." Although he remained in Schroder's employ for eleven years, he established—with their permission—his own global trading empire. As his commercial network expanded, he shrewdly invested surplus profits in Brazilian rubber, Parisian real estate, Indian tea, American cotton and railroads, Cuban sugar and tobacco, and Dutch spices. Each time, he accumulated a new fortune. Each time, he fortified his independent position. And each time he moved him closer to his ultimate objective—Troy.

Over the years, he emerged as a familiar figure on the Continental scene—at home in Paris, London, and Rome, as well as in Amsterdam, Hamburg, and Moscow. Like Ulysses, "many cities did he visit, and many were the nations with whose manners and customs he was acquainted."

He found London too dull and inhibited; Paris, too lively and uninhibited. Amsterdam had "a peculiar charm to me." Wherever he went, he put up a "brave show," as he called it. His showmanship was deceptive. Public relations, we would call it today. He stayed in the finest hotels but always in the least expensive suite, usually on the top floor (the elevator was still to be perfected). He ate in the most expensive restaurants, and always ordered the special of the day. Despite his growing wealth, as he himself observed, "I continued to observe the utmost economy." He never shed the memory of his "hapless and humble origins." But as a corollary, while he rebuffed those who sought a handout, he liberally dispensed money and gifts on family and friends and on people he felt in need, mindful of the generosity of the Texel islanders, Wendt and his friends in Hamburg, and others who helped him along the way.

For twenty years, until the age of forty-seven, he assayed the role of merchant prince. Yet during those years, Troy was near the surface. If he was not memorizing Fénélon in French and Russian, he was reading and rereading the ancient Greek writers; on his periodic visits abroad, he spent his leisure hours at museums. In London, for example, the British Museum, with its dazzling collection of antiquities from Greece, Rome, and Egypt, intrigued him, he said, "more than anything I have yet seen."

Yet obsessed as he was with things Greek, he studiously avoided learning Greek. His first objective on the road to Troy was to acquire financial independence, and he never permitted himself to forget this priority. Shrewdly, he recognized his weakness. Openly, he expressed the fear that if he learned Greek, hc would probably do so only at the expense of his commercial enterprises. The Greek language fascinated and haunted him. But he perceived that the study of Greek would, in turn, lead to Homer, not only Homer in modern Greek but Homer in its original tongue—ancient Greek. Once he embarked along this path, he would lose touch with reality.

In a letter to his father, Schliemann acknowledged that from Amsterdam to Ankershagen people envied his climb to the summit of the mercantile world and yet, he solemnly observed, "I have rarely been so discontented."

"Does happiness lie in the reichthaler?" he asked. "Does happiness lie in a fine house? Does happiness lie in fine food? Does happiness lie in a fine wine cellar? No. Indeed, not."

His manifest destiny notwithstanding, during these lonely years, Heinrich Schliemann immersed himself in the unpoetic world whose standard was gold. If gold was a measure of success, he would be successful. He matched wits with the most ruthless capitalists of the nineteenth century and was ruthless himself as the occasion demanded.

Before turning his back on Russia, on gold, and on the contemporary world, Heinrich Schliemann amassed a fortune of more than $18,000,000. The figure is an educated guess. The point, however, is that Schliemann was a character out of Alger before Horatio Alger set his first line to paper in 1867 and created the format of luck and pluck for the more than 100 books he wrote, which sold an estimated 30 million copies. Schliemann, of course, acquired his millions in an age before the erosion of the dollar's purchasing power, before the demands of an urbanized, industrialized society gave rise to a concept of the graduated income tax and the welfare state. In today's terms, Schliemann was probably worth, conservatively, tens of millions of dollars when he abandoned the counting house for the spade and pickax.

The turning point in Schliemann's acquisition of wealth, the event which transformed him into a multimillionaire, was the Crimean War. In 1853, Czar Nicholas I, whom Schliemann by then dramatically called "my Czar," described Turkey as "the sick man of Europe." The Czar ordered an operation. One of the prizes at stake in the Russo-Turkish confrontation was control of the Hellespont, just as it had been during the Trojan War. Britain, which then ruled the waves, allied herself with Turkey to maintain the status quo. The Royal Navy imposed a blockade on Russian ports, including St. Petersburg. In a maneuver designed to break the blockade, Schliemann and several other daring and enterprising merchants ordered large shipments of war materiel for delivery at Memel, the neutral Prussian port, for transshipment overland to Russia. On the eve of war, Schliemann invested his entire savings in the scheme.

"All my life I shall remember the morning of October 4, 1854," he later wrote. En route by carriage from Amsterdam to the Baltic port, he was crushed to learn that "the whole city of Memel had been consumed on the previous day by a fearful conflagration." At Memel, the worst rumors were borne out.

"The city," he said, "resembled an immense graveyard on which blackened walls and chimneys stood out like tombstones, mournful monuments of the fragility of human things." Memel looked like his beloved Troy after it was sacked and burned.

Distraught, Schliemann ran among the smoldering ruins in search of his shipping agent. Finding him amid the rubble of a burned warehouse, he anxiously inquired about his shipment. The agent pointed to the smoldering embers. "There," he said.

"The blow was tremendous," Schliemann recalled. Nine years of labor in Russia lay charred. "I was ruined," he said.

He consoled himself that, at least, unlike others, he was

free of debt. "I had no debts to pay," he explained, "for it was only the beginning of the Crimean War, and business being then very unsafe, I had bought for cash."

That evening, as a depressed, sullen, and solemn Schliemann prepared to catch the mail coach for St. Petersburg, he recounted his misfortune to other passengers when a bystander asked his name. "Schliemann," he said laconically.

"Schliemann!" exclaimed the stranger. "In all Memel, only Schliemann's merchandise survived the great fire!"

"For some minutes," for the first time in his life, the articulate Schliemann confessed, "I was speechless. The sudden transition from profound fright to great joy is difficult to bear without tears," he said. "It seemed incredible that I alone should have escaped from the universal ruin."

The fire had originated in the northern quarter of the city and was spread by a northerly gale. Schliemann's shipment, which filled the holds of two square-riggers, was stored only a couple of yards north of where the conflagration started and therefore was protected by the same northerly winds which destroyed everyone else's goods.

"My goods having thus been preserved," Schliemann said, "I speedily sold them to great advantage. I turned the money over and over again."

And, he should have added, "over and over and over and over again." With the windfall, Schliemann doubled his capital in a single year. Wily as ever, Schliemann was wary of revealing the details and, despite the tons of paper he left behind for future biographers in the form of correspondence, notebooks, diaries, and manuscripts, he left few clues about his role as war profiteer other than to confirm that he engaged "in a large business in war materiel"—nitrates, sulphur, and lead. "I was able to realize large profits," he said. He made no mention of gunrunning, although he hinted at the nature of his business in a letter to his father in which he said that his role as war profiteer ran against his grain, which it probably did. Self-deceptively, however, he consoled himself that the money amassed from mayhem would be spent ultimately on a great and noble purpose, the discovery of Troy. His rationalization paralleled that of a contemporary who, like himself, was largely self-taught, lived for a time in St. Petersburg, and died, like Schliemann, in Italy, a guilt-ridden merchant of death who expressed his hope in mankind's future by establishing a peace prize—Alfred Nobel.

There is, whispers aside, a fragment of evidence which points to the nature of his operations. Some years later, in 1871, after he withdrew from trafficking in arms and from other "speculations," as he called his commercial activities, and had embarked on his mission in life—the discovery of Troy—he received a letter from an arms dealer. The original letter does not appear to exist, but a segment of Schliemann's reply does. The reply begins: "I was very happy indeed to hear today of you through Mr. Gustav Schoeller of Paris, who offers me a joint-account operation in old French rifles. . . . But since I retired from business in spring 1864 my speculations are [now] purely of a scientific nature."

This paragraph was written seven months after the conclusion of the Franco-German War of 1870–1871. Apparently, his old associates thought Schliemann could assist in the disposal of obsolete military hardware to his newly acquired Aegean contacts, perhaps the Greeks or the Turks, or more probably, a combination of both.

But Schliemann was not merely a gunrunner; far from it. Essentially, he was, as he described himself, a speculator. Although uninterested in politics, Schliemann was a voracious newspaper reader. If he read of a serious fire—commonplace in an age of wooden construction—he tried to corner the lumber market nearest to the great conflagration. If a war appeared in the offing, he speculated in war materials—not just guns but also raw materials. For example, when he correctly surmised that America moved to the edge of civil war, Schliemann stockpiled cotton in a belief that the North, with control of the sea, would blockade the South, a primary cotton producer.

Schliemann speculated in anything and everything from real estate to printing paper. As a speculator, he indulged freely in the acceptable "dirty tricks" of the business world. Once again, however, he reveals only the tip of the iceberg. A letter from America, for example, urged him to plunge into American commerce, although it observed that "the banking business in New York is no doubt most advantageous if one is well acquainted with the ropes—the Yankees are most selfish and smart, and it takes a stranger some time to be well-versed in all their tricks, which are connected with that line of business." It was this letter, among others, which influenced his first journey to America. Schliemann had supreme confidence in his ability to play the market anywhere as well as anyone, either above or below the table, as conditions warranted.

During the Crimean War, for the first time, Schliemann abandoned his studies. Before the outbreak of hostilities, he studied the Scandinavian tongues and could speak and write fluently in Danish, Norwegian, and Swedish. He also broadened his Slavic base by adding Polish and Slovakian to his Russian. But his program of self-education halted during the war.

"I was so overwhelmed with work," he said with an air of genuine dismay, "that I could not even read the newspapers, far less a book." His problem, at the time, was typical of many men who make history—they are generally too busy to read or write it.

From the day of his arrival in Russia as Schroder's agent, Schliemann maintained a regular correspondence with his family—father, brothers, and sisters. Although he plied them with gifts and took an active interest in their lives, he never felt the impulse to revisit Mecklenburg. Indeed, for twenty years he conspicuously avoided it on his journeys by coach from St. Petersburg to Amsterdam. He feared, of course, another chance meeting with Minna, a meeting which would embarrass her and discomfort him. Then, too, there were the endless rounds of gossip concerning his father's sordid affairs. Clearly, Mecklenburg belonged to the past. Once, on a return trip to Russia by sea, from the deck of the ship, he could faintly make out the Mecklenburg seaboard and found himself "uninterested" in his native duchy. He was also contemptuous of it. He described the lighthouse at Travemunde as "little more than a smokestack," although, in his youth, he considered the structure the equivalent of the Pharaoh's lighthouse at Alexandria, one of the eight wonders of the ancient world.

Nonetheless, he maintained intimate contacts with Mecklenburgers. Three of his sisters married—Doris, the second, to a Mecklenburg official; Wilhelmine, the third, to a professor from Hesse-Cassel; and Louise, the youngest, to a Mecklenburg teacher. Elsie, the eldest, who bore the brunt of her mother's unhappiness, as noted earlier, was the only Schliemann child never to wed.

As for the two brothers, Paul, the baby of the family, who never lost his love for Mecklenburg's rural setting, was killed in an accident at the age of twenty-five. Louis, cut in Heinrich's mold—imaginative, dramatic, boastful, and independent-minded—set out for the American Wild West to duplicate his brother's success in the Russian Wild East. For a time, Heinrich and the family lost contact with Louis, who, like his older brother, was determined to establish his own independent position.

Suddenly, in 1850, Louis turned up in California, a wealthy, lusty young man who had amassed a fortune in the Gold Rush. In a letter to St. Petersburg, Louis recounted his adventures in California and urged Heinrich to join him in Sacramento "where the streets are paved with gold." Shortly thereafter, an official letter, bearing the strange imprint of The Great Bear Republic, advised him, as next of kin—in accordance with Louis' wishes—that his brother died of typhus and left behind "a large estate" which would require his presence to settle. The estate was valued at $350,000. Like Paul, Louis died at the age of twenty-five.

With his enterprises in Russia prospering, his curiosity about America whetted even as a grocer's apprentice, and anxious to insure that his brother was properly buried and, of course, that Louis' estate was settled in the family interest, Schliemann booked passage for the New World.

The Russian period of his life was sandwiched between two momentous voyages to the New World.

During his Russo-American interregnum, Schliemann wandered, like Odysseus, for almost twenty years, and appeared to move further and further afield from Troy. Yet, as Homer phrased it, "the omens were good for him and he would win an imperishable name among mankind." Despite the outward appearance of drift, as Schliemann himself observed, his hand was on the tiller. "In the midst of the bustle of business [and personal affairs], I never forgot Troy or the agreement I had made with my father and Minna to excavate it."

# V

⎍⎍⎍⎍⎍⎍⎍

⎍⎍⎍⎍⎍⎍⎍

# The Gold Coast

*I would rather be a paid servant in a poor
man's house and be above ground
than king of kings among the
dead.*

The Odyssey, BOOK XI

FOLLOWING AN OVERLAND journey to Rotterdam, the young
Schliemann crossed the English Channel and booked passage
aboard the *Atlantic*, "the most magnificent and grandest
steamer in all the world," one of the dazzling hybrids which
spanned the ages of sail and steam. A three-masted square-
rigger, she boasted "more than nine hundred horses' power,"
Schliemann wrote in his diary.

Before the vessel weighed anchor, with a few days to spare,
Schliemann whirled through England like a tornado: The
Thames was "majestic"; Kent presented, "as far as the eye
could reach, nicely cultivated fields intersected with neat looking villages and splendid cities"; the Crystal Palace in Hyde
Park, built almost entirely of iron and glass, a forerunner of the
stainless steel–goldfish-bowl skyscrapers of the contemporary
scene, was "stupendous"; Westminster Abbey, "divine"—no
pun intended; the Zoological Garden, "immense" and even included a hippopotamus.

Aeolus, the god of the winds, however, pursued Schliemann at sea with the same relentlessness that he pursued

Ulysses during his odyssey. As during the voyage of the *Doro-thea,* the cruise of the *Atlantic* turned into a sea-borne night-mare.

As they left Liverpool on December 28, a gale blew with such intensity that the pilot was unable to return ashore. The storm never abated. In mid-Atlantic, a mountainous wave struck the ship on the starboard with such force that the main-shaft broke. Without power, the vessel broached and threat-ened to turn turtle. The skipper, however, brought her about and, with jury-rigged sails aloft, she ran before the westerly winds and retraced her passage back to the British Isles, arriv-ing at the end of January, almost a month to the day of her departure. For the second time, Schliemann's voyage to the New World ended in failure. Schliemann himself thought that perhaps he was, after all, a Jonah, as the captain of the *Doro-thea* had laughingly suggested.

Perseverance, however, was an essential element in Schliemann's make-up. His ego never admitted failure. Un-daunted, he booked passage to America for a third time, em-barking from Liverpool eight days later aboard the *Africa.* After six days at sea, the *Africa* was caught up in a gale. By now, Schliemann despaired that he would ever complete the transoceanic voyage and perhaps, like many of the heroes of the Aegean past, he would "vanish beneath the dark blue wa-ters."

But at last, the storm calmed and they were sailing before a fair wind. A fortnight later, the New World beckoned. When the *Africa* was within three miles of "Zandy-hock," Schliemann's quaint, phonetic spelling of Sandy Hook, the sandspit guardian of New York's Lower Bay, the ship fired its cannons and sent rockets aloft "to give to the inhabitants to understand that we brought some highly joyful intelligence."

In an age without radio and telegraph—Cyrus Field would not lay his first cable across the Atlantic for another eight years —the intelligence, of course, was that the *Atlantic* had not vanished beneath the dark blue waters of her namesake.

As Schliemann rode through New York for the first time, he heard the newsboys shout from the street corners: "Extra! Read all about it. *Atlantic* is safe." In his diary, Schliemann noted that the newspapers, which cost two cents, sold briskly at fifty cents, probably a Schliemannesque exaggeration.

Already New York, in that kerosene-lamp and horse-and-buggy era, had established herself as the premier city of the new continent. Putting up at the Astor, "the grandest and most gigantic hotel I ever saw," Schliemann was favorably surprised to find the notoriously uncultured Americans at least ate well. "I find the American table extremely comfortable and tasteful," he wrote with an air of surprise. He apparently consumed the entire menu. "In the morning, I take ham and eggs, buckwheat cakes, fried hominy and chocolate," he said. "At dinner, oyster pies, soup, roast beef, roasted turkey, game, and pudding." At six in the afternoon, he was served "weak tea" and, at eleven in the evening, a supper of cold turkey and ham.

Few New Yorkers today would recognize the New York of Schliemann's day—"a nice, clean town"—but the skyscrapers were already stretching to the heavens. "The city has many, many elegant and even colossal buildings," he said with wonder. At the time, several buildings soared more than a dozen stories above the pavement. Yet the city lacked the grandeur of the great European capitals, he felt. Broadway impressed him, however, as "the broadest and most elegant street in town" and he discovered the theater district, but found that the "bustling spirit of the Americans does not permit them to think of theaters." He was favorably impressed to find that, unlike Europe, there was no prompter in the American theater. He visited the museums but found P. T. Barnum's museum, the most popular place in town, filled with "ludicrous humbug." The Yankees, he found, also took great delight in Negro minstrels. Misinterpreting American parochialism, he ascribed the lack of foreign newspapers in the Astor's reading room to "a fierce sense of patriotism."

Like any healthy young man in a strange land, the twenty-nine-year-old Schliemann engaged in the wholesome pastime of girl-watching. American women, he felt, were "beautiful and symmetrical at sixteen and eighteen and old and worn at twenty-two." In general, he discovered appealing qualities among New Yorkers. They were frank and communicative "and regarding industry and assiduity, there is hardly a people

on the earth's surface who surpass them." Even in 1850, New
York had developed a unique, pressure-paced lifestyle.

In that period, there were two routes to California—for
many, then as now, the Promised Land. Both were arduous,
both perilous: By overland stage or by sea and the rain forest of
the Isthmus of Panama—this was almost a half century before
the conquest of yellow fever and the opening of the Canal.
Schliemann's misadventures at sea notwithstanding, he chose
to put to sea again. The next vessel, the *Crescent City,* was
scheduled to leave for Panama in a month. A born tourist in an
age before tourism developed into a major industry—
Schliemann confessed that he possessed an "irresistible desire
to travel and to see the world"—he spent the time compiling an
American Baedeker punctuated by de Tocquevillean commentaries.

Schliemann took the train to Washington and discovered,
as early as 1852, what most Americans know today, that American railroads "do not take the least notice as to convenience and
accommodations for passengers." A novelty impressed him:
The seats in American coaches were two abreast and they
could be "turned over" so that four people could sit together in
a group. The train stopped overnight at Baltimore, and
Schliemann stuffed himself with oysters for supper and breakfast the following morning. Years later, at Troy, when he discovered oyster shells buried beneath Priam's Pergamus, his
thoughts flashed back to his Chesapeake Bay table.

He found Washington a delightful capital, laid out to
French specifications, and from the gallery of the Capitol
building he listened to the "powerful speeches" of Henry Clay
and Stephen Douglas. At issue, the slave question. Irresistibly,
the United States was being drawn into the vortex of civil war.

No visit to Washington by a distinguished foreigner—and
Schliemann, the youthful merchant with strong commercial
ties in Russia and Holland, considered himself of that distinc-
tion—was complete without a visit to the White House. The
residence of the thirteenth chief of state, Millard Fillmore, impressed Schliemann as "a most magnificent mansion." More
impressive than the architecture to his European eye, in one of
his rare political comments—Schliemann was almost com-

pletely apolitical—he observed that "there are no sentinels to watch and bar the doors and there exist no ceremonies to which the stranger has to submit to be presented to the first magistrate." The informality of the capital also surprised him and appealed to him as compared to the feudal-bound Europe of which he, a citizen of the Grand Duchy of Mecklenburg-Schwerin, was so familiar. Although Schliemann wrote in his diary that he spent one and one-half hours with Fillmore, there is no such record in the Presidential log; more likely than not, he simply joined the crowd which regularly paid its respects to the President, a custom established by Andrew Jackson and which has its counterpart today with the regular "open house" hours at the White House for visitors (sans the President).

After Washington, Schliemann visited Mount Vernon, astride the Potomac River ("Washington's mansion is a plain building"), and then Philadelphia ("regularly built, neater and cleaner than New York"). The archaeologist-in-the-making was already developing an acute sense of observation and an enthusiasm for travel and comparative studies which he would put to full use during the excavation of Troy.

Before embarking on the *Crescent City*, Schliemann, the reader and student, browsed through the bookshops of Greenwich Village and boarded the vessel with an armload of new books, including three which had just been published—Melville's *Moby Dick*, Hawthorne's *House of the Seven Gables*, and S. G. Goodrich's *The History of All Nations from the Earliest Periods to the Present Time*, the American equivalent of the Jerrer of Schliemann's youth.

As the sails of the *Crescent City* bellied out with the wind, in Homer "the ship flew across the deep blue water and the foam hissed against her bows as she sped onward." On deck, Schliemann opened Goodrich and was fascinated to read about the probability that Troy existed.

"Many learned and sagacious critics have denied the reality of the Trojan War," Goodrich wrote, "and regarded the poems of Homer as having no more truth at their foundation than John Bunyan's *Pilgrim's Progress.*"

But Goodrich took sharp issue with the critics and heatedly argued that "the reality of the Trojan War must be admitted."

He assailed the doubters for declaring Troy a myth "against strong evidence," a phrase which agitated Schliemann. Goodrich wrote:

> According to the rules of sound criticism, very cogent arguments should be required to induce us to reject, as a mere fiction, an historical tradition so ancient, so universally received, so definite, and so interwoven with the whole of the national recollections of the ancient Greeks, as that of the Trojan War.

Goodrich conceded, "However, beyond this historical fact, we can scarcely venture a step with certainty." After all, nobody had yet uncovered a shred of proof, not a sliver of tangible evidence that Troy ever existed—not a stone, not a potsherd, nothing.

Goodrich's commentary reminded Schliemann not only of Christmas past but also of his compact with Minna. Even in the New World, a fierce debate continued over the question of whether or not Troy ever existed. Why do the overwhelming majority of scholars insist that Troy was a myth, a beautiful, poetic myth to be sure, but nonetheless a myth? Why can't the experts see, like Goodrich, that Troy *must* have existed? In Schliemann's mind, there was only one way to resolve this controversy—somebody, spade and pickax in hand, must set out to uncover the debris of ages and restore Troy to the light. Only then would the argument against its existence be silenced.

For a man destined to find Troy and to establish modern archaeology as we know it today, however, Schliemann's personal odyssey continued to sweep him further and further from his true objective, or so it seemed. Now he was on a voyage to the tropics, as Schliemann described it in his diary, "the fatherland of the vegetable world," on the other side of the planet. When would he set out on the path leading to Troy? Why must the path be so circuitous? Perhaps he consoled himself by rereading *The Odyssey*—Schliemann was never without a copy of Homer in his pocket, the pages of *The Iliad* and *The Odyssey* so worn and underlined by pencil that they could be read only by someone who had memorized the verses in their entirety, as Schliemann had.

On arriving in Panama, Schliemann discovered that it was
an anthropological paradise and a sociological nightmare. The
rain forest, on the overland journey across the Isthmus, was by
saddle mule and canoe, "most surely one of the most interesting
journeys that I ever made in my life." As he crossed the spiny
Talamanca which are part of the Andean-Rocky mountain
chain, he was so absorbed in the heavy, moss-encased atmosphere of Spanish America that he lapsed into Spanish in his
diary (just as his notations on his travels in the United States
were written in English).

Schliemann, like others before him, found the jungle a
heaven and hell. From atop a steep mountain, involuntarily
shuddering as he looked down into the valley which lay two
thousand feet below, he viewed the grand majesty of the tropical world—coconut palms lifting their gorgeous tops to the
clouds, orange and lemon trees in profusion, butterflies the size
of pigeons in blue and yellow hues, birds of magnificent plum-
age, thousands of monkeys "from one foot in size to a man's
height" playing about and crying in the trees. The green man-
sions exercised Schliemann's penchant for hyperbole.

The tropics, he wrote, "sing the praise of the Almighty, an
immense Eden in which the descendants of Adam and Eve
seem to have retained the manners and customs of their primitive forefathers." So much for heaven.

As for hell, on a less romantic level, he complained, "I
perspire as if I am sitting in a Russian steam bath." He also
complained of the incessant rain, yellow fever, diarrhea, dysentery, ague, and, "above all, the terrors of myriads of mos-
quitos—like a crazy man, have I frequently weltered in the mud
without being able to free myself of this most horrible of
plagues."

The impact of the jungle on the people who dwelled within
it also disturbed him. He found the people a collection of races
and colors—Spaniards, Indians, and Negroes of pure and
mixed blood of every possible combination, a genetic wonderland. Yet all were bound by a common denominator. "Their
chief characteristic," the hard-driving Schliemann wrote with
disgust, "is a horrible laziness." The people, he discovered,
were at their happiest lying in a hammock or eating and drink-

ing. Their villages and towns were, in Schliemann's eyes, "miserable, dirty places." No Protestant work ethic here. A stickler for cleanliness and industry, Schliemann was repulsed by idleness, slothfulness, indolence, and sluggishness. What the tropics needed was a Reformation. Or did it?

To his great relief, on the Pacific Coast of Panama, from where Balboa had gazed out across the placid ocean three centuries earlier, Schliemann resumed the trip to California aboard the steamer *Oregon* whose berths, he sighed, are "very nice and clean."

The ship cruised northward along the "beautiful Mexican coast," "miserable little San Diego," "picturesque Santa Barbara," and at journey's end, the harbor of San Francisco, "sheltered by huge mountains and large enough to contain all the fleets of the globe."

He viewed San Francisco with mixed emotions. Schliemann wrote:

> In no country of the world have I found so much selfishness and such immense love of money as in this Eldorado. With an American, money goes over everything in the world, and the desire to attain it as fast as possible brings forth his indescribable, his boundless energy. His enterprising spirit, too hot for mature consideration, boldly goes ahead, and however frequently defeated by miscalculations, he as often tries to go ahead again. An American can never become daunted.

Yet for all his unconcealed envy and admiration for the industriousness of the "California Yankees," he also considered them, within the compass of the rush for gold, an unconscionable band of swindlers, liars, cheats, and sharpies. Gambling, to his horror, seemed to be the only relaxation of the day. The magnitude of the stakes and the number of casinos, "crowded with people, mostly miners, who lose here in a few minutes what they accumulate during years of privation," appalled him. So did the prices.

"Everything is very dear here," he said with untypical understatement. Eggs cost $1 *apiece* (he underlined the word in his diary); butter, $2 a pound; milk, $1 a bottle; veal, $1 a pound; beef—from the nearby Western range, and far better than at today's riotously inflated prices—as little as 30¢ a pound for a choice cut of steak.

From San Francisco, Schliemann set off for Sacramento and the mission which brought him to California. After much difficulty, he wrote his father, he found his brother's grave and gave the undertaker fifty dollars to erect a tombstone on the site bearing the Schliemann name. He also settled Louis' estate although, in his diary, as so often the case in all important financial matters, Schliemann was secretive and provided no information as to the scope of the financial settlement. But it was substantial: between a quarter- and a half-million dollars.

Heinrich recalled his brother's repeated advice that he deal himself a California hand. Schliemann, in a characteristically thorough manner, which was later reflected at Troy, decided to make a firsthand inspection of the gold fields to determine the authenticity of the Gold Rush. It was, he discovered with astonishment, genuine. "Even in the mud which hung to my boots I saw many particles of the precious metal," he said. "I am fully satisfied as to the enormous wealth of this country." Money was here for the taking, for the making.

With his excellent European contacts, Schliemann arranged to act as the Sacramento agent for the London house of Rothschild. Settling down in Sacramento, he opened a gold dust bank and, within a year, boasted that "there is barely one in a hundred thousand who has done as well as myself." Schliemann's gift for business, his gift for the acquisition of gold, was no less strong in the New World than in the Old World nor, as it later developed, in the Ancient World.

Like gold rushes everywhere, the California madness had a cosmopolitan overlay, drawing men from all parts of the globe. As in Amsterdam and later St. Petersburg, Schliemann's trump was his facility with language. Unlike other gold dust bankers, he conversed fluently in a dozen languages.

"My bank is jammed, crammed and rammed full of people from different nations and I have to speak all the day long in eight languages," he wrote in his diary. On some occasions, he spoke in more than eight languages. "In fact," he continued, "if I knew a hundred languages, it would not be sufficient to speak to every one in his native language."

Like a chessmaster who plays a dozen games simultaneously, Schliemann carried on different conversations at the same time, or so it appeared to his bewildered but grateful clients. English, of course. French, Dutch, Spanish, Portuguese, Finnish. Finnish? Yes, Finnish. Russian? Assuredly. Polish? Swedish? Ah, German? Naturally.

Oddly, Schliemann never displayed serious interest in East Asian languages, although his customers included many Chinese, largely from Canton and the Kwantung-Fukien coast of China. Later, on a world cruise, he visited all the East Asian capitals and still failed to develop mastery in any of the major languages—Chinese, Malay, Japanese or Hindustani, although he filled several copybooks with Hindustani homework. But later, in West Asia, as he searched for Troy, he added Turkish, Arabic, and Persian to his linguistic accomplishments. And in preparation for his work at Troy, he added ancient and modern Greek and Latin. In all probability, his disinterest in Chinese and other Far Eastern languages was the result of a lack of motivation. Motivated, he was driven to all sorts of apparently impossible accomplishments.

Whatever the case, the United Nations of the Gold Rush flocked to his doors and his banking enterprise flourished. In his diary, in the style of a budding sociologist, he cataloged the people with whom he did business. Schliemann privately observed that the Chinese were "honest and industrious"; the Mexicans "lazy and false"; Peruvians and Chileans "good natured and very industrious, particularly the latter"; Polynesians (Kanakers) "extremely lazy and always robbing."

Banking was a dangerous occupation in the Wild West atmosphere of California in the fifties. Schliemann and his two clerks armed themselves day and night with "Colt's revolving pistols, each of which can kill five men in as many seconds." An early riser, he awoke at daybreak. At 6:00 A.M., he opened his bank and kept the doors open until ten in the evening. "Every moment I expected to be murdered or robbed." He longed for the "tranquility of Russia," he said, where "I can sleep in my bed without any fear for my life or property."

In that lusty, brawling era, men usually died from lead poisoning or of yellow fever. Not once but three times, accompanied by chills, vomiting, and yellow rashes over his body, Schliemann came down with the fever. These bouts gradually drew him to the edge of death; on the third occasion, he realized that he must turn his back on California and her gold "for I feel I should not survive if I have another attack."

But what of Troy? If he perished amid the gold-strewn fields of the Pacific Coast, he was arrogant enough to believe that Troy might never be brought to light. As he wrote a friend in a private letter, of this he was convinced since his boyhood: "My mission in life is to find Troy and to prove it existed."

During his California sojourn, Schliemann never lost faith in his ultimate goal. The Great San Francisco Fire of June 4, 1851, is a case in point.

Arriving in the city that evening from Sacramento, Schliemann was asleep for perhaps a quarter of an hour, "when I was awakened by loud cries in the street: Fire! Fire!" He looked out the window and saw the hotel across the street aflame. No sooner did he run out of his hotel when it, too, caught fire as San Francisco's fierce "candlestick" winds spread the flames across the city. People panicked. Buildings collapsed. Iron railings melted in the intense heat.

As before at critical junctures in his life, good fortune guided him safely through the wall of flames and to the protection of Telegraph Hill. From this vantage point, he viewed the conflagration below. The roar of the firestorm, the exploding gunpowder in the town's arsenals, the crash of stone walls, and the cries of the people gave rise to the "spectacle of an immense city burning on a dark night." But what did Schliemann really see in the flames: San Francisco or Troy? The scene below him was a duplicate of Jerrer's illustration. It was a replay of the scene enacted 4,000 years earlier when the Achaean hosts emerged from their gift-bearing wooden horse, sacked noble Troy, and put it to the torch.

His repeated bouts with fever, "the enormous scale of my business and my large profits," and the burning of San Francisco confirmed to him that he must quit America. Schliemann was unaware of it at the time, but his firsthand observations of what happened to a city racked by fire—first Memel and then San Francisco—served him handsomely as he uncovered the origins of Aegean civilization and tried to pick up the pieces and put together the story of the Trojan War.

In the spring of 1852, Schliemann turned his back on the gold of California and retraced his steps across the Isthmus of Panama, en route to New York and Europe. The setting in Panama was unchanged: a poisonous climate, yellow fever, dysentery, "bad accommodations and stinking victuals"—yet faster and safer than the overland stage. He and his companions feasted on an "immense lizzard"—iguana—and were so hungry that they consumed it with an appetite "as if it had been roasted turkey." Several of his companions, worn out by the pursuit of gold, died on the return journey. The novelty of the rain forest had dissolved, and Schliemann and his companions "sank below the level of a beast," as he described it. They became listless, unkempt, lethargic, and disinterested in the world around them—like the Spaniards, Indians, and Negroes whom they had righteously criticized on their first trek through the jungle.

"We became so familiar with death," Schliemann wrote:

> . . . that it lost for us all its terror and we began to like it and to look upon it as a limitation on our suffering. Thus, we laughed and amused ourselves at the convulsions of the dying and crimes were perpetrated among us; crimes so terrible that now, at a later date, I cannot think of them without cold and trembling.

In pleasant weather, under ideal conditions, the sea-land New York to San Francisco run could be made in a month, give or take a day or two. Passengers departing from New York, for example, took a ship which was powered by sail and steam, for Chagres, Panama—a voyage of about ten days. From Chagres, they moved by dugout canoe and mule across the jungles of the Isthmus to Panama City—a trek of two or possibly three days. The run from Panama City to San Francisco, again under sail and steam, averaged eighteen days.

But the schedule was uncertain. The hurricane season in the Caribbean delayed sea traffic; time was lost in the rainy season when the trails across the Isthmus became impassable and the rivers, their banks swollen, turned unnavigable. But this was not all. If a connection was missed on either coast, the passengers huddled together on the fever-infested Panamanian shore an additional ten to eighteen days, waiting for a vessel. Being stuck in Panama City was scarcely bearable; at Chagres, unbearable. Accommodations were almost non-existent and food scarce at the latter port. Schliemann was stalled on the return journey and spent from April 26 to May 8, 1851, at Chagres waiting for a ship, "fully fourteen days in wet clothes . . . twelve days [camped] on a swamp, being night and day exposed to the rain which continued to fall upon us in torrents and against which we had no means to protect ourselves."

During this period, he wrote in his diary, "I lay more dead than alive." For a man recovering from repeated bouts with fever contracted in California, he was fortunate to survive this episode. Many of his fellow travelers, obviously, did not. Actually, Schliemann had missed his connection to New York by a few hours. The vessel weighed anchor at Chagres in midmorning and was well at sea by early afternoon. Schliemann arrived overland in late afternoon.

After California, New York was to Schliemann what Hamburg had been to the youth from Ankershagen. "New York! Oh! New York!" he wrote in his diary. "New York is a paradise for a man who comes from California."

The European within him surged to the surface. He promptly took the first available ship for England, which he now described affectionately as "Old England," a subconscious reflection of how rapidly he had aged and matured during his adventures in Panama and California. From London, he proceeded to Paris and, a man of means, there he soaked up the good life of the Old World as compared to the discomforts of the New World. When he tired of an "idle and dissolute life of Paris," he left for St. Petersburg. En route, for the first time in almost twenty years, he stopped briefly at Ankershagen and visited with family and friends. Fortunately, or perhaps otherwise, he never caught a glimpse of Minna. Visiting his childhood haunts, the secret treasure troves of Mecklenburg-Schwerin, "everything now appeared in miniature."

After America, Russia appeared as paradise lost. "This beautiful capital of Russia," he enthused. "This charming St. Petersburg. Nothing exceeds my joy to see myself here again." In the course of his journey, he completed his latest metamorphosis, from the robust adventurer of the California gold coast to the cultured German in the dazzling capital of all the Russias. The caviar was perfect. The vodka strong and good.

In St. Petersburg, his old friends received him with enthusiasm; among them, Catherine Lyschin, another "adorable creature," the niece of an extremely wealthy Russian merchant. He had met her briefly before his departure for the New World. During his Californian sojourn, in his mind and heart, Catherine gradually replaced Minna.

# VI

⎍⎍⎍⎍⎍⎍⎍

⎍⎍⎍⎍⎍⎍⎍

# The Lost Years

*It is fated that he should escape.*

The Iliad, BOOK XX

DESPITE THEIR VIRILITY and passionate nature, both Ernest Schliemann and his son Heinrich appeared to have shared a sense of sexual inadequacy or insecurity since both were attracted more often than not to young girls rather than young women. Heinrich Schliemann's affair with Catherine Lyschin is a case in point.

In 1850, four years before the Crimean War broke out, she captivated him. Catherine was sixteen at the time, Luise Schliemann's age when she married the Pastor. Impetuously, typically impatient and consuming, he proposed to her immediately. She rebuffed him roundly. However, on his return from the California gold coast two years later, with the jingle of nuggets in his pockets, she promptly revised her opinion of him.

After reaching St. Petersburg in July, Schliemann wrote his father jubilantly that "Catherine received me most kindly and everything appears to promise fair." Three months later, on October 12, 1852, they were wed.

During the first few months of their marriage, at least from

66

Schliemann's point of view, the marriage appeared destined for success. "I enjoy now all the comforts of a quiet domestic life," he wrote in his diary that snow-filled winter. He was, he said, the "happy husband of a Russian woman of great accomplishment, both of body and mind." For Schliemann, married life was two-dimensional, a union of bodies and minds. His infatuation with Catherine also turned into an infatuation with Russia and things Russian. Now he spoke of his friends as "my adopted Russian brethren"; the czar as "our Czar"; St. Petersburg as "our charming city." But their blissful relationship was short-lived as Schliemann, the romantic, slowly realized that Catherine was more interested in his money than in his body and mind. He pleaded with her to accompany him to the West on business trips, and promised her the keys to Paris, London, and Rome. But she preferred the isolation and insulation of Mother Russia and rarely ventured beyond its borders. She laughed at his childish obsession with Troy, and she took no interest in his linguistic accomplishments (since learning languages came so easily to him, he felt, like most people with a natural gift, that it should come just as easy to others).

Five days after their marriage, he wrote his father a joyful letter describing his bride as a model of perfection who "deserves great happiness." Eighteen months later, in a private letter to her, written during a business trip, he accused her of marrying him for his money. "You do not love me, you never did," he complained. "You have no sympathy for me. You refuse to share my joys and sorrows." In reply, she accused him of pinching the ruble, of possessing an explosive temper, and of being oversexed—probably a fair appraisal of his character and behavior.

Catherine, Schliemann confided to his eldest sister, drove him to despair and "to near madness."

Three years later, in 1855, she bore him a son, Serge, and thereafter turned him out of her bedroom. Her future was secure. From then on, their life was marred by daily recriminations and stormy encounters. He accused her of treating him "indifferently" and confessed that the two daughters she later bore him, Nadehsda and Natalya, were "forced out of her." By every measure, it was a wildly disastrous marriage.

Given his wealth, the unhappy connubial relationship cried out for divorce and a liberal, painless financial settlement. But divorce was almost unheard of in the Europe of his day. And for reasons of pride and loyalty, mixed with concern about the children, he bore the agony of the unhappy marriage —like his mother before him—for fifteen years before he turned his back permanently on her. Only then did he reorder his priorities: dissolve his commercial empire, renew the search for another Minna, and set out to fulfill his destiny, the discovery of Troy.

By 1858, six years after his return from the gold fields of America, the accumulation of a third fortune during the Crimean War, and his tormented marriage to Catherine Lyschin, Schliemann, unhappy and restless, wanted out—out of business, out of marriage, out of Russia.

Despite his intentions, however, he did not succeed in liquidating his business until 1863, and by then, he had amassed a fourth and final fortune—the largest of all—and he did so against his conscience, by profiteering during the American Civil War. Nor did he succeed in dissolving his marriage until six years later although, by then, it was a marriage in name only.

Thus, the period 1852–1869 was, in view of what lay ahead, his lost years.

For all his wealth, for all his popularity in the St. Petersburg circle of smart and clever people, Schliemann was a lonely man and, in this solitary interlude of his life, his loneliness descended to the lowest depths.

As in the past, Schliemann found relief from misery by throwing himself into unremitting work. From the beginning, he had avoided studying Greek, because he feared he would lose himself in that language. It would estrange him from the real world, an estrangement no practical businessman could afford. It was a genuine fear but now it no longer mattered. He wanted to escape from the counting house, from the ugliness of broken family life. Homer became his passage to freedom.

In 1856, as the Crimean War ended, Schliemann set vigorously to work on studying Greek. "Faithfully," he recalled, "I followed my old method."

But to his surprise, Greek proved more difficult for him than Russian, although he studied with two Greek teachers, one of whom, Theokletos Vimpos, was fated to play a significant role in Schliemann's later life. But, of course, Schliemann's definition of difficult defies the dictionary definition. In less than five months, he not only acquired a knowledge of modern, but ancient Greek as well, an astonishing feat.

Employing his old method, Schliemann purchased a modern Greek translation of *Paul et Virginia,* a familiar mentor, and read it through, comparing each and every word with its equivalent in the French original. When he completed this task, he knew at least one-half the Greek words the book contained. "After repeating the operation," he dryly observed, "I knew them all, or nearly so, without having lost a single minute by being obliged to use a dictionary." Thus, in his study of languages, as in his love life and business affairs, and later in his excavation of Troy, Schliemann always appeared in a hurry. He was always afraid, as he conceded, "to lose a single minute." In this sense, he was a man possessed by time and, inexplicably, by timeless Troy.

> In this manner it did not take me more than six weeks to master the difficulties of modern Greek. And I next applied myself to the ancient language of which in three months I learned sufficiently to understand some of the ancient authors, especially Homer, whom I read and re-read with the most lively enthusiasm.

Schliemann, wanderer and merchant, moving full circle, had again implanted his foot firmly on the road leading to Troy.

Thereafter, for the next two years, he occupied himself with reading the ancient literature of Greece, the bedrock of Western civilization—Aeschylus, Aristotle, Plato, Sophocles, Euripides, Aristophanes, Herodotus, Thucydides, and, above all, the poet who soared like an eagle above the rest, Homer. "I read the *Iliad* and *Odyssey* several times," he casually remarked as if they were the morning papers. And he read them in their original language, ancient Greek.

Always at loggerheads with the academicians, in studying

Greek, he took sharp issue with the language professors of his day. As for Greek grammar, he said, "I never lost my precious time in studying its rules," adding, by way of explanation: "I saw that boys, after being troubled and tormented for eight years and more in schools with the tedious rules of grammar, can nevertheless none of them write a letter in ancient Greek without making hundreds of atrocious blunders."

In his brusque manner of meeting a problem head-on to resolve it, he contended that a thorough knowledge of Greek grammar could only be obtained by practice, by reading the classics, and by committing choice pieces of them to memory. In sum, he learned ancient Greek as if it were a living language. This method, he said, was simple. Simple for Schliemann; it would be foolish for the average person to expect to master a foreign language as quickly as he did. Schliemann possessed a rare faculty for learning languages, but his method of self-teaching was not far removed from the modern way of teaching a language through tape recorders, plunging directly into the spoken word without regard for grammar—the method by which almost everyone learns his native tongue.

By the end of his self-styled, two-year cram course, he proclaimed: "I can write in ancient Greek with the greatest fluency on any subject I am acquainted with." He knew all the rules without ever studying them and whenever someone found an error in his Greek, "I immediately proved that I was right by merely reciting passages from the classics where the sentences employed by me occur."

Delving deeper into the origins of the glory that was Greece, Schliemann was drawn to the grandeur that was Rome. He embarked on an equally vigorous study of that other noble and dead language of Western civilization, Latin, whose study he had interrupted nearly twenty-five years earlier at the Gymnasium at Neu Strelitz. Schliemann again addressed himself to Latin as he did to ancient Greek, as if it were a living language. "Now that I knew both modern and ancient Greek," he said with delight, "I found the Latin language easy enough."

If only, he mused, the dissolution of his business and marriage were as simple as learning the stilled language of a stilled world.

Of the two problems central to his life at this stage, the withdrawal from the mercantile world was the simplest, or so it first appeared. In 1858, having lost himself in his Greek studies, as he feared, Schliemann abruptly and formally announced his retirement from commerce, a millionaire at the age of thirty-six. "I had money enough," he said. But like his mother before him, he hesitated before dissolving his marriage. Instead, he donned the hat of tourist and embarked on a *tour de horizon* in the vain and naïve hope that a change of air would dictate a change of heart in Catherine, ease the tensions between them, and lead to a reconciliation.

During his travels, he worked his way back into history. First, he toured Scandinavia and then Rome and the Pompeii of which his father spoke so eloquently in his childhood. Next Egypt, where he studied the Pyramids of Giza, and then up the Nile, beyond the great temple at Abu Simbel—then half-hidden by sand, and destined a century later to be transplanted to escape the rising waters of Aswan Dam. From Egypt, he followed the path of Moses to the first of the Promised Lands and he solemnly walked alone along the Via Dolorosa. Then onto Syria and the fabulous ruins of Baal-bek. Methodically, Schliemann soaked up the cultures and civilizations on the periphery of the Aegean world.

Finally, in the summer of 1859, for the first time in his life, he sailed across Homer's wine-dark waters and, in Athens, ascended to the Acropolis. Astride this majestic pinnacle of the ancient Greek world, he wept openly. In Athens, he suddenly found himself. Yet like Ulysses, on his return to Ithaca, Schliemann underwent further trials before he settled permanently in the land of his spiritual ancestors.

While in Athens, he received an urgent summons to return to St. Petersburg. A bankrupt merchant had brought suit against him in the commercial court. He had no recourse but to return to Russia to defend himself; after all, his family and residence were still in St. Petersburg. The case was cleared up with little difficulty—the merchant proved to be a scoundrel— but, in a final legal maneuver, the business associate appealed the case to the Russian Senate, where no lawsuit can be terminated in less than three years. Since Schliemann's presence was necessary to bring his defense to a successful conclusion, he reentered the business world. Defensively, with an intense sense of guilt, he protested that he reentered the commercial world against his innermost desires. "I had recommenced business much against my will," he said, "and merely in order to have some occupation and distraction while the tedious lawsuit was going on."

And it was business with a vengeance, on a massive scale, like a gambler rolling dice for high stakes, with abandon, as an amusement. The year was 1860 and Schliemann's imports for that twelve-month period soared to $2.5 million. The following year, with the outbreak of the American Civil War, his business turnover soared still higher. He speculated largely in cotton. "Heaven continued to bless all my mercantile undertakings in a wonderful manner," he said, "so that at the end of 1863, I found myself in possession of a fortune such as my ambition had never ventured to aspire to." He was now a multimillionaire, his great fortune established.

During this interregnum, he vainly tried to win back Catherine. But the abyss between them widened. The door to her bedroom remained double-locked. His third sojourn in Russia encompassed the unhappiest days of his life. A family man by nature, he was in constant torment. His quarrels with Catherine were bitter, sometimes violent. He became increasingly determined to sever his ties to Catherine, Russia, and the mercantile world. "I must free myself from this trap," he confided to a business associate. "I must return to my beloved Homer, to my beloved Greece."

The Russian Senate sustained the lower court and Schliemann won his case in December 1863. In 1864, he left Russia never to return. "Henceforth," he wrote, "I will devote myself entirely to archaeology, my ultimate goal."

Schliemann now entered a four-year period of additional travel, followed by formal education. In the spring of that year, he sailed for Tunisia and investigated the ruins of Carthage. Then back to Egypt and a reinterpretation of the great civilization of the Nile. Next to India and the Taj Mahal. From there he traveled to the holy city of Benares and to the foothills of the snow-trimmed Himalayas. He inspected the footprint of Lord Buddha at Ceylon, toured the massive Borobudur in central Java, strolled along the Great Wall in China, traveled to

Kamakura in Japan, crossed the Pacific and visited Mexico, the fountainhead of Aztec civilization.

In this manner, for two years, Schliemann remained abroad, absorbing the worlds of the past. Destiny was cruel. His bank accounts overflowed; yet, despite his hot-blooded nature, loneliness was his constant companion. Notwithstanding his desire to be done with her, in his loneliest hours, he corresponded with Catherine in the desperate off-chance of rebuilding their union, but his letters either went unanswered or were misinterpreted and answered with invective.

After two years of travel, in 1866, Schliemann settled in Paris and spent the next two years in the lecture halls and library of the Sorbonne.

Studying on an ad hoc basis, he enrolled in courses on ancient history and archaeology, then still in formative stages. He failed to complete the requisite courses for a degree and never got his baccalaureate. In 1869, however, after the publication of *Ithaca, the Peloponnesus and Troy,* he submitted the book to the University of Rostock, together with a dissertation written in ancient Greek, and the Grand Duchy's only university bestowed on its fellow Mecklenburger a doctorate of philosophy. Given the deep, pretentious, caste-ridden structure of Germanic society in that era, with its heavy emphasis on titles and degrees, Schliemann was in ecstasy. His doctorate provided him with the scholarly credentials he so sorely lacked as tangible proof that he had abandoned the crude and crass commercial world. "With unremitting zeal," he wrote, "I have ever since endeavored to show myself worthy of the dignity conferred on me." And he did. Later, honorary degrees showered down upon him.

In researching his first book on archaeology—the book which revolutionized Western thinking on Homer—he toured, as we observed earlier, the Troad or Trojan Plain, first visiting Bounarbashi, then Hissarlik. But in point of fact, on revisiting the Aegean in 1868 and undertaking the observations which led to the publication of *Ithaca, the Peloponnesus and Troy,* perhaps for symbolic reasons, he first set off for Mount Aetos on the island of Ithaca, astride the Ionian Sea, the final destination of Ulysses after his twenty-year odyssey.

When Ulysses returned, his father threw his arms about

him and called out, "The gods are still on Olympus after all!"
—a line which flooded Schliemann's brain as he climbed the
same mountain, following the footsteps of Ulysses as spelled
out by Homer. Thus, he "took the rough track through the
wooded country and over the crest of the mountain." Atop
Aetos, where Ulysses' citadel once stood, Schliemann got down
on his knees and, like Ulysses, "rejoiced at finding himself
again in his own land and kissed the bounteous soil."

Transported forty centuries backward into history,
Schliemann lifted his hands and prayed to the Naiades, the
tutelary goddesses of streams, springs, and fountains to whom
Ulysses prayed. "Nymphs, daughters of Jove," he cried out. "I
was sure that I was never again to see you, now therefore I greet
you with all loving salutations. . . . Advise me. . . . Stand by my
side and put your courage into my heart."

Schliemann wept unashamedly, as he had at the Athenian
Acropolis. And then the wiry, moustached, balding German,
nearing the fiftieth year of his life, his thin, gold-rimmed spec-
tacles as moist as his eyes, began to recite softly, in ancient
Greek, the twenty-fourth and last book of *The Iliad,* when
Priam visited the tent of Achilles and pleaded for the body of
his dead son, Hector, a god among men, so that he might give
Hector a proper burial.

> "Is my son still at the ships, or has Achilles hewn him limb
> from limb, and given him to his hounds?" Priam inquired.
> "Sir," was the reply, "neither hounds nor vultures have yet
> devoured him; he is still just lying at the tents by the ship of
> Achilles, and though it is now twelve days that he has lain there,
> his flesh is not wasted nor have the worms eaten him although
> they feed on warriors. At daybreak Achilles drags him cruelly
> round the sepulchre of his dear comrade Patroclus, but it does
> him no hurt. You should come yourself and see how he lies fresh
> as dew, with the blood all washed away, and his wounds every
> one of them closed though many pierced him with their spears.
> Such care have the blessed gods taken of your brave son, for he
> was dear to them beyond all measure."

As Schliemann recited these verses in ancient Greek,
which he often called "the most beautiful, most divine, and
most sonorous of all languages," itinerant peasants gathered

around him in wonder and listened in silence to the language of their forefathers. Many of them wept. When he ended his elocution, the emboldened Greeks grew closer. Amid shouts of "Thank you!" they offered him wine from their goatskins and large pieces of cheese. He proferred them money, and they refused to accept it. Among themselves, they asked, "Who is the stranger?"—the very same words the people of Ithaca asked four millennia earlier as Ulysses appeared before them after his odyssey.

As Schliemann looked across Aetos, he made his first true, scholarly, archaelogical discovery about Homer: The poet was geographically accurate. Schliemann could see Mount Parnassus, where Ulysses hunted wild boar in his youth; he spied the rocky islet in midchannel between Ithaca and Samos where Penelope's suitors waited to ambush her returning husband. Obviously, *The Iliad* and *The Odyssey* were not wholly fairy tales, like *Gulliver's Travels*. Homer was familiar with the terrain about which he wrote. "I found the local character of Ithaca to agree perfectly with the descriptions of the *Odyssey*," Schliemann wrote in his diary.

Indeed, Schliemann was so impressed by Homer's geographical accuracy that he decided, in his typically impetuous manner, to undertake his first dig where he stood. In the twenty-third book of *The Odyssey*, Ulysses, after his return, gave proof to his wife, Penelope, of his identity by explaining in detail how he constructed their nuptial bed, "a marvelous curiosity," hewn from a young olive tree growing within the precincts of their house, in full vigor, and about as thick as a bearing post.

Lighting on this descriptive passage, Schliemann put his intuition to work, for, as he repeatedly demonstrated, archaeology is not simply a science but also an art form. Without imagination, and the ability to make an intuitive judgment, an archaeologist is little more than a ditchdigger, a rubbish collector.

At five in the morning the following day, in mid-July, as the temperature soared above 100°F, accompanied by four workmen armed with spades and pickaxes, Schliemann reclimbed Mount Aetos. There, Schliemann selected a spot which, he said as if he held Long John Silver's chart, "I judged to have been where the olive stood, in full vigor and thick as a bearing post, around which stood the bridal chamber of Odysseus."*

The workers thought he was slightly irrational, like most foreigners. But he paid them, didn't he? And he was the stranger who recited Homer with passion and eloquence. So they dug, bemused, as he instructed. The hours passed, and they uncovered nothing. Schliemann, in a pattern familiar in search-and-rescue missions on land and at sea, ordered them to dig in ever-widening circles in the hope of picking up a track. Unlike many of the scholars of his day, Schliemann did not stand idly by as grand overseer but got down on his hands and also pawed the earth in search of clues.

As he studied the terrain, his eyes settled on a large stone with a slight curvature. Was the curve natural or man-made? With a pocketknife, he scratched around the base of the stone and discovered that it formed a semicircle. He summoned his workmen, borrowed a pickax and, mixing impatience with vigor, a style he abandoned later as he refined his methods, he literally savaged the spot. Four inches down, he struck an object which shattered under the pityless point of the pick. He extracted the fragments of a *krater* or vessel which, in his ruthless manner, he had smashed. As he held the fragments, he realized that the vase was far older than any he had ever viewed in a museum. It bore no inscription. Pursuing the excavation, he uncovered four more vases. Each contained human ashes.

In his very first effort as archaeologist, he had stumbled on to a necropolis, or city of the dead, a graveyard.

"It is quite possible," he later wrote, "that I have found the ashes of Odysseus and his faithful Penelope. Or their descendants." Quite possible; indeed, anything is quite possible. Hurried conclusions such as these, which got Schliemann into continual trouble with the academic establishment and delighted the popular press, were a Schliemann trademark. With a frag-

---

*Schliemann referred to Homer's cast of characters by their Greek names, although many of the protagonists, such as Odysseus, are perhaps better known in the West today by their Roman names—in this instance, Ulysses.

ment of evidence, a mere potsherd, he erected a towering
edifice. This inclination to dramatize his findings contributed
to his later fame and, more importantly, lifted the science of
archaeology from its launching pad and popularized it.

The refrain "quite possible" frustrated his critics and drove
them to exasperation. Yet however Barnumesque his imagination, he made a singular contribution to the patch-quilt history
of the origins of Western civilization; for, with each pronounce-
ment, he unfailingly matched his fantasy with something tangible—in this case, vases and ashes. Thus, throughout his archaeological career, Schliemann and the experts entered into
a strange confrontation. On the one hand, the authorities often
jeered at his proclamations from Mount Olympus; on the other
hand, they were frequently shaken by his finds. Some critics,
distastefully regarding their rival as an upstart, know-nothing
merchant, accused him of manufacturing his discoveries, as if
the finds would bear an imprint which, when turned over, read:
"Made in Japan."

But as the authenticity of his discoveries were confirmed
and reconfirmed by new techniques, his finds created an uproar
in scholarly circles. Cities which were not supposed to have
lived, lived; civilizations which were not supposed to have existed, existed. He forced the scholars to rewrite the history of
the origins of the Western World. The Homeric Age was not
Alice's wonderland.

Schliemann's first dig at Ithaca was merely an appetizer—
a preliminary test of his growing theory about the geographical
reality of Homeric poetry. The entrée was Troy. He quickly
returned to Athens, the base of his operations, read his mail,
studied the papers, checked the stock market quotations, repacked his bags, and sailed from Piraeus across the Aegean to
the Hellespont and straight to the village of Bounarbashi. It
was there, of course, that he discovered, at firsthand, that Lechevalier and many of the other authorities on Troy which he
had studied at the Sorbonne, were fakers. Bounarbashi no more
resembled the geography of Homeric Troy than a *krylix* a Cyclopean wall.

With this discovery, Schliemann rushed into print with
*Ithaca, the Peloponnesus and Troy.* Interestingly, his first work

on archaeology looked more like a bookkeeper's ledger than a book. It measured 5½ by 8½ inches and consisted of 213 pages with the type set in extra-wide margins.

The swiftness with which Schliemann published his findings was another trademark, a boon to the academic community in particular. By contrast, the publication of scholarly papers is often delayed by lack of funds, petty jealousies, or by a desire to create the impression of deliberation.

Not so in Schliemann's case. He had money, boundless energy and enthusiasm, confidence, and a compulsion which sought to reveal, not conceal, his discoveries. His books and private papers were also devoid of jargon, another trademark. He had no need to impress people by obscure language. And although irascible, of fiery temperament, and in a running confrontation with his academic critics, Schliemann's works are peppered with commentaries which he solicited from the scholarly establishment. He respected genuine scholarship and constructive criticism. He was aware of his limitations. But he neither forgave nor forgot the destructive critics, those who engaged in personal attacks, those who tarred him as "unscholarly," and worse.

On receiving from Leipzig an advance copy of his book on Ithaca and Troy, Schliemann sensed that since his childhood the currents had swept him inexorably toward the Aegean. Now, the great voyage of his life was moving on the flood.

# VII

⊓⊔⊓⊔⊓⊔⊓

⊓⊔⊓⊔⊓⊔⊓

# The Quest Resumed

*I want to go home, and can think of*
*nothing else.*

The Odyssey, BOOK V

WITH THE PUBLICATION, in 1869, of his theory on Troy,
Schliemann had found himself. "At last," he wrote, "I am to
realize the dream of my life, to visit at my leisure, the scene of
those events which have always had such an intense interest
for me, and the country of the heroes whose adventures had
delighted and comforted my childhood."

He had turned his back on gold, on "beloved Russia," and
on the "adorable Catherine." Admittedly in a crude fashion, he
had plunged into the embryonic world of archaeology. Yet for
a man of Schliemann's romantic drive, always in need of a
companion with whom to share his wildest dreams and most
intimate thoughts, something was missing. That something
was Minna.

Very well, if he could not have Minna, he would search for
a substitute, search for her as he searched for Troy. But, setting
his priorities in order, he first severed his last tie to Russia—
Catherine. After years of indecision—they had not slept as man
and wife for six years—he took the logical and final step, divorce.

79

In the Europe of the day, divorce was difficult to obtain and frowned upon; indeed, society was so strongly set against public disunion that when Schliemann mentioned it as late as 1880 in the introductory biographical sketch to his fourth and most important book, *Ilios: The City and Country of the Trojans,* his London publisher deleted the reference for fear that it would seriously affect reviews and sales.

During his first sojourn in America, Schliemann had taken out citizenship papers, most probably to gain a business advantage. Sheepishly, later, he sought to color his action by claiming that he acquired American citizenship automatically by his residence in the Great Bear Republic when it was admitted to the Union in 1850 as the State of California. Be that as it may, in America, as compared to Europe, divorce was relatively easy to obtain and the stigma was not nearly as great.

With this in mind, on March 13, 1869, he sailed for New York, took out his second papers and, thereby, joined the club. He remained a naturalized American citizen for the rest of his life, and his last will and testament, filed in 1889 in Marion County, Indiana, began thusly, "I, the undersigned, a citizen of the United States of America. . . ." In truth, however, Schliemann retained his citizenship for the same reason he acquired it, as a "flag of convenience." And it paid handsome dividends. As an American, he obtained his divorce; as an American, he was able to obtain his first *firman* or authorization from the Sublime Porte of Turkey to begin his Troy dig; as an American, he was in a stronger position to cajole Turkish and Greek officialdom as the occasion later arose.

At New York, in the process of completing the naturalization process, Schliemann learned that Indianapolis was the current divorce Mecca, the Reno of its day. With little lost motion, he set off by rail immediately for the Hoosier state, established residence at Indianapolis—the capital city whose name had a good Greek ring—purchased a house, and invested in a starch factory as an earnest indication of his intention to settle permanently in the Midwest.

For four months, he lived in the American heartland, pending receipt of divorce papers, employing a battery of five lawyers to develop his case, and introducing into evidence letters

from Catherine in which she flatly declared that "I energeti-
cally refuse to live with you," "I refuse to leave Russia for even
the shortest time," and "I herewith swear a solemn oath that I
shall never cross the Russian frontier."

Schliemann was a prolific letter writer, indeed an obses-
sive correspondent. The Gennadius Library at Athens, where
Schliemann's private papers are today stored, is a veritable
Schliemann Archive; among them, 155 letters alone written
during the Indianapolis interlude. Many of these contain pene-
trating observations about America and the American way of
life as viewed through the eyes of a seasoned Continental traveler.

Everywhere in America, even in the Midwest, Schliemann
wrote his father, for example, he found that the foreigner was
immediately accepted, unlike Russia, where "a foreigner is
despised." Life in Indiana was parochial, unworldly, insulated,
and, horror of horrors, "no classical education existed" and
French wine was "difficult to obtain." As in California, he
wrote, the American passion was for acquiring material wealth
—this from a man who was to be repeatedly maligned later for
lusting solely for gold. But the American concept of the dignity
of labor impressed him. Not only were the Americans far more
industrious than any other peoples he had observed, but they
had no compunction against getting their hands dirty and "one
can easily make a living here providing he is willing to work."

As for the American concept of democracy, he found it
"rough and naked" and diplomatically observed that the party
system was ideally suited and responsive to "lateral influ-
ences." As an overall judgment, looking ahead with an insight
which was rare for a man who invariably looked backward, he
forecast that because of its energy and industriousness, the
United States "is bound to eclipse all the empires of history."

A month before his arrival in Indianapolis, Schliemann
put into motion the obverse side of his divorce strategy—remar-
riage. In February, on the eve of his departure for America,
Schliemann wrote Vimpos, his old Greek tutor in St. Petersburg
and now the Archbishop of Athens, and confided in his determination to excavate Troy and to restore the splendor and radi-
ance of the Homeric Age. Against this background, he con-

fessed to the Archbishop that he was also in search of a companion for life. He did not want to embark on this adventure alone. He wanted a wife with whom to share his triumph. He solicited the Archbishop's assistance. Schliemann's specifications for a new mate were pure Dumas with a dash of Verdi. He wrote:

> She should be poor, but very well educated. . . . She should be an enthusiast of Homer, and therefore a girl of the Greektype. . . .
> She should have black hair . . . if possible, she should be beautiful. [The uncharacteristic qualification, "if possible," revealed an element of doubt.]
> Finally, she should be perhaps an orphan or the daughter of a scholar who is compelled to eke out a meagre living as a governess.

With such a companion, a new Minna, hand in hand, they would set out to discover the mythical city of Troy in the fabled land of the legendary Trojans.

# VIII

# The Search for Penelope

*You shall have a woman who shall go up
into your bed.*

The Iliad, BOOK VIII

THE RELATIONSHIP Schliemann calculatingly arranged with
Sophia Egnostromenos promised from the outset to be of extraordinary dimensions. It more than fulfilled its promise.

In response to Schliemann's request, the archbishop sent
him a collection of photographs of prospective brides, including the portrait of Sophia, the sixteen-year-old daughter of the
prelate's cousin. She was the seventh and youngest child of
George and Victoria Egnostromenos. Her father operated a successful upholstery business. The family lived in Athens and
maintained a small country house at Kolnos, the birthplace of
Sophocles, the playwright son of a munitions maker who was
known in his day as "the favorite of the Graces and Muses." The
young girl, with large brown eyes, black hair, round cheeks,
and acquiline nose, drew Schliemann's attention as he sat in
his armchair in Indianapolis and pondered his future. The
others, he rejected out of hand.

After several weeks of hesitancy, Schliemann wrote the
Archbishop on April 26 rejecting all his offerings. Sophia, he
conceded, appeared to be the most pleasing of the lot—compas-

sionate, refined, and lively. Ah, there was the rub: lively. "She is too young for an old man of forty-seven," he said. As in a man approaching climacteric, he unashamedly confessed to the Archbishop that he felt impotent and had not engaged in sexual intercourse since he and Catherine separated six years earlier. Expressing his fear at Sophia's "liveliness," he concluded that young girls probably were more interested in the sexual aspects of marriage than companionship. Perhaps he should look for a widow, a woman of experience, closer to his age, who knew what to expect from a late marriage.

His letter was no sooner deposited at the post office in Indianapolis than, the following day, Schliemann—after a torturous night—wrote Vimpos again and confessed that the first letter was a ruse and that "I have already fallen in love with her picture." Soliciting more information about Sophia, he asked about her father, about her education, and her familiarity with Homer "the language of our ancestors."

Within the next few weeks, he made up his mind. In a letter to his father on May 18, he wrote that because of his infatuation with things Grecian and Greece, "I believe I can be happy with a Greek girl only." Then he disclosed that he had found her.

On June 30, 1868, the Marion County Court of Common Pleas, located in the temporary courthouse at Court House Square, in downtown Indianapolis, granted the plaintiff a divorce. Schliemann, describing himself as overjoyed, wrote Vimpos that he was leaving immediately for Athens.

Schliemann sold out his Indianapolis interests, packed, and left for Greece via New York, whose bustle and traffic continued to "dazzle and bewilder me." As an indication of his disenchantment with the mercantile world, he wrote on July 18, that "the commerce of the whole universe appears to be concentrated here." Six days later, notwithstanding the prospect of building a fifth fortune, the brilliantly successful entrepreneur with immense capital at his disposal, turned his back on the opportunity and sailed for the Aegean in search of a companion with whom to share his search for Troy.

On September 2, Schliemann's ship docked at Piraeus; the gangplank was no sooner lowered than he rushed off to visit the school where Sophia was studying to observe her in her natural habitat, first in the classroom, then at home. The arrival of the mustached, slim, bespectacled, middle-aged German of medium height caused a sensation at the institute. The girls twittered and giggled. The nature of his mission was hardly a secret; there are few secrets among the voluble Greeks. Among her classmates, he picked out the blushing young girl immediately. She was more attractive than her photograph, which was scarcely a surprise. Photography was then in its infancy, and people sat rigidly at attention, tense, fearfully staring ahead.

The following day, meticulously attired in a black suit with vest, a black string tie, black Homburg, and carefully polished black shoes, looking more like a preacher or undertaker than a prospective bridegroom, he and Vimpos drove by horse and carriage through the heat of the waning Greek summer to the Egnostromenos home.

It was an awkward moment for Sophia, for her parents and relatives, and for Heinrich. Only Vimpos felt at ease.

After perfunctory introductions, the small group filled the sitting room. They made idle talk, sipped wine, and nibbled excessively rich Greek pastries, especially the honey and nut delight, *halva*. Stiffly, Schliemann discoursed on his travels; suddenly, abandoning pretense and caution, in his thin, high-pitched voice, he posed three questions to the young Sophia.

The drone of voices faded, glasses were put down, and everyone listened attentively as Schliemann addressed himself for the first time to his prospective companion for life. Schliemann was not interested in whether Sophia could cook, sew, or rear children. Rather, he first asked her whether she enjoyed travel, and then, whether she knew the date Hadrian, the Roman emperor, visited Greece. Next came the crunch, the ultimate question: Did she know Homer? Could she recite passages from memory?

Here was a trial which rivaled the ordeal of a Papagena.

In a warm and melodious voice, she demurely replied, "yes," to the first question, provided the correct date (125 A.D.) to the second, and—breathlessly— answered "yes" to the third. Her parents beamed, an uncle coughed, the Archbishop, at Schliemann's side, put his arms around his old St. Petersburg friend, and the room filled again with sounds of idle chatter, the pouring of wine, and the clatter of pastry dishes. Sophia survived the first barrier.

During the next three days, Schliemann repeatedly visited the Egnostromenos home, and each visit was the occasion of a family-style reunion. One evening, joining the family circle for dinner, he presented them with copies of his new book, *Ithaca, the Peloponnesus and Troy*. After regaling his listeners with stories of adventure from Moscow to the Gold Coast, he spoke passionately about the mission which lay ahead: unearthing Troy. Every Greek believed in the historical validity of the Trojan War; Schliemann did not have to prove that. Although they considered his project a bit far-out—with his money he should sit in the sun and enjoy himself—they took his plan in stride. But as he spoke with rising animation, there surfaced the real Schliemann, the knight in search of the Holy Grail, the adult-child in pursuit of a dream, the man of eternal youth.

During these visits he was increasingly enchanted by Sophia and increasingly frustrated by the convoy of relatives with whom she traveled. Exasperated, he wrote a note and asked whether he could speak to her alone so that "we can get to know each other."

A meeting was arranged, and in their first private encounter, the middle-aged man put to the girl, thirty years his junior, a question which went to the heart of the matter. "Why," he asked, "do you want to marry me?"

What kind of answer did Schliemann expect? A barefaced lie that "I am madly in love with you?" If Schliemann hoped to flatter himself by proferring this question, he was sorely disappointed. Or was he, like Diogenes with his lamp, simply in quest of honesty? If so, the answer had the ring of authenticity. It was brutal. "Because my parents want me to do so," she replied evenly, adding, "and because you are so rich."

Schliemann was aghast. His make-believe world crumpled and crumbled. Ashen-faced, he returned to his hotel. "You answered like a slave!" he rebuked her in a letter. "You hurt me. I am simple and honorable, and if you agree to marry me, it must be because we can share our joys and sorrows together, excavate the past, and share our enthusiasm for Homer." He signed the note imperiously: Heinrich Schliemann, Doctor of

Philosophy. He also announced his imminent departure for Paris.

If Schliemann was shaken by the reply, so was Sophia's family, which viewed millionaire Schliemann as a worthy patron. In her unsophisticated mind, Sophia thought the answer would please him. In an age when marriages were often prearranged, her reply was framed as evidence of her loyalty to her family and her admiration for his position and intellect.

At the family's dictation, Sophia wrote a letter expressing sorrow at their misunderstanding and his impending departure. "I thought it was the right and proper answer for a young girl," she explained, adding, "my parents and I will be most happy if you could visit us tomorrow." But how to address the letter, that was the question. Dear Henry? Too familiar. Dear Dr. Schliemann? Sounded like a surgeon. A happy medium was struck. The letter's salutation read: "Dear Mr. Henry."

Schliemann sulked at his hotel for several days, reconsidered, and revisited the Egnostromenos' home. Displaying impetuosity and impatience, he requested her immediate hand in marriage and proposed they marry within a fortnight. A fortnight? There was so much to arrange, so many relatives to take into account, Victoria Egnostromenos, her mother, pleaded. Schliemann was adamant. The mother retreated.

On September 23, within three weeks of his second arrival in Greece, Heinrich and Sophia were married. Archbishop Vimpos presided at the High Nuptial Mass in accordance with the services of the Greek Orthodox Church.

Like a little boy, in his first letter to Mecklenburg, Heinrich enthusiastically wrote: "I fell in love with her while I was still in America." He went on to sing a paean of joy. But, he conceded, the bride had one serious defect—"Sophiton, my dear Sophia, speaks only Greek." Brimming with confidence, he forecast that she would learn four new languages within the next four years. In truth, Sophia proved an apt pupil and added German and French to her linguistic achievements. As they moved into an increasingly English-speaking environment, she taught herself English.

At the conclusion of the wedding reception, at 2:00 A.M., the bridal couple left on their honeymoon, embarking on a tour of

Europe aboard the appropriately named Greek steamer, *Aphrodite*. As they sailed, Sophia's relatives and friends, in the tradition of the Greeks, continued their feasting, singing, and dancing to mark the occasion.

Sophia's honeymoon was no more pedestrian than the questions Schliemann put to her that day in front of her parents. It was a whirlwind courtship through Sicily, Italy, Germany, and France. With Heinrich self-cast in the role of guide, they attended a seemingly endless procession of operas and plays; spent hours and days visiting museums and ancient ruins; and, in a more conventional fashion, dined in the most expensive restaurants and made purchases in the finest boutiques. In some places, Schliemann was mistaken for her father. In other places, she was taken for his mistress.

Just before Christmas, their honeymoon was crowned with a magnificent ball at his Parisian residence at 6, Place St. Michel. On that occasion, with the mansion decked in holly and lanterns, Schliemann presented her to his friends and associates.

"Sophia could make any man happy," he wrote his father from Paris. "She loves me with Greek passion and I love her no less. Together we speak only Greek, the language of the gods."

Clearly starry-eyed during her first trip into the outer world, Sophia developed into as ardent a letter writer as her husband. She wrote home about the wonders of Rome, Pompeii, Venice, and Naples; was overwhelmed by the Sistine Chapel; and was stunned by the magnificence of the Louvre.

The whirlwind honeymoon tour appeared endless. They never rested. Schliemann never let her attention span focus for too long on anything or anyone, including himself. He ran faster and faster, in Lewis Carroll's phrase, to stand still. He behaved like a man walking on a high wire for the first time. He was deliriously happy and feared the happiness was transitory. For her part, she could hardly catch her breath. They rarely dined alone. Nightly, their table was crowded with friends—notably scholars and writers such as Ernest Renan, a celebrity in his time. Schliemann introduced her to a society that she never knew existed. He looked up Greek friends for her and hired a cook who could prepare an occasional Greek dish.

Simultaneously playing the roles of mother, daughter, wife, mistress, matron, hostess, and student was too much for her. Sophia lost weight and tired easily. Their life style was too swift. The pressures were too intense. One evening, as they prepared to go to the opera, she suggested that he go alone because she felt unwell. He remained at her side and comforted her. When she felt better, he briskly said in a tone of finality, "Good, now we can leave for the opera."

Sophia exploded; she declared her independence. She was an individual in her own right. She was not a mail-order toy doll. He could not crank her up with a key. She refused to go, drove him from the room, and bolted the door.

During the opera—Gluck's *Orfeo ed Euridice*—Schliemann did not hear a note. Catherine had locked him out, too; she had locked him out forever. Was this the beginning of another tortuous round in the pattern of Catherine? Terrorized, tormented, he recognized he was impulsive, restless, and domineering. He realized, too, that he desperately needed her warmth, her strength, her intimacy, and her companionship.

At the conclusion of the opera, enveloped in fear, he returned to Place St. Michel. He almost was compelled to drag himself home. His throat dry, overcome by dread, he slowly turned the doorknob to their bedroom. Would the door open? He paused as he tightened his grip on the knob. The door swung gently open. He was overcome. He slowly approached her, dropped to his knees, placed his head in her lap, and sobbed. Their marriage, which started patently on unequal terms, had stabilized itself as a listing ship rights itself with a shift of cargo. Sophia and Heinrich Schliemann had found a common ground as equals. They would remain on this ground for the rest of their lives. Henceforth, they would laugh and cry, share their joys and sorrows, agree and disagree, and love together with the sublime unity of one on one. Henceforth, too, his blustering aside, she would dominate him. He would rant and rave at fate, at his critics, and then, more often than not, comply with her wishes.

The French physicians suggested that Sophia, wan and pale, return home. She needed Greek food, Greek air, and the Greek pace of life to restore her strength and vitality. Her first visit away from home and country, she was desperately home-sick.

During this period of readjustment and reaccommodation between husband and wife, Troy remained close at hand. Indeed, their honeymoon in Paris was extended by the reluctance of the Turkish government to grant Schliemann a *firman* to excavate the hill at Hissarlik. No excavation could be undertaken within the Ottoman Empire without such a document. From the Turkish point of view, the problem was simple enough. Why would anyone, ostensibly in his right mind, seek permission to dig up a barren hill in a remote region in northwest Turkey unless—ah—unless there was buried treasure beneath it? Or was his real purpose to spy on Turkey's new fortifications at the Hellespont? Common sense dictated that there was a deeper motive behind Schliemann's request other than his open declaration that he sought only to find a mythical city.

In 1868, following his first visit to Hissarlik, Schliemann had made discreet inquiries into the hill's ownership. Half of the hill, he learned, was owned by two Turks who used it as a sheep pasture. The other half was owned by two Englishmen, the Calverts. Frederick Calvert was British consul at the Dardanelles and his brother, Frank, was the honorary American vice-consul there. Both were archaeology buffs, especially Frank, who had written extensively on the area.

Explaining his plan to excavate Hissarlik, Schliemann had entered into intense correspondence with the Calverts. They enthusiastically endorsed his project and gave him carte blanche permission to excavate the hill at will.

Indeed, Frank Calvert pressed Schliemann to begin excavations in the summer of 1869 but, in a letter dated April 14 that year, Schliemann explained that "we must wait until next spring" because, first, he was in the process of securing a divorce and, secondly, the terrible heat and pestilential fever in the area made a summer excavation next to impossible. Schliemann did not mention his third reason, his desire to remarry before setting out for Hissarlik—and Troy.

Frank Calvert, like Schliemann, had studied the existing literature on Troy and he, too, upheld the theory of Lechevalier, which placed Troy at Bounarbashi. But later, especially through the arguments of Maclaren, Calvert converted to the Troy-Hissarlik theory. Thus, when Schliemann first established contact with Calvert, he discovered that Calvert had become a "valiant champion" of the Troy-Hissarlik theory and this, in part, strongly influenced Schliemann. Indeed, Schliemann, in his first book on Priam's citadel, *Troy and Its Remains,* published in New York in 1875, noted in detail that Frank Calvert brought to light at Hissarlik *"before* my visit" some remains of the Macedonian and Roman periods, uncovering, for example, a part of a wall which, according to Plutarch, was built by Lysimachus. While Calvert shared Schliemann's enthusiasm for digging up Troy, however, he lacked the funds and forces necessary to complete the great project. Accordingly, Calvert went out of his way to help Schliemann launch his plan. Even with Calvert's permission to dig up his half of the hill, Schliemann required a *firman*, and Calvert interceded on his behalf to obtain the proper documents from Constantinople.

Schliemann approached the project with boyish enthusiasm. In their correspondence, Schliemann peppered Calvert with questions which pointed up, in his mind, the nature of the dangerous adventure he planned. In December, for example, he wrote out a list of twenty questions for Calvert:

> I am very susceptible of fever; is there much apprehension of same in spring . . . ? Have I to take a tent and iron bedstead and pillow with me from Marseille for all the houses in the Plain are infested with vermin? . . . Do I require pistols, dagger and rifles . . . ? What sort of hat is best against the scorching sun?

Calvert's replies are equally amusing:

> The fever months commence about September. . . . There are two ways of managing this: The one is to rent a village house at Chiblak; have it thoroughly scoured, whitewashed, then with a reserve of insect powder destroy any of the vermin which may have escaped—[thus] a person may live in peace. The other is a tent which would be pitched at the site of Ilium Novum. The only question would be whether the nights would not be too cold

in early spring for tent-life. Perhaps you might wish to combine the two plans . . . You can bring with you any arms if they will afford you any feelings of security. As to myself, I carry my gun with me wherever I go. . . . Any hat that you can wind—a white muslim—round in the form of a turban will do.

Against this backdrop, on Christmas Eve, following their Parisian honeymoon ball and the physicians' suggestion that Sophia return to Athens because of her delicate health, a letter arrived from Frank Calvert. "At last," Schliemann shouted as he rushed into Sophia's arms waving the letter. "The *firman* is granted."

# IX

The Dig Begins

*On the rich plains of Troy,
far from his home.*

The Iliad, BOOK XVI

WITHIN A MONTH after receiving Calvert's letter, the newlyweds packed their bags and sailed for Greece, arriving February 9, 1870.

Sophia's mother and father, her brothers and sisters, and droves of uncles, aunts, and cousins, descended on Piraeus in a great wave to welcome her home. At the dock, they encountered a polished, highly refined young lady of the world, attired in the latest Parisian fashion, buttoned shoes, ruffled collar and sleeves, and a fabulous bonnet with a white peacock feather. Overnight, the baby of the family had matured into a matron. She looked as if she had just stepped out of a Renoir canvas.

The elation surrounding the return of the Schliemanns was short-lived. Among the letters waiting for Heinrich on his arrival at Athens was another note from Frank Calvert. The news was disconcerting. The Turkish government had changed its mind. No *firman* would be granted for the time being. But, Calvert assured him, ultimately he would obtain a permit, and he should remain patient.

Of all Schliemann's characteristics, for good or evil, the

quality most remote and repugnant to his nature was patience. He was the obverse of Talleyrand's dictum, "Above all, not too much zeal." To him, zeal was the essence of life. Accordingly, Schliemann flew into one of his periodic tantrums, while Sophia's relatives looked on askance. So he did not receive his *firman.* So what? He had money, leisure, and their dear Sophithon. What difference did it make whether or not he received a *firman.* Turkey! That barbaric land. Why would such a nice man like that want to dig up Turkey? If he had to dig, there was plenty to dig up in Greece.

By now, however, Sophia had learned, like the lion tamer, how to contain the beast when it roared. After gliding him into a private room, she sought to console him by pointing out that Calvert was convinced that he would get his *firman* in time. "If you are going to live and work here," she said, "you must master patience."

After sitting in the Athenian sun for several weeks and making exploratory trips within Greece to occupy his time, the little patience Schliemann possessed evaporated completely. Without warning, one evening he ordered her to pack. "Where are we going?" she inquired.

"To Hissarlik," he said. "To Troy."

Hissarlik was Turkish territory; she was a Greek national. The relationship in those days between Athens and Constantinople was on a par with the gingham dog and the calico cat. Sophia balked. "Very well," he declared. "I'll go alone."

Schliemann had "lost" almost fifty years. Inwardly, he felt, he could not afford to lose another day.

Early in April, Schliemann sailed alone for the Hellespont. There, he organized a small work party and abruptly ascended the lonely, uninhabited hill at Hissarlik—without a *firman.* For the second time, trembling with anticipation, he climbed the scrub-covered hillside. "Ever since my first visit," he wrote in his diary, "I never doubted that I should find the Pergamus of Priam in the depths of this hill."

The hill rested on a plateau lying about 80 feet above the Trojan Plain, which, in turn, was another 82 feet above sea level. At its crest, the northwestern corner of the hill rose slightly, an area about 700 feet in breadth and 990 feet in length. It attracted Schliemann's eye. "This," he wrote, "presented a likely place to start." Just as simple as that.

Schliemann's behavior was akin to visiting the Alps, Himalayas, or the Rockies—selecting an isolated hill and declaring forthwith that beneath it lay a lost city.

"In my first visit to the area I endeavored to prove," he said, "both by the result of my own excavations and by the statements of *The Iliad* that Homeric Troy cannot possibly have been situated on the heights of Bounarbashi, to which place most archaeologists assign it." Fair enough. But what made him so sure he would find Troy beneath Hissarlik? Faith? Intuitive judgment? The geographic reality of Homer?

Whatever the case, he issued his first order of the day, the order of each subsequent day he spent atop the lonely pinnacle, wind-swept, barren, and isolated. "Dig," he directed with the ring of impatience in his reedy voice.

The first pickax cracked open the dark earth. The crew started to remove the dust of thousands of years. The dig was on.

Two feet. Six feet. Fifteen feet. Another foot down and—crack!—a pickax struck a hard object. Like a madman, Schliemann rushed to the spot, seized the worker's pick, and attacked the spot like Ahab driving his men forward in search of the White Whale. "I laid bare a wall of huge stone," he wrote, "six and a half feet thick." Then he made a disturbing discovery. Seven and a half feet deeper, this wall apparently rested on another wall, quite dissimilar in construction. Schliemann was in a state of delirium. Troy! "I have found Troy," he cried out as the workers assented gravely.

"Probably the palace or Pergamus of Priam," he wrote in his notes. "I cannot rest until I excavate the whole hill."

Initially, in 1868, without turning over a spade of earth, Schliemann proclaimed to the world that he uncovered the site of Homeric Troy. Now, two years later, after a few spadefuls of earth, he promptly announced that he had actually discovered Troy. No inscriptions, no artifacts, no plastic art, no tangible evidence except for a wall of immense stones which only a Cyclops could lift into place.

Schliemann's first excavation at Troy ended as abruptly as

it began. He was digging on the side of the hill owned by the two Turks who maintained their sheepfold on the spot. The Turks descended on him in anger and demanded that he stop digging up their pasture land.

First Schliemann tried diplomacy. He politely requested permission to continue the excavation, something he should have requested before he began. The Turks refused. Then he tried to entice them into a deal. The Turks conferred among themselves, Schliemann wrote, "but they would only grant me permission to dig on further on condition that I would at once pay them 12,000 piasters for damages [$2,640] and, in addition, they wished to bind me, after the conclusion of my excavations, to put the field in order again."

Schliemann was furious. In the manner of the millionaire, who believes he can buy anything—well, almost anything—he countered with money. "I'll buy your half of the hill—how much?" Schliemann asked. But the Turks refused to sell at any price. A frightful row ensued, and Schliemann retreated in despair. His appetite for Troy was whetted by what it fed on; the sight of the wall turned him into a fanatic.

Back in Athens, he unfolded the story of his discovery to Sophia, wrote the Calverts, and then decided again to take matters into his own hands. He visited Constantinople and gained an audience with Safvet Pasha, the Minister of Public Instruction (Works). Schliemann lost control of himself. He fumed and fussed. The answer was firm: No. No *firman*. For months to no avail, Schliemann, like a shuttlecock, traveled back and forth between Athens and the capital of the Sublime Porte.

There was Troy before him, but when he stretched out his hands, it acquired a dreamlike character "as in our sleep when we are pursuing an object and we never catch it because as often as we reach out it escapes us again." Was Troy destined to be another Minna?

His despair was brightened momentarily by Sophia's announcement that she was pregnant. "We shall name the boy Hector," he said triumphantly, and with finality. As it developed, Sophia gave birth to a raven-haired girl in May 1871. Well, if they did not produce a Hector, at least they had an Andromache and thus she was christened, with her father wav-

ing his vest-pocket thermometer, testing the baptismal water to
make sure it was at room temperature.

Otherwise, 1871 was a frustrating year. In his agony, he
turned to a familiar stratagem, one which had never failed him
in his lifetime. His conversations with Turkish officialdom
were always conducted in either German or French. Perhaps a
touch of flattery would work. Moreover, by learning their language, he would demonstrate to the Sultan's court the intensity
and genuineness of his desire to uncover Troy. After all, Troy
was part of the history of Turkey as well as that of Greece. The
Turks, of course, knew he did not speak their language beyond
the few words the conventional traveler acquired in the course
of a journey.

With his usual melding of enthusiasm, determination, and
calculation, Schliemann set about to learn Turkish. He purchased exercise books and a dictionary. He locked himself in
his room. Three weeks later, he emerged and wrote a letter, in
fluent Turkish, requesting another meeting with the Minister
of Public Instruction. Indeed, he became so fluent in Turkish
within two years that a high-ranking authority scratched a
postscript on one of Schliemann's notes, which read: "Among
our people, only a very highly educated person could write such
an elegant letter as this." First in Holland, then in Russia, and
later in California—now in Turkey—Schliemann employed
language as a secret weapon.

He also employed business acumen to get the hill at Hissarlik into the public domain. He connived with Safvet Pasha, "in
the name of science," to have half of the hill owned by the
Turkish farmers expropriated by the government in return for
3,000 piasters ($660) in compensation. From Safvet Pasha's
standpoint, this was a precautionary matter in the event treasure was found there.

Yet even with his new-found fluency in Turkish,
Schliemann ran into fresh trouble. "I met with new and great
difficulties," he recounted, "for the Turkish Government is col-
lecting ancient works of art for their recently established Museum at Constantinople, as a consequence of which the Sultan
no longer grants permission for making excavations." However, through Frank Calvert's persistence, Schliemann met the

American chargé d'affaires to the Sublime Porte, John P. Brown, another antiquity buff, who two years earlier, had published a book on the history of Constantinople. Brown interceded on behalf of Schliemann, the American citizen, and the Turkish authorities relented. On September 27, 1871, after the loss of still another year, Heinrich Schliemann returned to Hissarlik—this time with a *firman,* an excavation plan, and Sophia on his arm.

The Turks, still suspicious that Schliemann was Long John Silver with a map of Treasure Hill, if not Treasure Island, assigned an observer to his expedition. Under the terms of the *firman,* Schliemann wrote with exasperation and indignation, "I was to be watched by a Turkish official whose salary I have to pay during the time of my excavations."

But Troy was at hand.

"I hope," Schliemann wrote in his diary, "finally to solve the great problem as to whether the hill of Hissarlik is—as I firmly believe—the citadel of Troy."

# X

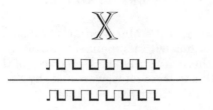

# The View from Hissarlik

*Heaven delivers into my hands the city of
Ilium.*

The Iliad, BOOK XXI

ON A CLOUDLESS Wednesday, October 11, 1871, as the Aegean Sea
sparkled and a light westerly fanned Hissarlik, Heinrich and
Sophia Schliemann and eight Greek workmen climbed the
desolate hill—armed with spades, pickaxes, and eight wheelbarrows Schliemann had purchased earlier in France for carrying away debris. In a state of high excitement, at the crest of
the hill, Schliemann ordered a brief rest, which was unlike
him. He wanted to savor the moment he had dreamed of since
childhood. He had reached the end of the elusive rainbow.
"The view from the hill of Hissarlik," Schliemann wrote jubilantly in his diary, "is extremely magnificent."

With Sophia at his side, he continued tenderly:

Before me lies the glorious Plain of Troy, which, since the
recent rain, is again covered with grass and yellow buttercups.
On the north-northwest, at about an hour's distance, it is
bounded by the Hellespont. The peninsula of Gallipoli here runs
out to a point, upon which stands a lighthouse. To the left of it
is the island of Imbros, above which rises Mount Ida of the
island of Samothrace, at present covered with snow. A little

more to the west, on the Macedonian peninsula, lies the celebrated Mount Athos with its monasteries, on the northwestern
side of which there are still to be seen traces of that great canal
which, according to Herodotus, was made by Xerxes, in order to
avoid sailing round stormy Cape Athos.

In Schliemann's mind, the wasteland of the Trojan Plain
was a proscenium on which the first recorded scene of the first
act of Western civilization unfolded. The succeeding acts on
the plain had a familiar echo—the clashing of armies and the
agonizing screams of a living hell, the battlefield.

During Schliemann's era, for example, the West occupied
and fortified Gallipoli, opposite the Plain, as a block to Russian
expansionism. Schliemann would have been stupefied to know,
so fickle are politics, that less than fifty years later, at terrible
cost, the West would try and fail to seize the plain as part of a
strategy to force open the Dardanelles so that it could supply
Russia with war materiels in the struggle against his own Germany. And seventy-five years after he started his excavations,
Schliemann would have been even more astonished to learn
that, reverting to its historic policy, like the Achaean confederation poised against Troy, the West would dispatch another
powerful fleet into the Aegean—the United States Sixth Fleet—
to keep the plain and its environs out of hostile (and in this
instance, once again, Russian) hands—the Truman Doctrine.

Schliemann wrote as he scanned the horizon:

Returning to the Plain of Troy, we see to the right of it, upon
a spur of the promontory of Rhoeteum, the sepulchral mound of
Ajax; at the foot of the opposite Cape of Sigeum that of Patroclus, and upon a spur of the same cape, the sepulchre of
Achilles; to the left of the latter, on the promontory itself, is the
village of Yenishehr.

Beyond the plain lay, of course, the shores of the Aegean
across which the armada of the proto-Greeks sailed on its invasion of the Troad, the land of the Trojans.

But wait, did that fleet sail? Was the Trojan War fought?
Was there ever a Troy? What tangible proof was there to support this history? Of course, Schliemann, with his childish,

indomitable faith in Homer, believed unquestionably that Troy lay beneath his clay-streaked boots. All he needed to do was dig it up and prove his case. And dig he did, starting where he left off a year earlier.

That evening, his workers returned to their neighboring village of Renkoi and spread the word that the crazy foreigner, the one with the pretty young Greek wife, paid 9 piasters a day (about 22 cents) to dig up Hissarlik. On Thursday, Schliemann's work force increased to 35. On Friday, his labor force rose to 74 able-bodied men. Thereafter, it fluctuated between 80 and 150 men.

The lack of wheelbarrows, a novelty in Turkey, created a problem: How to remove the debris? The workers resolved it in their own fashion, returning on Saturday with fifty-two large wicker baskets.

Initially, all the workmen were Greeks. Devoutly religious, however, they refused to work on Sunday. So on the seventh day, when the Greeks rested in accordance with the Biblical injunction, Schliemann employed Turkish workers, who observed the Moslem Sabbath on Friday. As for himself and Sophia, they worked without rest, seven days a week, like the pagans of the civilization they sought to unearth.

"The difficulties of making excavations in a wilderness like this, where everything is wanting, are immense and they increase day by day," Schliemann recorded. The founder of modern archaeology was coming to grips with the reality of the task which confronted him. Because of Hissarlik's steep slope, the removal of the debris developed into a serious engineering problem.

"The rubbish cannot be thrown directly down the slope," he observed, "for it would, of course, only have to be carried away again." Impatient as usual, he complained after a week on the site that the work "proceeds but slowly and is very tiring, as the rubbish has to be carried a long way off."

To speed up the work, he rented four carts at 20 piasters a day, each drawn by a pair of oxen.

"I work with great energy and spare no cost, in order, if possible, to reach the native soil before the winter rains set in, which may happen at any moment," he wrote.

In this passage from his on-location diary are clues about Schliemann's character and how he viewed his project. The phrase "I spare no cost" is a slap in the face to his critics and later biographers who portrayed him as touched by gold fever. His belief that he would strike virgin soil "any moment," as fast as the winter set in, is evidence of his belief in instant archaeology and instant excavation, that with a few shovelsful of earth he would restore the dead city to life. But he was quickly disabused of this idea.

The further down his men dug, the more Cyclopean stones they discovered, walls built upon walls. Occasionally, they uncovered a copper coin. Schliemann identified his first finds as Greek and Roman in origin, belonging to the first centuries before and after Christ. He was contemptuous of them. Within a Trojan timeframe, these objects were minted only yesterday. He considered such finds a nuisance since it meant that he must dig deeper and this delayed his discovery of Homer's Troy. By now, of course, he realized that the wall he had unearthed the year before was totally unrelated to Priam's city.

He complained:

> The number of immense blocks of stone which we continually come upon cause great trouble and have to be got out and removed, which takes up a great deal of time, for at the moment when a large block of this kind is rolled to the edge of the slope, all of my workmen leave their own work and hurry off to see the enormous weight roll down its steep path with a thundering noise and settle itself at some distance in the Plain.

Aside from Sophia, nobody understood what he sought and this compounded his problem. He wrote:

> It is an absolute impossibility for me, who am the only one to preside over all, to give each workman his right occupation and to watch that each does his duty. "Nikolas Zaphyros, whom I pay 30 piasters [$.66] a day, is invaluable to me in paying the daily wages of the workmen, for he knows every one of them, and is honest. Unfortunately, however, he gives me no assistance in the work, as he neither possesses the gift of commanding, nor has he the slightest knowledge of what I am seeking.

So completely enveloped in the work was Schliemann, and so exhausted was he by nightfall, that the compulsive letter writer and diarist wrote up his notes only when it rained. "I naturally have no leisure here, and I have only been able to write the above because it is raining heavily and therefore no work can be done," he explained October 18. "On the next rain day, I shall report further on the progress of my excavations."

His next diary entry is dated eight days later. By then, he had reached an average depth of thirteen feet. To his delight, he no longer came upon the ruins of Roman buildings. Instead, he found layers of mussel shells, shark vertebrae, and oyster shells (which reminded him of Chesapeake blue points) and "very many fragments of pottery."

Describing the potsherds as "rubbish," he hurled them over the hill. Only later, much later and far too late, Schliemann learned that potsherds were the footprints of the past and that with every fragment of pottery that he discarded, he obliterated a clue to the past. But Schliemann can hardly be faulted; this was in an age of primitive archaeology, and it was only through early trial and error that Schliemann and his colleagues developed and refined the methods which form the basis of modern archaeology. Thus, some years later —indeed, thirteen years later—in discussing the "results of the latest researches and discoveries on the site of Homer's Troy," which was published in 1884 at New York under the German title, *Troja,* he conceded that "at that time archaeologists had not given yet any attention to the fragments of ancient pottery they found." Schliemann, however, discovered that the fragments were virtually indestructible and he never overcame his wonder at how thick, lustrous, black pottery, exposed to 4,000 years of frost and heat, rain and sunshine, could still be quite fresh.

Displaying the flexibility of scholarship, when he erred, he openly reversed himself. If anything, Schliemann did not consider himself infallible; on the contrary, and this set him apart from many of the academics of his era. Thus, later we find him castigating those who did not understand the scientific value of potsherds and lecturing on their value. He wrote in *Troja:*

Even when in 1876 I made large excavations at Mycenae, the delegate of the Greek Government, the Inspector of Antiquities, Mr. P. Stamatakis, pronounced the immense masses of fragments of highly important archaic pottery which we brought to light and which far exceeded in interest anything of that kind ever found in Greece, to be useless *debris,* and urgently insisted that they should be shot from the hill with the real rubbish; in fact I could not prevent this being done with quantities of such fragments. It was then that I telegraphed to Athens, begging the Minister of Public Instruction, as well as the President of the Archaeological Society, Mr. Philippos Ioannes, to stop this vandalism. Finally I invoked the aid of the Director General of Antiquities, Mr. P. Eustratiades, and of Professor E. Carotches, and I owe it solely to the energy of these worthy scholars, that the Archaeological Society was at last induced to put a stop to that outrage, and to command Stamatakis to preserve all the fragments of pottery. Since that time people have begun to regard pottery as the cornucopia of archaeological knowledge, and to employ it to determine approximately the age of the sites where it is found.

And then in the egotistical, bombastic manner which ruffled so many people, he quickly, imperiously added: "Science will, therefore, be grateful to me for having saved the really enormous masses of fragments of most ancient Mycenaean pottery from certain destruction." The comment was unnecessary, but it served to fill his urgent need for recognition, to compensate for the sense of inferiority he had acquired in his youth.

Neither Schliemann nor any of his successors, including the members of the famed Cincinnati Expedition to Troy in 1939, ever found a trace of writing in Homer's Troy. It is "quite possible," as Schliemann was fond of saying, that he inadvertently destroyed the written records of ancient Troy, if there were any. Even as late as World War II, when the first Linear B tablets were found on the Greek mainland by Carl Blegen, the dean of American archaeologists, they were almost overlooked as bits of scratched clay. Parenthetically, the tablets were not deciphered until more than a decade later and then by an amateur archaeologist, like Schliemann—the late Michel Ventris, who combined his love for the past with an enthusiasm for cryptography.

Gradually, Schliemann learned of the value and inde-structibility of potsherds. When he first detected these frag-ments at Troy, he confessed that "all are of such excellent clay, and burnt so hard, that I at first believed them to be of stone, and only perceived my mistake after having carefully exam-ined them."

In this manner, Schliemann stumbled on. Step by step, he destroyed everything in his path, from potsherds to buildings, in search of tangible evidence that Troy existed. "Unfortu-nately," he wrote in his diary that November, "we are obliged to destroy the foundations of a building, 59 feet long and 43 feet broad, of large wrought stones, which, by the inscriptions found in or close to it, seems to have been Hellenic." Similar entries dot his field journals.

At a depth of 30 to 33 feet, he uncovered still another stra-tum of houses hewn from very large blocks and "mixed with immense quantities of coarse hand-made pottery." Over the hill went everything.

Schliemann was perplexed. Instead of removing the top of Hissarlik and finding Troy beneath its crest, he found traces of different cities and civilizations at different depths. A Novem-ber 3 entry in his diary, for example, mirrors his amazement:

To my extreme surprise, on Monday, the 30th of last month I suddenly came upon a mass of debris in which I found an im-mense quantity of implements made of hard black stone, but of a very primitive form. On the following day, however, not a single stone implement was found but a small piece of silver wire and a great deal of broken pottery of elegant workmanship, among others the fragment of a cup with an owl's head.

I therefore thought I had again come upon the remains of a civilized people and that the stone implements of the previous day were the remains of an invasion of a barbarous tribe, whose domination had been of but short duration. But I was mistaken for on Wednesday the stone period reappeared in even greater force and continued throughout the whole of yesterday. Today, unfortunately, no work can be done owing to the heavy down-pour of rain.

I find much in this stone period that is quite inexplicable to me, and I therefore consider it necessary to describe everything as minutely as possible in the hope that one or other of my honoured colleagues [now that he had a doctorate he considered himself a member of The Establishment] will be able to give an explanation of the points which are obscure to me.

He found lances, hammers and axes, knife blades, saws, needles, bodkins, and spoons fashioned from bone. "I cannot explain how it is possible that I should find things which, to all appearance, must have been used by the uncivilized men of the stone period, but which could not have been made with the rude implements at their disposal." He also found more and more humming tops or whorls for which he used the descriptive German word, *carrouselen.* "The question then forces itself upon us: *For what were these objects used?*" he asked.

Anxious to explain what he could not explain, Schliemann gave rein to his imagination. "Primitive canoes, such as I frequently saw in Ceylon, formed out of a hollowed trunk of a tree, are often met with here in miniature, made of terra-cotta, and I presume that these small vessels may have served as salt cellars or pepper boxes." When he found a black, cigar-shaped object cut from marble, his imagination disappeared over the horizon. He described it as a priapus or phallic symbol "just such as I have seen in Indian temples." He also hastily, and erroneously, added, "I consequently have not the slightest doubt that the Trojan people of the stone period worshipped Priapus as a divinity."

In his confusion, Schliemann also stumbled onto a verity of the Trojan War, that it was a civil war among people of the same race, religion, culture, and probably language. "It is probable that these ancient Trojans are the ancestors of the great Hellenic nation, for I repeatedly find upon cups and vases of terra-cotta representations of the owl's head which is probably the great, great grandmother of the Athenian bird of Pallas-Athena."

Athena, the goddess of wisdom, was born out of the head of Zeus, one of the dozen Olympians and was often portrayed in Homer and elsewhere as an owl. Thus, in *The Iliad,* Homer refers to "the goddess Athena with the owl's face."

With an eye on the calendar and the descent of winter, to no avail, Schliemann sought to increase the tempo of his excavations. In the middle of November, he lamented that "unfortunately, I have lost three days; for on Sunday, a day on which the Greeks do no work, I could not secure the services of any Turkish workmen, for they are now sowing their crops; on two other days I was hindered by heavy rains." Then he bitterly complained that the work was being interrupted not only by Sunday and rain, but also by endless Greek festivals. Yet he had reached a depth of 33 feet and found colossal ruins, which he "positively" identified as ancient Troy.

As he progressed, the work became more difficult. He jotted in his notebook on November 24:

> This morning, I worked for three hours with sixty-five workmen in removing a single threshold [huge stone block] by means of ropes and rollers.
>
> But these difficulties only increase my desire, after so many disappointments, to reach the great goal which is at last lying before me, to prove that *The Iliad* is founded on fact, and that the great Greek nation must not be deprived of this crown of her glory.
>
> I shall spare no trouble and shun no expense to attain this result.

But, inwardly, doubts grew. The more he studied the confusing Stone Age strata he uncovered the more uncertain he became about finding Troy. Defensively and deceptively, he lowered his sights. He abandoned hope of uncovering tangible evidence. "My expectations are extremely modest," he consoled himself. "I have no hope of finding plastic works of art."

Then, as a form of self-encouragement, he restated the theme of his life: "The single object of my excavations from the beginning is only to find Troy, whose site has been discussed by a hundred scholars in a hundred books, but which as yet no one has ever sought to bring to light by excavations."

His doubts about finding Homeric Troy grew with the growing number of Stone Age implements he found. At first, unknown to Schliemann, in digging straight down, like an elevator passing a floor and terminating in the basement, Schliemann had passed the stratum in which Priam's Pergamus was located. He was traveling backwards in time and space to the Stone Age which preceded the Greek Bronze Age. He made the initial error of thinking that Homeric Troy was the basement when, in point of fact, the site had been occupied by primitive man long before the epic Trojan War unraveled.

In his diary, he weakly and unconvincingly contended that "if I should not succeed in finding Troy, still I shall be perfectly contented for having brought the deepest darkness of prehistoric times to light and enriching archaeology."

He wrote these words sitting at a makeshift desk in a crudely built peasant hut in the Turkish village of Chiblak, a mile and a quarter from Hissarlik, where he and Sophia had established their temporary headquarters.

"I fear the object of our excavations, to find the Pergamus of Priam has failed," he gloomily confided to Sophia.

"Patience, dear Henry, patience," she counseled repeatedly.

"But," he insisted with anger in his voice, not at Sophia but at the Fates, "we have reached a period long before the Trojan War, perhaps thousands of years older than the deeds of Achilles."

Yet his doggedness in the face of adversity, his strong will and determination would not permit him to accept defeat. Reflecting the instability of the romantic and the visionary, his moods of despair blended with moods of triumph. He wrote several days later:

> The discovery of the Stone period, instead of discouraging me, has only made me the more desirous to penetrate to the place which was occupied by the first people that came here. And I still intend to reach it even if I should have to dig another fifty feet further down.

Before his great work ended, he dug deeper, bodily removing the whole hill at Hissarlik and laying it bare to the sunlight. Before his great work ended, he spent not one year but fourteen years on the site of Homer's Troy.

As November drew to a close and winter rapidly encased the Trojan Plain, accompanied by strong winds and torrential rains, Schliemann abandoned his dig. "Unfortunately," he wrote, "I find myself now compelled to cease excavations for winter. But I now most firmly believe that I am already among the ruins of Troy."

Sophia and Heinrich packed their few belongings, bade farewell to the Turkish villagers and Greek workmen, and promised to return in spring. Over a nondescript road, they set off by horse and carriage for the Dardanelles and thence to Piraeus by boat. Sophia now realized that she was married to an extraordinary man, a man who was as at ease in an unwashed Turkish shack in Chiblak, "in the middle of nowhere," as in his sumptuous, ornately appointed Parisian town house at Place St. Michel.

In the final entry in his diary for the year, November 24, 1871, Schliemann made known his suspicion that he had not only found Troy but different cities and civilizations representing different periods of history.

As I find ever more and more traces of civilization the deeper I dig, I am now perfectly convinced that I have not yet penetrated the period of the Trojan War, and hence I am more hopeful than ever of finding the site of Troy by further excavations.

If there ever was a Troy—and my belief in this is firm—it can only have been here, on the site of Hissarlik.

# XI

⎍⎍⎍⎍⎍⎍⎍
─────────────
⎍⎍⎍⎍⎍⎍⎍

# The Base Camp

*In all his glory, he rages like a maniac;*
*confident that Zeus is with him he*
*fears neither god nor man.*

The Iliad, BOOK IX

"ON APRIL 1, 1872, at six o'clock on the morning of a glorious day, accompanied by my wife," Schliemann wrote in his field journal, "I resumed the excavation." Based on his previous experience at Hissarlik, repeatedly turned over in his mind during a comfortable winter in Athens, Schliemann mapped a detailed strategy for his "Trojan campaign," as he called the project.

Rather than continue an almost intolerable existence in the nearby village of Chiblak—"this place of vermine"—or confine himself to the inconvenience and impermanance of tent life, he decided to erect his own settlement at the dig— three buildings of wood, and one, for Sophia and himself, of the marble blocks he had uncovered the year before. Within three weeks of their return to the site, the first makeshift house was completed. It consisted of three rooms, plus a magazine and kitchen. The building, he observed in his journal, "cost me $200, including the covering of waterproof felt." The stone house was not completed until late November. He planned to move in with the advent of winter but, perhaps recalling his own hard winter in Amsterdam as a destitute youth, "I was compelled," he said, "to let my foremen occupy it, for they were not sufficiently provided with clothes and wrappers, and would have perished through the great cold."

As a consequence, he added, "my poor wife and I have therefore suffered very much." The north wind blew with such violence through the openings of the wooden house that "we were not even able to light our lamp in the evening, and although we had a fire on the hearth, the thermometer showed 23 degrees Fahrenheit, and the water standing near the hearth froze in solid masses," he recorded.

Characteristically, he penned a footnote: "We have nothing to keep us warm except our enthusiasm for the great work of discovering Troy." And, perhaps, he should have added, the warmth of each other's bodies. But winter is short-lived on the Trojan Plain and, with its passing, in mid-February, Schliemann exuberantly reported, "We have glorious weather."

In ensuing years, the camp at Hissarlik turned into a semi-permanent settlement. Two more barracks were erected, one serving as a dining hall, "and was called by that proud name," although it consisted of little more than rude planks. When the wind blew strongly, it was impossible to light a candle at the table. The other barrack served as a storehouse for the antiquities which he brought to light and which were to be divided between the Imperial Museum at Constantinople and himself in accordance with his *firman*.

His camp also boasted dwellings which appeared as a throwback to the tale of Ali Baba and the forty thieves of Bagdad. Among the principal objects Schliemann uncovered in 1872–1873 were *pithoi*—coarse, red jars, seven feet high, embedded in the soil in a vertical position. Intact, unpolished, without handles, ornamented with four broad projecting bands, the *pithoi* were employed by the Trojans as storage bins for grain, olive oil, wine, and water. The enterprising Schliemann placed these jars on the campsite where they were used by the workers as a nineteenth-century version of quonset huts. One jar housed one man and "it even lodged two of them in rainy weather," Schliemann said.

Food was plentiful at the dig, but it lacked variety. Mutton was always present but vegetables were limited to potatoes and spinach, the former shipped from the Hellespont, or Dardanelles, about six to eight hours' distance by horse carriage, depending on the weather and, therefore, the condition of the road. Schliemann found it inexplicable that the villagers of the Troad, Greeks as well as Turks, shunned potatoes, although the soil was well adapted for their cultivation. In the summer, however, their diet was supplemented by locally cultivated hog beans, kidney beans, and artichokes.

For reasons of loyalty and sentimentality, Schliemann never forgot the house of Schroder, which launched his mercantile career, and by the same token they never forgot him and his accomplishments. Periodically, Schroder shipped him a supply of "Chicago corned beef," oxtongues, English cheese, and peaches. On one occasion, they sent him 240 bottles of English pale ale. Hoarding the shipment like an Ulbricht below the Rhine, he stretched the supply so that it lasted for almost half a year. By experimentation, he discovered that the locally produced wine of the neighboring villages was cheap, abundant, and of good quality. With the usual touch of exaggeration, he announced that the wine of the Troad "excelled the very best Bordeaux" and he loyally maintained that "I prefer it to any French wine."

Mindful of his bouts with fever in California and Panama, the fear of contracting swamp fever never left him. All the conditions for the formation of malaria were present in the Troad although, at the time, the cause of the disease was unknown; it was not until eight years later, in 1880, that Alphonse Laverne, working in Algeria, first recognized the anopheles mosquito as the source of the disease in man. After paying Schliemann a visit at Hissarlik, a physician friend from Berlin later wrote that:

> ... the Trojan Plain is a notorious region of fever, nor can any one be astonished at this. Large swamps and marshes extend in all directions. Several rivers and rivulets disappear in them and fill the subsoil with their water. Shortly before my arrival, the Scamander had overflowed its banks and had inundated the plain far and wide. In the first week of April the whole land on

its west side was still coated with thick silt and mud: all the roads were covered up, and stagnant water stood in many places. Then the evaporation commenced and in the evening a stinking fog lay over the plain.

Although the cause of the disease was not known, quinine, derived from the chinchona tree in tropical America and Asia, was recognized as an effective preventative and cure. Sophia's health was of particular concern to Schliemann, and he insisted that she take a daily dose of quinine. Even so, they periodically contracted fever and, on one occasion, in the summer of 1872, they were forced temporarily to close the camp. He noted in his diary August 14:

> Since my report of the fourth of this month, I have continued the excavations with the utmost energy, but I am now compelled to stop the work this evening, for my three foremen and my servant, who is also my cashier, have been seized by malignant marsh-fever, and my wife and I are so unwell that we are quite unable to undertake the sole direction throughout the day in the terrible heat of the sun.
>
> Tomorrow we shall return to Athens.

That night, he and Sophia packed their cloth bags and left at daybreak by horse for the Dardanelles. But Sophia was hardly back in "civilization"—her beloved Athens—among her family and friends, and she no sooner cradled young Andromache in her arms, when she and her unpredictable millionaire husband repacked their belongings and within a month returned to the Trojan Plain. The dig resumed on September 10.

During their breathers at Athens, Heinrich spent the better part of each day writing up his notes and maintaining his mountainous, global correspondence. Assiduously, he studied the stock market reports each morning in the London *Times,* usually two weeks late, and kept a professional eye on his investment portfolio.

During journeys between Athens and Hissarlik, he constantly replenished his stock of quinine and, since the Troad possessed neither an apothecary's shop nor a physician,

Schliemann increasingly found himself assaying the role of a Schweitzer, if not a barefoot doctor.

Rude, bombastic, and demanding as he was in the developed world—Athens, Paris, The Hague, London, Berlin, and St. Petersburg—in the impoverished, underdeveloped world Schliemann showed compassion and humanity for the stream of "wretched creatures" who ventured to the camp for medical assistance, especially the victims of malaria. Schliemann confided in his diary that he did not understand "anything about medicine" and expressed fear of committing a "great mistake" in treating his patients. But he could not turn his back on their agony.

He recalled that in Central America, when he succumbed to fever, a physician saved his life with a dose of sixty-four grains of quinine (one can almost visualize Schliemann swallowing the quinine a grain at a time and recording their number in his diary). "Hence I give a similar quantity here," he wrote, "but only in one dose when the case is a very bad one; the quantity I generally give is four doses of sixteen grains." And as his fame as physician spread, he was daily called upon not only to cure men, but also camels, donkeys, and horses. As a veterinarian, he usually prescribed a tincture of arnica. Only once, in his private correspondence, did he display impatience. He grumbled:

> My valuable time is now claimed in a troublesome manner by sick people. But . . . it breaks my heart to see the unfortunate wretches die away. . . . Therefore I beg you to please send word to your apothecary to send to me, in care of the American Consul James [sic] Calvert [at the Dardanelles] a tin-box of quinine made up in powders of four grains each. I am now perfectly convinced that with four grains of quinine in the morning as a preventative, a man is fever-proof even in the most poisonous climate. I think even two grains are enough.

In the villages of the Troad, the local priest among the Greeks served as parish doctor and, ignorant of medicine and lacking drugs, the priest rarely employed any other means to cure an illness than bleeding, which, Schliemann observed, often killed the patient. Wrinkles on either side of the lips of children showed that the priest repeatedly bled them. As for himself, Schliemann hated the custom of bleeding and he never recommended it. Instead, he usually prescribed, in non-fever cases, a dip in the salt water of the Aegean. Ever since his Dutch days, he attributed the healing of his chest lesions to his immersion off Texel and to the salt-laden air of Amsterdam. As a result, he became a pathological advocate of ocean bathing; for the remainder of his life—whenever the opportunity presented itself—each morning, he took a dip in the sea. As a result of his ministrations, the concept of salt-water bathing caught on in the Troad and, he boasted, "even women who fancied that it would be their death to touch their bodies with cold water," now took to the sea. Yet throughout his stay in the Troad, he complained, not one of his patients thanked him for his effort. "Gratitude does not appear to be one of the virtues of the present Trojans," he said.

On one occasion, in May of 1872, a seventeen-year-old girl from the village of Neo Chori was brought to him, her body covered with ulcers. Gaunt, coughing, her left eye covered with a large ulcer, the telltale scars of excessive bleeding around her lips, he gave her a spoon of castor oil and ordered her to take daily sea baths. He wrote May 23:

> I was quite touched when early this morning the same girl appeared on the platform, threw herself on the ground, kissed my dirty shoes, and told me, with tears of joy that even the first sea bath had given her an appetite, that all the sores had begun to heal directly, and had now disappeared, but that the left eye was still blind.

The girl had walked three hours from her village to thank him, and he remembered the incident as the first and only time he received an expression of gratitude for his medical endeavor. But his experience in the marketplace made him so wary and inordinately suspicious of human motivation that he dryly commented, "I still am not quite sure whether it was a feeling of pure gratitude that induced the girl to come to me, or whether it was in the hope that by some other means I might restore sight to the blind eye."

In addition to the presence of malaria, other horrors made the Troad anything but a nineteenth-century tourist attraction. During the first three days of the 1872 excavation, for example, in digging into the hill, Schliemann came upon a nest of snakes, among them a remarkable quantity of small, brown, deadly vipers, the *antelion,* which are scarcely thicker than an earthworm. "It seems to me," Schliemann wrote in his journal, "that, were it not for the many thousands of storks which destroy the snakes in spring and summer, the Plain of Troy would be uninhabitable, owing to the excessive numbers of this vermin." The snakes plagued the site, hiding among the stone walls and building blocks Schliemann uncovered. On one occasion, while working in a pit 36 feet from the surface of the hill, Schliemann was astonished to see his workmen take hold the reptiles with their hands and hurl them out of the way; indeed, one man was bitten twice by a viper without seeming to trouble himself about it. Schliemann was horrified, but the man laughed, and explained "that he and all his comrades knew that there were a great many snakes in this hill and they had therefore all drunk a decoction of the snakeweed which grows in the district, and which renders the bite harmless."

Henceforth, Schliemann and Sophia fortified themselves daily not only with quinine but also with the snakeweed mixture. The speculator and businessman surfaced in Schliemann and he also wondered aloud "whether this decoction would be a safeguard against the fatal effects of the bite of the hooded cobra, of which in India I have seen a man die within half an hour; if it were so, it would be a good speculation to cultivate snakeweed there."

But, like winter, the reptilian phase was of short duration. "The snakes seem to have been enticed out of their winter quarters by the warm weather which has set in," he recorded with relief on May 11, 1872. "It is ten days since I have seen any."

Yet the problem of snakes arose in an unexpected manner late in the summer. The camp was thrown into an uproar when he uncovered fragments of terra-cotta serpents, whose heads were sometimes represented with horns. Like the Trojans of antiquity who inhabited the site, the villagers of his day still considered this a symbol of great significance "for even now there is a superstition that the horns of serpents, by merely coming into contact with the human body, cure a number of diseases, and especially epilepsy." His assurances notwith-standing, he could not convince his laborers that there were no such things as serpents' horns.

Nor did he and Sophia ever become reconciled to the "im-mense numbers of insects and vermin of all kinds" which plagued the region. The nineteen-year-old Sophia especially dreaded a centipede known locally as "the insect with forty feet" which periodically fell from the ceiling of their barrack and, according to the villagers, whose bite was said to be fatal. The centipede was probably the scorpion, which is as common-place in Asia Minor as in Central America.

With the torrents of spring, the Trojan Plain was enveloped in deep grass and red and yellow flowers. As the swamps dried, the fear of snakes gave ground to the annoyance of millions of croaking frogs each evening and to the locust swarms which descended on the region. One evening Schliemann described himself as "astonished to see all the walls of my barracks, up to the roof, covered with a black mass which seemed to be moving." The following morning, he found that the masses were locusts. The racket made by the frogs and locusts was often drowned out in the middle of the night by the shrieking and screeching of the numerous owls which inhabited the plain. Throughout their years in the Troad, the Schliemanns never grew accustomed to the periodic outbursts of "horrible screams," as they described them, which rent the night around the bleak and lonely hill of Hissarlik. Schliemann's journals and copybooks are dotted with quotations from Homer, and it is reasonable to believe that the presence of screaming owls probably recalled to his mind the passage in *The Iliad* when:

> . . . the ghosts came trooping up from Hades—brides, young bachelors, old men worn out with toil, maids who had been crossed in love, and brave men who had been killed in battle, with their armor still smirched with blood; they came from every quarter and flitted round the trench with a strange kind of screaming that made me turn pale with fear.

These varied living conditions notwithstanding, Schliemann, caught up in his magnificent obsession, drove the men forward in a frenzy. He raged like a maniac against delay. But no matter how hard he drove his workers, he drove himself the harder; they knew it and respected him for it, even if they felt he was slightly unbalanced like most foreigners.

Work commenced regularly at sunrise, and continued until half-past five in the evening. For this twelve-hour day, his workers received about 22 cents (9 piasters). The daily rate increased with the season, rising during the hot summer months to 45 cents. The din of the pickax and shovel was broken during the day only by the foreman's shout, *"Paidos! Paidos!"* a word of uncertain derivation which had passed over into Turkish and meant "time for rest." In the spring, the shout *"Paidos!"* was heard only at dinner-time, midday. The rest period lasted one hour but, as Schliemann proudly pointed out, "as the days become longer, I allowed, after the Easter holidays, another half-hour at half past eight for breakfast; this latter break was increased to one hour during the summer." In that setting, only striped pajamas and leg irons were missing. But such working conditions were completely acceptable in the nineteenth century; indeed, in the industrialized West, the sweatshop was coming into its own; trade unions were nonexistent; and the economic principle that the greater the purchasing power of the people, the greater the profit-making capacity of the entrepreneur was unrecognized.

Schliemann followed this work pattern up to and including his last dig at Troy in 1890 when, as a man of almost seventy and broken in health, he still maintained the strict pace he set for his young, able-bodied work gangs. Actually, he worked harder. In the evening, when the men, exhausted, either returned to their villages or slept in the open on the site, Schliemann spent hours preparing his reports, writing letters, planning the next day's work, and studying and cataloging the objects excavated during the day. For that matter, he also usually rose earlier than his men so that he could take a dip in the Aegean before the workday started. With Sophia nightly by his side, it is hard to believe that he had much energy left for lovemaking. But he was a man of enormous energy and on the site of Priam's Pergamus, the Troy of his childhood dreams, adrenalin flowed freely in his veins.

The extent of this stimulation, this release of energy, is revealed in a letter written the previous November to an English friend, as he reached the lower depths of the hill. He said:

> I do not know what to think. But to see that at the very utmost I am, in twenty-three feet, in the rubbish of people who lived 1500 years before Christ . . . bewilders my mind. Perhaps I have not even reached yet the layers of rubbish of the epoch war of Troy. . . . But all this confusion of ages instead of discouraging me, only stimulates me the more to go ahead and to reach the virgin soil at any price.

Schliemann's camp, like his gold dust store in California, was a veritable League of Nations. Based on his experience of the year before, he supplemented his Levantine Greek work gangs with Turks and Levantine Jews. As the men labored through the day, a curious, godly vignette emerged: Troy was being resurrected by a mixed band of Greek Orthodox Catholics, Moslems, and Jews under the direction of a pagan sired by a Protestant minister. "*The Iliad* is my gospel," Schliemann said.

In character, as in Germany, Holland, Russia, and the Americas, Schliemann was impressed by industry, enterprise, and imagination. The Turks, for example, he found the hardest workers and therefore his favorite employees. From a managerial perspective:

> They work much better than the Greeks, are more honest, and I have in them the great advantage that they worked on Sundays and on the numerous saints' days when no Greeks would have worked at any price.
>  Besides, as I could always be sure that they would work on with unremitting zeal, and never need to be urged, I could let them sink all the shafts and assign to them other work, in which no superintendence on my part was possible.

Hard work deserved a reward and, accordingly, Schliemann paid the Turks a slightly higher wage than the Greeks.

For linguistic reasons in particular, he was fascinated by his Jewish laborers, "who likewise worked much better than the Greeks."

These were the descendants of the Spanish Jews expelled from Spain by Ferdinand and Isabella at the end of the fifteenth century. Despite their wandering and the vicissitudes of their fortunes, they never forgot the Spanish language in which, to Schliemann's amazement, they still conversed among themselves, employing a vocabulary of Cervantian contemporaneity.

"It is a wonder that the Spanish language could have been so well preserved here for four centuries, in the mouths of a people who do not write it with the Latin alphabet but solely with Hebrew characters, whenever they have to correspond among themselves."

Fluent himself in Spanish, Schliemann delighted in talking with them. He employed a Spanish-speaking Levantine Jew as his agent in the Dardanelles for procuring fresh supplies, forwarding his mail, and similar duties. Schliemann always wrote to him in Spanish, but the man invariably replied in Italian and confessed that he did not know how to write Spanish with Latin characters, as from his childhood he had been accustomed to using the Hebrew alphabet to write Spanish.

The 1872 camp was no sooner organized than Schliemann was confronted by mutiny.

A taskmaster's taskmaster, he observed that smoking on the site interrupted the work schedule and he warned, "I therefore forbid smoking during working hours." The men ignored the outrageous order and smoked in secret. Schliemann, however, was not to be denied. It was his hard-earned fortune which was being spent on excavating the hill. At dawn on April 25, a few days after the first house was erected on the site, Schliemann announced: "Smoking will not be permitted and transgressors will be dismissed and never taken on again."

Enraged, seventy of his independent-minded Greek workers declared that they would quit unless they were permitted to smoke as much as they pleased. The men walked out of the camp, confident that Schliemann would relent since, obviously, he could not do without them and, already aware of his impatience and industriousness, "that during the beautiful weather it was not likely that I would sit still a whole day."

But Schliemann, who had outfoxed some of the most cunning merchants of the era, outfoxed the mutineers with ease. He sent his foremen far and wide that night to recruit new workers; the following morning they returned with 120 men of mixed nationality. Ever to press an advantage, another of his commercial attributes, he not only prohibited smoking during work but bragged that "I have even lengthened the day's work by one hour to half past six in the evening."

Good foremen and an ample supply of drinking water were essential to the smooth operation of the camp—"one foreman is worth ten or more good workmen," he often said—and on his return to Hissarlik he promptly reengaged Nicholas Zaphryos, who had served as foreman the year before. Schliemann paid him handsomely, about $2.70 a day, and considered him a man cast in the Schliemann mold—honest, industrious, and enterprising. "He is perfectly honest," Schliemann said, "and as a purser and major domo in a large camp in the wilderness or in explorations, he can never be excelled." But honesty and industry aside, Schliemann was captivated by Zaphryos' spirit of private enterprise. For in effect, Zaphryos operated a company store.

> His wages are the least advantage he has with me, for he derives enormous profits from the shop which is kept on his account by his brother, and in which he sells bread, tobacco and wine on credit to my workmen, whose debts to him he always deducts in paying them on Saturday evening.

Another favorite among his foremen was Georgio Photidas who for seven years had worked as a miner in Australia. Homesickness brought him back to his native Greece and when he heard that Schliemann was excavating Hissarlik, he came "on speculation" (at his own expense) to offer Schliemann his services. Once again, the industrious spirit captivated Schliemann. Mindful of his own youthful struggle for survival, he hired Photidas on the spot when the young man assured him that "my accepting his services was a question of life and death to him and his wife." The young man, it developed, was down to his last piaster. At the time, Schliemann considered his experience as a miner, tunnelmaker and pit man a bonus. Shortly thereafter, to his joy, he learned that Photidas could read and write Greek; thereafter, he became Schliemann's Bob Cratchit.

"He is thus able to copy my Greek reports," Schliemann wrote enthusiastically, "for I had hitherto found nothing more intolerable than to have to write out in Greek three times over my long reports about one and the same subject, especially as I had to take the time from my sleep." Carbon paper was yet to be invented.

Others drifted into camp from time to time to offer their services, including a sea captain whom Schliemann immediately hired as a foreman. After his adventures at sea, Schliemann had great respect for sailors. "I find," he said, "that the gift of command is rarely met with except among seamen."

As for drinking water, he solved this problem by employing a man and a boy exclusively for the purpose of fetching water from the nearest spring, a distance from the dig of 395.6 yards (Schliemann, of course, measured it). The boy's job was to fill the barrels; that of the man to load two of them at a time on a donkey and to convey them to the site. "So great was the consumption of water that in hot weather," Schliemann recalled, "the man could hardly fetch water enough, though ten barrels were in constant use."

In the village of Neo Chori, where Schliemann's fame as a physician had spread and where he frequently bought fresh food for the camp, he found a kindred spirit, Konstantinos Kolobos, the owner of a grocery shop, who, he observed admiringly, "although born without feet has nevertheless made a considerable fortune in retail business." Here, Schliemann's true character again surfaces. He is attracted to the man because of his commercial success despite a difficult start in life. Also because, like himself, Kolobos is a self-taught, natural-born linguist. Although Schliemann makes no reference to the Hopping Peter of his boyhood, he writes about Kolobos, who, clearly, was a Schliemann in the rough. in almost the same affectionate terms.

His talents are not confined to business; they include a knowledge of languages; and although Kolobos has grown up among the rough and ignorant village lads and has never had a master, yet by self-tuition he has succeeded in acquiring the Italian and French languages, and writes and speaks both of them perfectly. He is also wonderfully expert in ancient Greek, from having several times copied and learnt by heart a large etymological dictionary, as well as from having read all the classic authors, and he can repeat whole rhapsodies from *The Iliad* by heart.

What a pity that such a genius has to spend his days in a wretched village in the Troad, useless to the world, and in the constant company of the most uneducated and ignorant people, all of whom gaze at him in admiration, but none of whom understand him.

Brigands infested Greece and Turkey in this period as the authority of the decaying Ottoman Empire waned with ever-increasing rapidity. In point of fact, not only was the rot already visible, but the 600-year-old empire crumbled within a generation after Schliemann completed his last Trojan campaign.

Of particular concern to Schliemann in establishing his camp was the penchant of the brigands to kidnap and hold for ransom wealthy men, especially itinerant foreign travelers. More often than not, even though the ransom was paid, the captive's throat was slit. "I was afraid of a like fate at Hissarlik," Schliemann freely acknowledged. To round out his camp, he therefore organized "Schliemann's irregulars," a band of eleven Bulgars and Albanians. Later, when Bulgaria and Albania, like Greece, wrested their independence from Ottoman rule, Schliemann dissolved the army. "To such men I would not now entrust myself," he said. Yet he needed protection, and he turned to Constantinople for help. The local Turkish civil governor was authorized to assign him eleven gendarmes, "the surest men he could find." Schliemann paid each man $13.50 a month. They were men of powerful frame, well-disciplined, and armed with rifles, pistols, and daggers.

"Their firearms were not precisely of the latest invention," Schliemann, the ex-gunrunner observed with understatement, "for they had for the most part only flintlocks." But they did include several Minie rifles which were used in the Crimean

War and of which Schliemann, as a war profiteer, was acutely aware. "These shortcomings, however, were made up by the courage of the men," he said, "and I trusted them entirely."

Three of the gendarmes accompanied Schliemann each morning, weather permitting, for his ritualistic sea bath in the Aegean, a distance of three miles. "As I always rode at a trot, they had to run as fast as they could to keep up with me," he said. "These daily runs being, therefore, very fatiguing to the men, I paid them an extra ten cents every morning as extra wages."

Comic overtones aside, Schliemann's decision to maintain an armed patrol was not generated by flight of fancy, however active his imagination. In 1878, six years later, while on location, a band of armed Circassians attacked a village only twenty minutes' walk from Schliemann's camp atop Hissarlik. In the ensuing fire fight, two intruders and two defenders were slain.

Schliemann's irregulars also served as a security detail and kept an eye on the workers during the day and on the barracks containing antiquities and field equipment during the night. The latter included forty iron crowbars, two screw jacks, 100 large iron shovels, an equal amount of pickaxes, fifty large hoes, battering rams, chains, two windlasses and 100 wheelbarrows, most of them with novel, iron wheels. "All of this equipment," he vaunted, "is of the best English manufacture." He also maintained, for removing debris, twenty mancarts, that is, carts drawn by one man in front and pushed by two men from the rear, and several horse and ox carts, all of local design and construction and still in use today in the Troad.

Thus armed, figuratively and literally, the great work of recovering Troy, "this grand enterprise," as he also called it, began in earnest.

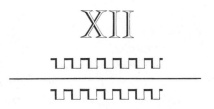

# XII

# Troy Discovered

*"He rushed across the plain like a winter
torrent that has burst its barrier in
full flood."*

The Iliad, BOOK V

DURING THE PRECEDING WINTER, Schliemann had adopted a novel
plan for excavating Troy. To what extent he was influenced by
the digging and opening of the Suez Canal, the most celebrated
engineering triumph of his century only four years earlier, is
not known. But instead of painstakingly peeling back the top of
Hissarlik layer by layer until he reached his Trojan wonderland, Schliemann decided to dig a big ditch right through the
hill. In a private letter to the Calverts in the winter of 1871, he
hinted at his strategy. "I shall merely limit myself to cutting
through the mountain a tremendous trench 98 feet broad and
at least 400 feet long," he wrote. The big ditch was necessary,
he explained, because, "it is above all things necessary for me
to reach the primary soil, in order to make accurate investiga-
tions." Schliemann obviously viewed Troy as the most ancient
settlement at Hissarlik, the first settlement. Therefore, he reasoned, by reaching virgin rock, Troy would reemerge from the
bowels of the earth, a ghost town from antiquity, and, in the
process, his beloved and maligned Homer would be vindicated.

As simple as the plan seemed, he had serious misgivings

*125*

about the strategy. He realized that by cutting a swath through the hill he would, willy-nilly, be compelled to destroy everything in his path "which does not belong to the Heroic Age." His concern, however, was not with the embryonic science of archaeology. Instead, he worried that the scheme would generate new difficulties with the "ignorant authorities," for the *firman* expressly stipulated that he must "respect the walls of the ancient celebrated city" and, he reasoned, "the Turks will think that those tremendous post-Trojan walls belong to the ancient city whereas I see that they belong to a posterior age."

Whatever the case, he implemented the strategy in the spring of 1872 in order, he confidently asserted, "to be sure of thoroughly solving the Trojan question this year." Little did he realize that instead of solving the question, his excavations at Hissarlik raised a whole array of new questions which to this day have never been answered.

Against this backdrop, he undertook to erect a horizontal platform on the steep northern slope of the site which rose at an angle of 40° to a height of 105 feet perpendicular, and 161 feet above the surrounding sea-level Plain of Troy. The platform extended the length and breadth of the hill. The scheme involved a stupendous undertaking at a time when the steam shovel, the backhoe, the trench digger, and other earth-moving machines were still to be invented. A French engineer, familiar with de Lesseps' triumph at Suez, inspected Schliemann's site and concluded that his work gangs would have to remove at least 100,000 cubic yards of earth to push their "canal" through the hill.

To make the work easier, after removing the earth so that it rose perpendicularly to a height of about 8.5 feet from the bottom of the hill, and after that at an angle of 50°, Schliemann continued to loosen the debris forming the walls of his trench in such a manner that the angle always remained the same. But as the work progressed, it became increasingly dangerous.

"In spite of every precaution, I am unable to guard my men or myself against the stones which continually come rolling down, when the steep wall is being picked away," he noted in his journal. "Not one of us is without several wounds in his feet," he said.

The shouts of *"Guardo! Guardo!"*—like the cry of "Timber!" in a logging camp—echoed through the site as the work gained momentum. Even so, many stones rolled down the steep walls without the workmen noticing them, and Schliemann said at the end of each day's work, "I fervently thanked God for the great blessing that another day has passed without accident."

On May 23, tragedy was narrowly averted. A buttress of large stones, supporting the trench platform, collapsed as six men worked below it. "My fright was terrible and indescribable," Schliemann said. "I quite believed that the six men must have been crushed by the mass of stones; to my extreme joy, however, they all escaped, as if by a miracle." The following month another tragedy was even more precariously averted. Schliemann and forty men worked together for three hours in 90° with huge levers and a windlass to loosen an earthen wall sixteen feet high, sixteen feet wide, and ten feet thick, when suddenly an adjoining earth wall fell of its own accord and buried Photidas, the foreman, and a workman. As the wall collapsed, 100 cubic yards of stone and earth dropped on them.

Frightened, Schliemann and the others set to work immediately to rescue the men. "We had scarcely begun," he said, "when we heard them moaning beneath the weight of earth, for several logs had been upset, and, lying lengthwise, they still partly supported the earth, so that the men had breathing space left."

But their release could not be effected without great danger to the rescuers, owing to several large gaps in the cracked earthen wall. The men had to be cut out. Schliemann, the man of action, did not hesitate. He leaped down to the spot and with his knife cut out Photidas while two other men followed his example and cut out the other worker.

And so, in this manner, the grand enterprise proceeded.

Essentially, Schliemann's excavation consisted of a series of transverse cuttings, which laid open sections of various strata from the surface of the hill, to the virgin soil fifty-three feet below. Thus, the work of one day often yielded objects from almost all the strata, a great jumble of objects, a cornucopia of archaeological finds. Little wonder that he was often confused by what he uncovered. Worse, he was impatient, the curse borne by a man possessed. Ruthlessly, he destroyed walls, buildings, temples, whatever stood in his way, if he felt that the ruin obstructing his trench did not relate to "sacred Troy." Since the site, it later developed, had been inhabited by man for more than thirty centuries, and was the location of city superimposed upon city, Schliemann's path to Troy was repeatedly blocked by ruins which he felt compelled to disintegrate.

Schliemann was aware that in his wake he left a trail of destruction, like a tornado on the plains of Indiana, as he pressed his trench through the hill. His field journals and published reports of the expedition are dotted with expressions of continuing dismay. Thus, at one point he conceded:

> As it was my object to excavate Troy, which I expected to find in one of the lower cities, I was forced to demolish many interesting ruins in the upper strata, as, for example, at a depth of twenty feet below the surface, the ruins of a prehistoric building ten feet high, the walls of which consisted of hewn blocks of limestone perfectly smooth and cemented with clay.

And at another point he wrote, "I was also forced to destroy a small channel made of green sandstone, eighteen inches broad and seven inches deep which I found at a depth of about thirty-six feet below the surface and which probably served as the gutter of a house." When he stumbled across the foundation of a temple built in the classical Greek age, Schliemann confessed, "In order to bring Troy itself to light, I was forced to sacrifice the ruins of this temple." And when he came across an edifice dating from 1000 B.C., he solemnly wrote, "To my regret, however, it must be pulled down to allow us to dig still deeper."

Arbitrarily, however, whatever struck his fancy, in ad hoc fashion, he preserved, even though it was not Trojan. Thus, when he came across a stone bastion, composed of large, finely hewn blocks, not joined by either cement or lime, although he recognized it as the work of Lysimachus, the successor of Alexander the Great, he worked cautiously around it. "It is certainly very much in our way," he conceded. "But it is too beautiful and venerable for me to venture to lay hands upon it, so it shall be preserved."

Later, to his horror, he discovered that Troy did not occupy the first strata of the hill and that to reach this Stone Age settlement he had actually destroyed part of Troy. But he was learning fast. A year after he commenced his big ditch, in 1873, he already recognized that he had been overly destructive and therefore modified his blockbusting technique. "In consequence of my former mistaken idea that Troy was to be found on the primary soil or close above it," he lamented in his journal, "I unfortunately, in 1871 and 1872, destroyed a large portion of the city."

As noted later, these admissions of error laid him open to his critics. With relish, they assaulted him. It was left to his friend and supporter, Rudolf Virchow, a prominent professor of pathology and anatomy, to take up Schliemann's defense on his return to Berlin from his first visit to the dig in 1879.

Like Daniel in the den, Virchow delivered his defense of Schliemann at a meeting in Berlin of the Society for Anthropology, Ethnology, and Pre-historic Archaeology. He said:

> Schliemann's excavations will for a long time to come give testimony, not only to the gigantic height of these masses of ruins, but also, as I believe, to the incredible energy of the man, who has with his own private means succeeded in removing such enormous masses of earth. . . . You would, indeed, scarcely believe that a single man in the course of a few years could have accomplished so great an undertaking.

Biting the bullet, he flatly declared:

> On this occasion I would stand for Schliemann against a reproach which, though plausible in itself, falls to the ground on closer consideration—the reproach that he has not excavated from the surface, layer by layer, so as to obtain a complete plan for each successive period.
>
> There is no doubt that the manner in which he has excavated, by making at once a large trench through the whole hill, has had, in the highest degree, a destructive effect on the upper layers. I allow that this has been a kind of sacrilege. . . . But, undoubtedly, if Schliemann had proceeded in such a way as to remove the ruins stratum by stratum from the surface he would, owing to the vastness of the task, not even today have reached

the layers in which the principal objects were found.
  He only reached them by at once extracting the nucleus of the
great hill.

And the principal objects he found after reopening the dig
in the spring of 1872 remain to this day among the great finds
in the history of archaeology. He discovered a lost world, a
preclassical civilization in the Aegean which was never
thought to have existed. He uncovered a new Stone Age. And he
uncovered the Bronze Age about which Homer wrote so eloquently.

With pickax and spade, extending his ditch through the
hill at Hissarlik, he found a nest of cities, one superimposed
upon the other, seven in all—an archaeological kaleidoscope.
He recovered stone implements, terra-cotta idols, odd-shaped
goblets and *kraters* or drinking bowls, double-necked jugs, copper and bronze weapons, and thousands of spinning tops or
whorls and smooth-surfaced, ornamented balls whose exact
use in antiquity still troubles archaeologists in the contemporary period.

Working with Sophia at his side, he retrieved from the
earth more than 100,000 objects.

Schliemann, of course, was unprepared for this archaeological fallout. Simple-mindedly, he expected to dig into the
hill and find Homer's Troy. Presto! Instead, he found a mosaic
of human history stretching back to the dawn of civilization
and beyond. Somewhere in the strata of successive civilizations
was his coveted Troy. But which stratum? This question dogged
him until his death and, as reflected in his journals and correspondence, he went to his grave without truly knowing which
of the cities he found was Troy.

Cataloging the objects was an awesome task. As with his
destruction of ruins which lined his way in the search for Troy,
Schliemann's critics had a field day over his failure to catalog
his finds properly. Philip Smith, his American editor and the
author of several works on ancient history, was outraged by the
critical abuse heaped on Schliemann. "The marvel is that Dr.
Schliemann should have been able to preserve any order at
all," he said.

The work of the day, he observed, often yielded objects from almost every layer. At the end of the day's labor, after a light supper of mutton and spinach, in the light of a flickering, hot kerosene lamp, Schliemann and Sophia processed their collection. "With little competent help save from Madame Schliemann's enthusiasm in the cause," Smith continued, "the objects thrown on his hands from day to day could only be arranged and depicted very imperfectly."

The haphazard nature of the operation is illustrated by the June 18, 1872, entry in Schliemann's field journal. Earlier that day, at a depth of thirty and a half feet, among the yellow ashes of a house which was destroyed by fire, he found a bundle of thick wire. Together with a heap of potsherds, whose significance he was gradually beginning to appreciate, he laid the coil "carelessly upon my table.

"But when the lamp was knocked down accidentally," he said, "a silver wire, which held the packet together, broke, and out fell three bracelets."

The wrist bands had been welded together by the heat of an intense fire. On closer inspection, to his astonishment, the packet further contained a gold earring, decorated with three rows of stars on both sides, two sets of leaf-shaped silver earrings, and three earrings of electrum (an alloy, four parts of gold to one part of silver, which had been introduced as currency in Asia Minor seven centuries before Christ). The find was wholly accidental.

Without a staff of any description, Schliemann was fearful that his workers would overlook an object of archaeological value. "I am, above all things," he said, "obliged to take care that nothing escapes me." He therefore offered his workers a reward of ten *paras* (about a half cent) for "every object that is of the slightest value to me," he said. Especially, he advised the men to maintain a lookout for terra-cotta figures with symbols and inscriptions.

In spite of the enormous quantities of objects that were discovered, his workmen occasionally attempted to decorate unornamented finds, either for the fun of it, to bemuse Schliemann, or for the reward. "The sun, with its rays, is the special object of their industry," Schliemann complained. "I, of

course, detect the forged symbols at once, and always punish
the forger by deducting two piasters from his day's wage."

Most of the objects he brought to light were shattered, especially the fragile terra-cotta figures, and he devoted considerable time to repairing them. With regret and candor, he attributed much of the damage to his impatience. He admitted:

> Unfortunately, owing to the great extent of my excavations,
> the hurry in which they were carried on, and the hardness of the
> debris, by far the greater portion of the terra-cotta vessels found
> by me in the depths of Ilium were brought out more or less
> broken.

Clearly, as reflected in his impatience, the grand enterprise
intoxicated him.

This deepening obsession led, at times, his imagination to
do cartwheels. One late afternoon, he found, at thirty-three
feet, a small pot, about two inches high and with three feet. The
mouth of the opening was about one-third of an inch in diameter. He no sooner cradled it in his hands than he rushed to a
series of conclusions, one following the other, the sort of sweeping deductions associated with Arthur Conan Doyle whose
Sherlock Holmes would appear on the European scene in less
than a generation. "I presume," Schliemann intoned, "that this
small and wonderful Trojan vessel was used by ladies for holding scented oil, which we know was applied after the bath."
Thus, in rapid-fire order, he presumed: 1) the cup was Trojan
in origin; 2) used by women; 3) used after the bath; 4) filled with
oil; 5) with scented oil. Little wonder that the critics with a
vested interest—either in the non-existence of Troy or its location at Bounarbashi—exploited his flights of imagination.

Schliemann's first major find was unrelated to Homer's
Troy; it belonged to the classical Greek period.

In the course of extending a third platform horizontally
into the hill, Schliemann sighted the edge of a carved marble
block in an earth bank. After careful digging—unusual for him
—he uncovered a block of triglyphs about six by three feet, with
a metope, in high relief, of Phoebus Apollo, the sun god, one of
the twelve Olympians, son of Zeus and Leto, raised by Poseidon.

Apollo held in his hands the reins of the four immortal horses who journeyed through the universe endlessly. Schliemann, Sophia, and the workers were stunned by its beauty.

"The anatomy of the horses is so correctly rendered that I frankly confess that I have never seen such a masterly work," Schliemann exclaimed. For once, he was not engaging in hyperbole. When a copy of the metope appeared in the European press, the art world was dumbfounded. Professor H. Brunn, the director of the Munich Museum, in a letter to Schliemann, hailed the composition as "a work of art which displays the greatest skill in solving one of the most difficult of artistic problems." The team of four horses did not appear to move on the surface of the relief but, instead, created the optical illusion of emerging straight out of the marble itself through the ingenious portrayal of the horses in a half turn. "I rejoice to see such a treasure," Brunn wrote.

As a result of this incident, Schliemann's Trojan horizon expanded. For the first time, perhaps, he was moved by *ars gratia aris*, sans the Metro-Goldwyn-Mayer lion. From then on, his romance with the preclassical Aegean period notwithstanding, Schliemann, during his periodic revisits to Hissarlik, scoured the hill for other metopes. As late as 1882, after spending two months in the same spot removing, with the help of twenty-five laborers, the enormous mass of debris which he and his workers had thrown down the slope a decade earlier, he reluctantly reported that "no second metope was found there, nor any other sculpture of great interest, only a marble female head of the Macedonian period." Typical Schliemann: "only."

If the art custodians were excited by his Phoebus Apollo, the archaeologists were jarred. Neither Homer nor any of the other Greek and Roman classical writers made mention of a temple to the sun at Troy either in the pre-Hellenic or Hellenic periods. Schliemann's intuitive judgment was probably correct. He believed the metope was an ornament adorning the propylaeum or eastern gate of a temple which, naturally, is lit at dawn by the rays of the rising sun.

Many of the other principal objects he excavated puzzled him, and Schliemann openly said so. He recognized his limitations. "I call particular attention to the fact that for a layman it is next to impossible to distinguish which is Trojan brick debris and what is Trojan brick masonry," he said on one occasion. And on another, he confessed, "I am puzzled by this and state only the facts."

In addition to the numerous owl-faced figures he found in 1871 and correctly identified as the image of Ilian Athena, the tutelary goddess of Troy, his other startling discoveries included the figure of a hippopotamus, jade axes and clay whorls and balls adorned with clockwise and counterclockwise swastikas. Each of these discoveries generated widespread controversies in his day.

Discovery of a bright-red, clay hippopotamus, an animal worshipped in Egypt and more likely to be found in the Upper Nile than in the Scamander, provided evidence of a trade link between Egypt and the Troad, either by sea or overland, an exciting development. Similarly, when Schliemann uncovered twelve green jade axes and one cut from white jade, his discovery created a sensation among Orientologists. One professor, on hearing the news, concluded that the implements came from China by a process of primeval barter over the "roof of the world," from Kashmir to Afghanistan to Persia to the Troad. He said:

> I am writing you perhaps some dreams more dreamy, you will think perhaps, than any dreams I wrote [previously]. At any rate, while you are giving realistic life to the ancient tale of Troy, strive to do something, too, for this more venerable witness to the brotherhood and intercommunication of the human race in the age of Kronos than of Zeus.

And then he raised a question: "Was it a jade stone that Kronos swallowed?"

Kronos, a Titan, was a member of the first race to inhabit the earth, according to Greek mythology. Kronos, who slew his father Uranus, was fearful that one of his own children would one day in turn slay him. So he swallowed each of his offspring after birth. Rhea his wife, also a Titan, overwhelmed by grief, sought to outwit him. When their child Zeus was born, she wrapped a stone in swaddling clothes and told Kronos that it was their newborn son. He promptly swallowed it. In time, as Uranus feared, Zeus drove him from the universe. Zeus was destined to rule over Homer's Troy, the Heroic Age. Indeed, was it a jade stone Kronos swallowed?

But the discovery of the hippopotamus and jade objects was overshadowed by a more sensational find, especially for Germany, the emergent empire in search of a place in the sun.

In the Teutonic pantheon of gods, the swastika is the symbol of Donar, perhaps better known in the Anglo-Saxon world by his Scandinavian name, Thor. Beyond that, however, the swastika was an ancient symbol of unknown origin which has been found on the temples of the Hindu gods, on the Indian subcontinent, and on the tents of American aborigines on the plains of North America.

In the Sanskrit epic, *Ramayana,* King Rama mounted his seaborne invasion of India and Ceylon in boats which bore the swastika emblem on their prows. The Sanskrit relationship to the swastika and the obvious linguistic links among Sanskrit, Greek, and Latin gave rise to the belief in Europe that these languages were divergent later forms of some one prehistoric tongue and people, the Aryans. A generation before Schliemann's birth, Sir William Jones, the first great Western Sanskrit scholar, noted the resemblance between Greek and Latin and Sanskrit and concluded that all three "spring from some common source." He added that the German language was probably of the same origin. Thus, by the mid-nineteenth century, the Sanskrit word Aryan, which means "excellent" and "honorable," came to designate the family of Indo-European languages or Indo-Germanic languages which had a Sanskrit base.

Schliemann's discovery of swastika symbols at Troy stirred the academic and political worlds.

Confusion between race and language notwithstanding, many Germans, including Schliemann, considered themselves of Aryan stock and Schliemann's recovery of so ancient a Sanskrit and Teutonic symbol as the swastika gave rise to speculation that the Trojans were Aryans. Schliemann himself declared, with his usual finality, "All that can be said of the first settlers of Hissarlik is that they belonged to the Aryan race."

In Schliemann's mind, doubtlessly, the discovery of the Aryan symbol at Troy linked his native Germany with his Trojan dream. Naturally he was elated and, for a time, he toyed with the idea of establishing a society in Germany to finance the excavations. He also entertained the hope that perhaps the German Emperor, Wilhelm I, or Bismarck, the Iron Chancellor, might underwrite his grand enterprise as part of the *kulturkampf* campaign then in vogue in the newly federated Germanic states.

Schliemann, the cosmopolitan, would have been horrified to learn that his find was later used by militant German nationalists and racists as evidence that the Germanic tribes of northern Europe were of "pure Aryan descent." Indeed, a little more than a generation after Schliemann's death, in 1920, Adolf Hitler settled on the swastika as the emblem of his Nazi movement. In *Mein Kampf,* this would-be, latter-day Kronos wrote, "In the swastika we see the mission of the struggle for the victory of Aryan man."

But by the time Hitler adopted the symbol, anthropologists, enthologists, and philologists were already consigning the term *Aryan* to the dustbin of science as an imprecise term.

In the light of the misuse of the term by the Nazis, it is worth footnoting that one of Schliemann's close friends, Professor Max Muller of Oxford, the most influential Orientologist and comparative philologist of the period, demonstrated that the primitive Aryans who inhabited southwestern Asia were, if anything, a pastoral and unwarlike people.

Later, upon unearthing skeletons at the dig, Schliemann turned them over to his other equally close academic friend, Rudolf Virchow, then Germany's leading professor of pathological anatomy. Virchow reported that the skulls were preeminently dolichocephalic, that is, long-headed, and therefore, as to their racial origin, he said, "We have the choice between Aryan, Semitic, and Hamitic." A definitive judgment, he said, could not be made from a purely anthropological viewpoint. But, Virchow continued, it was reasonable to believe that since these people were in contact with other races—as demonstrated, for example, by the clay hippopotamus and the jade ax heads—they were "exposed to being mixed in blood." So much for the concept of the racial purity of the warlike Aryans even in Schliemann's day.

The disinterment of the skeletons excited Schliemann no less than the discovery of the swastika symbols.

Three complete skeletons were found in the lower depths of Hissarlik, the first at a depth of forty-two and a half feet below the surface of the hill. Schliemann had yet to master his impatience; he never would. "The skull especially is in a good state of preservation, but has unfortunately been broken in our excavations," he wrote in his journal. "However, I can easily put it together again."

The skeleton was of a young girl. Alongside the body, he found a finger ring, three earrings, a dress pin, and several gold beads. For the second time, he found a trace of gold at the site, a hint of things to come. The skeleton was a welcome sight. Since Troy had been sacked and burned in the aftermath of heated combat, skeletons should be found although Schliemann knew that in the Heroic Age, according to Homer, the dead were burned and their ashes placed in urns. Later, he found two more human skeletons, those of warriors with corroded copper helmets on their heads and broken lances at their sides.

As Schliemann studied his finds and the layer upon layer of ruins running vertically up the walls of his big ditch and along the horizontal platforms he built into the hill at right angles from the ditch, he realized that he had fulfilled his boyhood dream. He had found mythical Troy. Overwhelmed, on June 18, 1872, he wrote triumphantly in his journal: "I am among the ruins of Homeric Troy!"

But the entry betrayed him. Among the ruins, yes; but which ruin was his Troy? Clearly, he was uncertain as to which stratum contained the Troy of Homer's poetry, an uncertainty which he never truly resolved in his own mind. Over the years, he vacillated between the second and third cities as Priam's Troy, and toyed briefly with the idea that it might be the sixth city; after his death, modern archaeology identified forty-six strata in the hill and singled out the seventh, Schliemann's sixth, as Homer's Troy.

As he studied and restudied the strata each day, took measurements, collected artifacts, and wrote up his notes, he realized that the different strata were the place markers of different cities, different ages, and different civilizations. Like the striations on a bullet, each stratum had its own individuality. In recognizing this situation, Schliemann earned the sobriquet, "founder of modern archaeology." Belzoni and Layard unearthed ruins before him, the dust of the ages was brushed from Pompeii in his infancy, but Schliemann was the first archaeologist to maintain, however crude and imperfect, notes on his finds, each object numbered and, more importantly, the first to record the depth at which the object was recovered. This was the beginning of the *science* of archaeology, the application of stratigraphy to the study of the worlds of the past. "Every object I find is to me a page of history," he wrote. And the history he wrote at Hissarlik filled volumes.

The *first* settlement at Hissarlik, belonging to the late Neolithic Age, he scratched almost immediately as Troy, although this settlement, built on virgin rock, was the principal object of his big ditch strategy. The first city appeared to him of longest duration because its ruins, fifty-three feet from the surface of the hill, extended unevenly from thirteen to twenty feet in height. At first glance, Schliemann thought it was Homeric Troy, but his doubts multiplied when he failed to find an example among the ruins of a double cup from which, according to faithful Homer, the protagonists of *The Iliad* drank freely. He did find, however, single cups, numerous stone implements, and primitive pottery. The houses of this first settlement were crudely built of stone—large and small—joined with earth. Schliemann was unable to date his find, although modern archaeology assigns this New Stone Age settlement to 3500 B.C.– 2500 B.C. "Primitive Trojans," Schliemann called the inhabitants. The first city was destroyed or abandoned, he surmised, and built over by another people. It may have been destroyed by an earth tremor, he speculated (as do modern archaeologists), for when the walls of the stone and mud houses fell, everything in the houses was crushed by immense blocks of stone. Schliemann was acutely aware of the presence of earthquakes in the region even in his day, and in his journal a decade later, he reported with satisfaction "a slight shock of earth occurred on April 1, 5 h 15½ m p.m."

Upon the site of the destroyed city, new settlers of a different civilization, manners, and customs built the *second* city for, in the succeeding layers, Schliemann found neither the style of architecture nor the pottery of the first settlement. How could he be so sure that the hill was now occupied by a different people? For the answer, a momentary digression is necessary.

Schliemann's friend, George Denis, an art historian who also wielded a pickax and shovel, provided him with the simple answer. Denis wrote him:

> The several styles of art of the same race at different periods are bound to one another like the links of a chain; and it is impossible for a people, after having wrought out a style of pottery which had acquired among them a sacred and ritual character, to abandon it on a sudden, and adopt another style of a totally different character. A people may develop, perfect, but can never utterly cast aside its own arts and industry, because in such a case it would deny its own individuality. When we find, therefore, between two styles of art so many and such strongly pronounced discrepancies, that it becomes impossible to perceive the most remote analogy between them, it is not enough to attribute such diversities to a difference of age, or stage of culture; we can only ascribe them to different races.

Schliemann's second city was located at depths of thirty-three to forty-five feet below the surface. The houses of the period were built of clay molded into blocks while moist and hardened in the sun or by fire; in plain talk, brick. This city, unlike the first, also had fortifications. Even then, apparently, the art of war kept pace with the art of civilization. The second settlement was well preserved because its houses were gutted by a great conflagration—Memel and San Francisco spring to mind—and the walls of unburned brick, as a result of the intense heat, received a sort of brick crust or actually became burned brick. This stratum was flecked with red, yellow, and, occasionally, black wood ashes; every stone Schliemann found bore the marks of the "fearful heat to which it has been exposed." The extent of the holocaust was confirmed by a stream of melted lead and copper which ran through the whole strata at a depth of thirty-nine feet. This, he felt, was the true Troy.

"The lost ancient people who inhabited this stratum were Trojans," he declared. Everything seemed to fit in accordance with Homer. Within the second layer, he uncovered double cups, Cyclopean walls, and the base of a stone lookout tower which he promptly identified as the Great Tower of Ilium. The tower was forty feet thick and twenty feet high. Climbing to the top, he commanded a view of the Plain of Troy and the Aegean Sea as well as the offshore islands of Tenedos, Imbros, and Samothrace. "I therefore presume that it is the Great Tower of Ilium which Andromache ascended because she had heard that the Trojans were hard-pressed and the power of the Achaeans was great," he said, recalling his Homer.

Schliemann sank twenty shafts and learned that none of the early cities exceeded the precincts of the hill. Thus the Troy of Homer, as he identified it, was disappointing with respect to its size. Calculating that "this pretty little town with its brick walls" can hardly have housed 3,000 inhabitants, he found it difficult to reconcile it with Homer's picture of Troy besieged for ten years by an Achaean confederation of 110,000 men, "which could only at last be captured by a stratagem"—the Wooden Horse.

But he assuaged his hurt by observing that all prehistoric cities were "but very small." The most famous Acropolis of all, that of Athens, he pointed out, was limited to a small, rocky plateau 900 feet long and 400 feet wide at its broadest part. Mycenae, on the Greek mainland, Agamemnon's city, was also exceedingly small in area; so was the Acropolis at Thebes. Therefore, he concluded, the Acropolis or citadel of the second city—called Pergamus by the Trojans—was essentially a strong point with the people dwelling in villages on the surrounding plain. Here, within the Pergamus, were the temples of the gods, among them that of Athena the owl-faced goddess. His discovery of so many vases and jars shaped like an owl's head confirmed this assessment.

The *third* city was built on the ruins of the preceding settlement and occupied a depth of between twenty-three and thirty-three feet from the surface. The new inhabitants leveled the ruins of the second city, filling in the cavities and ravines with stones and other materials—in many places only with ashes or clay. Clearly, Hissarlik, overlooking the plain, the sea, and the Hellespont, was of unestimable strategic value to the peoples of antiquity. Indeed, to this very day, the nuclear missile age, the Hellespont or Dardanelles is still among the half-dozen most important straits on the planet.

Once again, Schliemann detected a different style of architecture and pottery in the third layer and, therefore, the possession of the hill by a different people. As was the second settlement, the third city was also destroyed by a conflagration. Schliemann labeled it "the Burned City." Indeed, the heat was so intense that its brick houses and fortifications were partly vitrified by means of the silica they contained. The bricks of the third city had suffered so much from fire that they had decayed into formless masses, and Schliemann rarely found a well-preserved one. As a result of these observations, he became confused. The Burned City, he reasoned, must have been the Troy which was sacked by the Achaeans after they poured from the Wooden Horse, slew Priam, recovered their Helen, and bore Andromache, Hector's wife, into slavery.

Schliemann, accordingly, now reassigned the Great Tower of Ilium from the second to the third city and, finding a stone walk at its base, identified it as a "splendid street" which, perforce, must lead to Priam's Pergamus. Once again, like a madman, he destroyed everything in his path. "I was most unfortunately compelled to break down three of the largest walls of a more recent house," he said. But the result of his destruction this time surpassed his expectations "for I not only found two large gates, standing twenty feet apart, but also two large copper bolts belonging to them." Was this the famed Scaean Gate through which the Wooden Horse was dragged?

"I now venture positively to assert that the great double gate which I have brought to light must necessarily be the Scaean Gate," Schliemann declared imperiously. His certitude notwithstanding, Schliemann's intuitive judgment never abandoned him. A year later, still tracing the splendid street from the Gate to the Tower, he stumbled on the most remarkable of all the structures he would ever discover at Hissarlik, a mansion which boasted corridors forty feet long and six feet wide and rooms twenty-four feet by twelve feet. Jettisoning his thesis about the second city as Troy, in his enthusiasm, he promptly identified the mansion as "Priam's Palace," the palace which Homer described as "adorned with polished corridors, in which were fifty chambers built of polished stone, all side by side." It was here, according to the ageless poet, that the sons of Priam slept with their wedded wives and the sons-in-law of Priam slept beside their chaste brides.

Schliemann, in assigning the third or Burned City to the Homeric Age, freely admitted that he contradicted himself. To further confuse matters, in 1879—seven years later—he reversed himself again and declared, "The Burned City is not the third, but the Second City. I hope that these contradictions may be pardoned when it is considered that I have here revealed a new world for archaeology," he wrote in his journal. But his hopes were, as noted later, to be crushed by the critics. Schliemann's problem, and that of every student of Troy since, was to make the enormous accumulation of ruins at Troy agree with the known chronology of the Aegean. To this very day, there is no agreement among the authorities as to the precise time frames of the various strata.

As businessman-turned-archaeologist, Schliemann labored at Hissarlik with a sense of inadequacy, ever mindful of the experts who hovered in the background. "Hence," he said, "I frequently ventured upon conjectures which I was obliged to give up on mature consideration." But whether the second or third city, he and Sophia were convinced that they had found Troy.

In assigning Homeric names to his finds—Priam's Palace, the Scaean Gate, the Great Tower of Ilium—he defended himself with eloquence. In a letter to a friend, dated August 1, 1872, he wrote:

> I flatter myself with the hope that, as a reward for my enormous expenses and all my private annoyances and sufferings in this wilderness, but above all for my important discoveries, the civilized world will acknowledge my right to re-christen this sacred locality; and in the name of the divine Homer I baptize it with that name of immortal renown, which fills the heart of

everyone with joy and enthusiasm: I give it the name of "Troy" and "Ilium," and I call the Acropolis, where I am writing these lines, by the name of the "Pergamus of Troy."

But Schliemann should have known his civilized world better; in matters of human emotion, a civilized world is no more civilized than an uncivilized world. The critics would have a field day with his nomenclature.

In the next stratum, he brought to light the *fourth* city at a depth of thirteen to twenty-three feet below the hill's crest. As in the second and third city, he uncovered owl-shaped idols; primitive, bronze battle-axes; terra-cotta vases with tripod feet; double-handled goblets; stone hammers and saddle querns of trachyte. "The only difference is that, in general, the pottery of the fourth city is coarser and of a ruder fabric, and that we find here an infinitely larger quantity of rude wheel-made terra-cottas and many new forms of bases and goblets." The art of the preceding settlements was in decline. The fourth city or settlement was also a third larger than the third, and the masses of shells and cockles he accumulated in the debris of the houses were so stupendous, that, Schliemann wrote, "they baffle all description."

"A people which left all their kitchen refuse on the floors of their rooms must have lived in a very low social condition," he said.

Schliemann's Trojans, like himself, were scrubbed, orderly, and meticulous, or so he liked to believe.

But in assessing the stratum of the fourth city, he concluded that Homer was correct in declaring that Troy was not wholly destroyed because, in Homer's words, "it is fated that Aeneas should be saved in order that the race . . . may not utterly disappear." Schliemann's pickax and spade confirmed the survival of the race, whatever its name, for he found that the southeast corner of the burned city had not been destroyed by the fire and that it became the starting point for the building of the new, fourth city.

Above the strata of ruins of the fourth city, he found a layer of debris six and a half feet thick, evidently consisting of the remains of houses built of wood and clay. This marked the *fifth* settlement. That the people of the fourth city, accustomed to stone and earth houses, should suddenly have abandoned their architectural style seemed "incredible" to him and therefore, he correctly concluded, a new people had established a hand-hold on the strategic site. In the fifth city, he no longer found stone axes. Moreover, the ever-present, spindle-type whorls were of inferior quality.

His commentary on the *sixth* city is of special significance since it is now generally recognized as the stratum of Homeric Troy. The sixth city puzzled him as no other. Within this stratum, he found vast quantities of "very curious pottery," partly handmade, partly wheel-made which, in shape, texture, color, and fabric, were "so utterly different from all the pottery of the preceding prehistoric cities that I hesitate to refer it to prehistoric or historic times." As neither the Greeks nor the prehistoric peoples who preceded them at Hissarlik had ever made such monochrome pottery—or grayware, as it is now called—and especially since the pottery occurred in abundance, it indicated that a strange new people had settled at Hissarlik.

"But who were they?" he asked in his journal. He speculated that they were "Lydians," whom Herodotus and other classical writers reported as having colonized the Troad around 700 B.C. Their buildings were built in the style of the *megron* found commonly on the Greek mainland, long and narrow with pitched roofs. For the first time, Schliemann found the bones of horses among the ruins. These people must have had chariots.

The *seventh* city, close by the surface, had scanty interest for him. This was a Greek city. Everything about the ruins, six and a half feet below the outer crust of the hill, was Greek, the architecture (uncemented stone blocks), the masses of marble and granite columns, the millions of fragments of sculptures, the mosaic floors, an aqueduct, and the inevitable theater capable of holding 5,000 people. This was the city of Homer's day, of classical Greece, of Greece in her glory. Both Greek and Roman writers referred to it as Ilium or Troy. Schliemann felt this was a travesty since it impinged on the "real" Troy. Accordingly, he rechristened the seventh city "Novum Ilium" (curiously, he gave it a Roman name) to distinguish it from the pre-Hellenic Ilium of Homer.

Once again, Schliemann appealed to his readers and critics. He wrote:

> If my memoirs now and then contain contradictions, I hope that these may be pardoned when it is considered that I have here revealed a new world for archaeology, that the objects which I have brought to light by the thousands are of a kind hitherto never or but very rarely found, and that consequently everything appeared strange and mysterious to me.

In fact, many of the objects he uncovered remain "strange and mysterious" to the present. The famed Cincinnati Expedition in 1938, after seven years of excavatory work and analysis, for example, failed to solve the riddle of the thousands of spindle whorls found on the site.

Exhausted by their summer-long effort, weakened by recurring bouts with pestilential fever, and anxious to see Andromache, their daughter, the Schliemanns closed their camp at the end of September and returned to Athens—Sophia with a sigh of relief—for another brief period of rest and rehabilitation. By now, of course, Schliemann realized that his dig raised more questions than it answered. There was much more work to be done. But he had reason to be contented for the first time in his life. Unanswered questions notwithstanding, he had not only proven that Troy existed but that he had found it.

He pontificated in his usual offensive manner:

> Everyone must admit that I have solved a great historical problem, and that I have solved it by the discovery of a high civilization and immense buildings upon the primary soil in the depths of an ancient town, which throughout antiquity was called Ilium and declared itself to be the successor of Troy, the site of which was regarded as identical with the site of the Homeric Ilium by the whole civilized world of that time.

By his excavations, Schliemann established, for the first time, the existence of an independent Aegean civilization, a precursor to the classical age of the Greeks. He had uncovered a prehistoric, late New Stone Age and a Bronze Age. Schliemann himself recognized that he was not simply dealing with the Heroic Age as depicted by Homer and the classical writers but with a pre-Hellenic and prehistoric civilization, a world unheard of in his day and age.

Yet it was left not to Schliemann but his friend and mentor, Frank Calvert, to hit on the underlying truth about Schliemann's excavations in 1869–1873 which would be confirmed generations later by modern archaeology.

Calvert argued that Homer would have mentioned a New Stone Age if it had existed at Troy and that, as he speaks of none, there could have been none. Consequently, Calvert continued, none of the cities of the lower strata through which Schliemann's trench traversed and which contained stone implements possibly could be Troy. They were something else; what they were, he did not know. He concluded that even the stratum lying below Novum Ilium—the sixth city—"must be more than 1,000 years older than the Trojan war."

Schliemann was annoyed by Calvert's analysis which appeared in the *Levant Herald* on January 25, 1873, on the eve of Schliemann's return to Hissarlik. Years later, almost twenty years later, he would come around to Calvert's point of view. But he died before he learned that his cherished Troy was the sixth city which modern archaeology identifies as Troy VIIA. Impetuously, Schliemann had bypassed it completely in his frenzy to reach virgin soil and his sacred Troy.

All illustrations are from the original engravings from Schliemann's *Troy and its Remains* (London: John Murray, 1875; New York: Scribner, Welford and Armstrong, 1875) and his *Mycenae* (New York: Sribner, Armstrong & Co., 1878). The engravings are by James D. Cooper and J. W. Whymper.

VIEW OF HISSARLIK FROM THE NORTH.

After the Excavations.

Schliemann, systematically cutting into the face of Hissarlik, uncovered different cities at descending levels. *James D. Cooper*

BLOCK OF TRIGLYPHS, WITH METOPÉ OF THE SUN-GOD.
From the Temple of Apollo in the Ruins of Greek Ilium.

A block of triglyphs with metope of the sun god Apollo, discovered by Schliemann in a pile of rubble at the level of Troy as a Greek city in the classical period, long after the Trojan War. *J. W. Whymper*

TROJAN BUILDINGS ON THE NORTH SIDE, AND IN THE GREAT TRENCH CUT THROUGH THE WHOLE HILL.

A view of the great trench which Schliemann cut through Hissarlik. He may have taken his idea from the digging of the Suez Canal which occurred during the same period. *J. W. Whymper*

Samothrace.

Imbros.

Dr. Schliemann's Houses.

Plain of Troy, seen through the great Trench.

Later but Pre-Hellenic Buildings, partly over the limits of Priam's Palace.

Hellespont. Plain of Troy. Scamander.

Greek Tower (where the sun stands).

Place where the Treasure was found.

Wall of Troy Scœan Gate, and Paved Road to the Plain.

Paved Road.      TOWER OF ILIUM.

THE SCŒAN GATE AND PAVED ROAD, THE TOWER OF ILIUM, CITY WALL, PALACE OF PRIAM,
AND THE WALLS OF A TOWER OF THE GREEK AGE.
From the South-East.

The third city, Schliemann's "Burnt City," exposed to the sun for the first time in four thousand years. Here the Schliemanns discovered fabulous treasures. *J. W. Whymper*

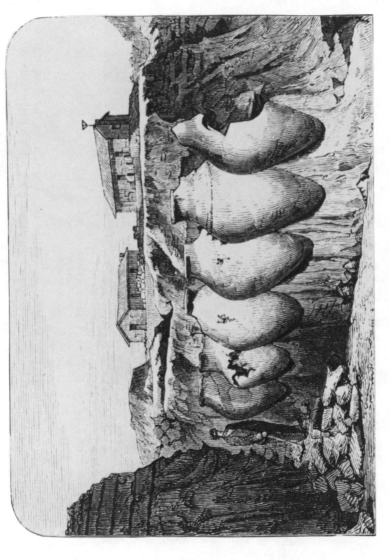

B. THE MAGAZINE, WITH ITS COLOSSAL JARS,

In the depths of the Temple of Athena.

Schliemann admires the colossal jars recovered beneath Greek Troy. American archaeologists suggest that the jars, which contained water and olive oil, served as food cachés during the siege of Troy. *J. W. Whymper*

Dr. Schliemann's Houses and Magazine.

Plain of Troy and Hellspont.

Upper Helot.

Palace of Priam.

Scæan Gate.

Tower of Ilium.

THE TOWER OF ILIUM, SCÆAN GATE, AND PALACE OF PRIAM.

Looking North along the cutting through the whole Hill

Ancient Troy lies exposed. The wooden houses atop the hill were built by Schliemann and served as field headquarters during his "Trojan Campaign," as he termed his excavations. *James D. Cooper*

GATE OF THE LIONS. The Principal Entrance to the Acropolis of Mycenae.

The famed "Lion Gate," the clue which led Schliemann to believe that just beyond lay the graves and buried tresures of Mycenae's Heroic Age. *J. W. Whymper*

ICHNOGRAPHY OF THE ROYAL TOMBS WITHIN THE CIRCLE OF THE AGORA.

The grave circle at Myceane, whose fantastic treasures of gold and jewels surpassed even those found by the Schliemanns at Troy. *James D. Cooper*

No. 474. Massive Golden Mask of the body at the south end of the First Sepulchre. Size 1 : 3, about. (For description, see page 312.

Massive gold mask recovered by the Schliemanns in the Mycenae grave circle. To this day, scholarly debates rage over the discovery: is this the face of Agamemnon, who led the Achaean hosts against Priam's Troy? *J. W. Whymper*

THE TREASURY CLOSE TO THE LIONS' GATE. Excavated by Mrs. SCHLIEMANN.

Sophia standing triumphantly at the entrance to "Mrs. Schliemann's Treasury" at Mycenae. This excavation, which she personally led and supervised, brought her fame as the first woman archaeologist in history. *J. W. Whymper*

# ITHAKA

# DER PELOPONNES

UND

# TROJA.

ARCHÄOLOGISCHE FORSCHUNGEN

VON

## HEINRICH SCHLIEMANN.

Νῦν δὲ δὴ Αἰνείαο βίη Τρώεσσιν ἀνάξει
Καὶ παίδων παῖδες, τοί κεν μετόπισθε γένωνται.
ILIAS XX, 307—308.

NEBST 4 LITHOGRAPHIEEN UND 2 KARTEN.

LEIPZIG,

COMMISSIONS-VERLAG VON GIESECKE & DEVRIENT.

1869.

Title page of Schliemann's first published work on Troy. In this book he pinpointed the location of Troy and the grave circle at Mycenae before turning over a spadefull of earth.

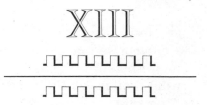

# XIII

# Priam's Treasure

*The city of Priam was famous the whole
world over for its wealth of gold and
bronze.*

The Iliad, BOOK XVIII

SCHLIEMANN SPENT December 25, 1872, in Athens—with Sophia
and young Andromache by his side—with the pagan, ornamented tree in their sitting room reminiscent of his childhood
at Ankershagen. It was the most pleasant Christmas he remembered since that day, forty-three years earlier, when he turned
over the pages of Jerrer's *Universal History*. And yet, contented
as he was, beneath the surface restlessness flickered. He had
found *his* Troy. Had he found *Homer's* Troy? "I wish I could
prove Homer to have been an eye-witness to the Trojan War,"
he wrote. "Alas, I cannot."

Schliemann had pursued his ghostly Troy from childhood,
and now that he clutched it, inexplicably, it eluded him.
Clearly, he must return to Troy and continue to search the
debris until he uncovered something tangible to prove conclusively that his Troy and Homer's Troy were one and the same.
Only in this way could he exorcise the specter of Troy which
had haunted him through so many Christmases past.

Something tangible. But what? Schliemann did not know.
An inscription, perhaps. He had searched in vain for an al-

phabetical language amid the ruins ever since he had launched his grand enterprise but, he confessed, he was no longer sanguine about the possibility of finding inscriptions. "If it seems that neither the Trojans nor their successors possessed a written language," he said consolingly, "we must, as far as possible, replace it by *monuments figures.*"

He had uncovered architecture, art, and artifacts, but nothing sufficiently spectacular to prove his case. How about the one signpost which, above all, men could read—gold? *The Iliad* is dotted with references to the yellow metal—gold brooches, gold armlets, gold double cups, gold chains, gold daggers, and gold bowls.

Homer told of the shield of Nestor, who fought at Troy, "the fame of which ascends to heaven for it is of solid gold." He sang of Hector whose "bronze spear tip is fastened to the shaft by a ring of gold." These are monuments figures the world could understand. Through them, Homer's Troy could speak and tell its story of the Heroic Age, at the daybreak of Western civilization.

Leaving Andromache behind in Athens with Sophia's parents, Sophia and her impulsive Heinrich departed for Troy within a fortnight of Epiphany. "I returned here on January 31 with my wife, in order to continue the excavations," he wrote in his field journal. He returned with an engineer and artist in tow—the engineer to make ground plans, and the artist to copy the objects in India ink so that Schliemann could reproduce the drawings in Athens "by means of photography," one of the wonders of the century. "But," he complained on February 22, "we have been repeatedly interrupted by Greek church festivals, thunderstorms, and also by the excessive cold, so that I can scarcely reckon that I have had as yet more than eight good days' work."

When the weather cleared and the festivals slowed, however, the excavation at Hissarlik regained its old rhythm. In the month of February alone, the Schliemanns and their 158 workers removed 11,000 cubic yards of debris from the site. Schliemann concentrated on the temple of the classical period he had uncovered the previous summer, his theory being that the Greeks probably built this house of worship on the exact spot where the Trojans in antiquity had built their own temple to Ilian Athena, their patron goddess.

As the work progressed, the old intoxication returned. "Since my report of the first of this month I have continued the excavations with great zeal, favored by glorious weather and an abundance of workmen," Schliemann wrote in mid-March. His spirits were lifted higher when the work gangs uncovered three inscriptions. Alas, all belonged to the Greek period, but at least they confirmed that the temple was, indeed, dedicated to Athena. But there was no trace of an inscription in the bowels of the dig, and no trace of gold.

In the spring of 1873 the Muses appeared to put the Schliemanns on trial. A whole series of disasters engulfed them. One night, for example, as March waned, he, Sophia and their foreman, Photidas, narrowly escaped being burned alive. For six days, the temperature had dropped and, in the bedroom which he and Sophia shared on the north side of their wooden barrack, nightly they lit a fire in their makeshift, primitive fireplace. The stones of the fireplace rested on the floor boards and, whether it was due to a crevice in the cement joining the stones, or for some other reason, the wooden floor caught fire. Schliemann accidentally awoke at three in the morning and was horrified to find the floor aflame. The room was filled with smoke and the north wall was beginning to catch fire; a few seconds would have sufficed to burn a hole into it, and the flimsy, wooden house would have gone up in flames in less than a minute since a strong wind gusted from the north.

As off Texel when the *Dorothea* sank, or aboard the *Atlantic* when she almost broached in mid-Atlantic, or when he leaped into the trench at Hissarlik to free the foreman who was buried alive, the man of action came into play, his fear notwithstanding. "In my fright I did not lose my presence of mind," he recalled. "I poured the contents of a bath upon the burning north walls, and thus in a moment stopped the fire in that direction."

Sophia, awakened when Schliemann leaped out of bed to fight the blaze, cried out, "Fire! Fire!" Photidas, asleep in the adjoining room, awoke and summoned the other foremen from the stone house. Schliemann said:

In the greatest haste they fetched hammers, iron levers and
pickaxes; the floor was broken up, torn to pieces, and quantities
of damp earth thrown upon it, for we had no more water. But,
as the lower beams were burning in many places, a quarter of
an hour elapsed before we got the fire under control and all
danger was at an end.

As a result of the incident, mindful of the holocausts he had
witnessed at Memel and San Francisco, if not his Burned City
in the depths of the dig, during the following week, Schliemann
rearranged the camp, shifting the location of the different
wooden structures so that in the event of another fire, the whole
camp would not burn to the ground.

Since January he and Sophia had "ransacked"—
Schliemann's word—the hill without finding a trace of writing
or any significant monuments figures which conclusively
proved he had found Homer's Troy. Troy may have been
Schliemann's rainbow, but there certainly was no pot of gold at
the end of it. They grew weary, both physically and mentally.
Hissarlik was a far cry from Athens, even farther from Place
St. Michel. They began to tire of searching for tangible evidence of the discovery of "godly Troy."

Gold was found, but they did not find it. Nor did they learn
of it until the following December, when the story came to
light. The fire was no sooner extinguished when, on March 31,
at a depth of thirty feet on the east side of Priam's Palace, two
of Schliemann's workers uncovered an owl-headed vase filled
with objects of pure gold and two smaller hoards of gold ornaments. Secretly, they moved the loot from the site and shared
it between themselves. The brighter of the two had his part of
the loot melted down by a goldsmith who then reshaped it into
a broad, heavy necklace with flower ornamentation in the
Turkish fashion. The other worker showed the objects to his
wife. Several months later, long after Schliemann had left Hissarlik, the woman boldly paraded one Sunday with gold earrings and gold pendants of strange design. Exciting the curiosity and envy of the villagers, the woman was denounced to
the authorities and the Turkish constabulary arrested them
both, threatening to hang her husband if they did not explain
the origin of their gold.

Terrified, the man and wife confessed. Their part of the treasure—a cache which included a bar of electrum, gold earrings, bracelets, and pendants—was recovered and shipped to the Imperial Museum at Constantinople.

During this period, as they despaired of finding a trace of Trojan writing or a significant monuments figures, Sophia's father passed away and she hurried back to Athens to attend the funeral. George Egnostromenos' death gave both of them pause for thought. Schliemann, alone at Troy, missed her companionship. He had nobody to talk to, nobody to row with. He grew despondent. He had found Troy. Why must he continue this seemingly endless quest? What more did he want? "We are weary," he wrote a German friend in May. And in a letter to John Murray, his London publisher, he confided that the "hardships here are beyond our strength, and we have decided to discontinue this excavation June 1." In his field journal, he estimated that since his preliminary dig in 1870, he and Sophia had removed more than a quarter of a million cubic meters of earth by wheelbarrow, mancart, and oxcart. The days, weeks, and months had rolled into years. For the first time, without Sophia at his side to encourage and comfort him, Schliemann admitted that he was tired and depressed.

Distraught following the burial of her father, Sophia had no desire other than to return to Troy and to rejoin her Heinrich, the most exciting man, the only man, in her life. Only he could comfort and console her. On her return, she and Heinrich embraced tightly. That evening, standing on the circuitwalls of Troy, Heinrich and Sophia looked down into the core of the dig at the bottom of which lay the Burned City of their dreams, with its walls and foundations visible. In their melancholy mood, they probed the meaning of being which has eluded all men since the beginning of time. For her, as Homer put it, there was no ransom that could bring her father to life again. For him, again in Homer's words, like the drowning man who reviews his life in the fleeting second before death takes him, Schliemann realized that he had triumphed in life beyond his greatest expectation.

It was now May, and as their self-imposed deadline approached, an unusual find injected buoyancy into their sinking hopes. A silver vase, slightly more than seven inches high, was unearthed. Nestling within it was an elegant cup of electrum. Both vessels bore the marks of the intense heat to which they were exposed in the conflagration which scorched the Burned City. Electrum is not mentioned in *The Iliad,* but it occurs three times in the *Odyssey.* Nearby, a metal helmet was also found, the chloride copper content of the object so high that "it fell into minute fragments when it was being taken out," Schliemann said.

The find notwithstanding, the orderly minded, obstinate Schliemann intended to stick to his plan to break camp sometime before mid-June. In another letter in this period, he wrote that since he and Sophia had achieved "the great idea of our lives," he would definitely quit the site June 15.

In the excitement and confusion which followed, the date cannot be pinpointed with accuracy. What is known is that shortly before he reached his deadline, sometime between the end of May and mid-June, the search was rewarded. One morning during that period, he and Sophia routinely returned to the main site and descended to a depth of twenty-eight feet. They had trod this path often. And, as on countless other occasions, the sun splashed brilliant rays of light over Hissarlik.

As Schliemann moved along at this level, the declination of the sun at that precise moment sent a shaft of light ricocheting off the trench wall and, for the fraction of a second, it blinded him. Half-paralyzed, he abruptly stopped. Another ray of light rebounded into his eyes. Heinrich tugged at Sophia's arm and her gaze followed his. Immobilized, they stood hand in hand.

Two gangs of day laborers worked nearby. Twenty years earlier, during his California interregnum, Schliemann witnessed the terrible hypnotic effect of gold on the men who panned for it.

"Go at once," he told his wife, "and shout *paidos.*"

"Now?" she queried. "It is only seven o'clock."

If anything was likely to arouse the suspicion of the workers, it would be the cry of *paidos* only a few minutes after the start of the day's work. Why would this piaster-pinching, hard-nosed, German merchant-turned-archaeologist give the workers an extra rest period? With the cunning of Odysseus,

Schliemann's mind wrestled with the problem just as it had always done to stay a step ahead of business competitors. Very well, then, he would cast himself in the role of crazy foreigner, a caricature close to the heart of peasants.

"Tell them that today is my birthday, and that I just remembered it," he said. "Everyone will get his wages for the day without working. Tell them to go back to their villages. Hurry. Hurry. Shout *paidos.*"

Sophia emerged from the dig, shouted *paidos,* and laughingly provided them with the specious reason. The workers were amused. Foreigners are, indeed, crazy; the whole aimless dig in the hill is crazy. With Sophia leading the way, they abandoned the site. As if in a Shakespearean play, the scene was marked: *Exeunt* all but Schliemann.

The sun, meanwhile, climbed higher in the heavens and the object, which had glistened only minutes before, dissolved and blended back into the debris of the site.

Schliemann, on his knees, his throat dry, his forehead perspiring and his pulse accelerating, scratched and clawed the spot as Sophia returned with a large red shawl. Finally, using a stout knife, he loosened the object from its bed as stones and dust tumbled from above. It was a tarnished copper bowl slightly more than a foot in length. Behind it gleamed a treasure trove of gold objects. He had found Priam's Treasure, in Homer's words, "a treasure of gold and bronze."

As Schliemann savaged the spot, Sophia, alarmed, pointed to upper reaches of the trench. Schliemann later said:

> I cut out the treasure with a large knife, which it was impossible to do without the very greatest exertion and the most fearful risk of my life, for the great fortification-wall, beneath which I had to dig, threatened every moment to fall down upon me. But the sight of so many objects . . . made me foolhardy, and I never thought of any danger. It would, however, have been impossible for me to have removed the treasure without the help of my dear wife, who stood by me ready to pack things which I cut out in her shawl and to carry them away.

Her heart pounding as her blood pressure rose, Sophia made several "casual" trips back and forth between the dig and their house, her red shawl laden with monuments figures.

Back in their wooden house, Schliemann announced to the foremen that Sophia had a touch of fever and that they did not want to be disturbed. "Nothing serious," he said. "She needs rest and a cold water pack." Too bad; it ruined his birthday.

Locking the door behind them, they stood transfixed in the presence of the cache of gold and silver scattered on the fire-scarred floor. This was the supreme moment of their lives, a moment they would replay over and over again in their minds until darkness veiled their eyes. Spread before them was a king's ransom—a treasure trove half-real and half-mythical—which had lain buried in the hill for thousands of years.

The treasure held them spellbound, in rapture. The room contained 8,772 objects running the gamut from gold diadems to bars of silver to copper and bronze lanceheads and battle-axes. "Priam's Treasure," Schliemann murmured in a daze as he recalled the scene from *The Iliad* when Priam sought to ransom the body of his dead son, Hector, and offered Achilles, the victor, the booty of a king. "Weigh then the gold," Priam said, and, Homer continued:

> . . . as he took ten full talents; also two shining tripods and four cauldrons; and also a most beautiful goblet, a rich possession which the men of Thrace had presented to him when he went thither as ambassador: even this the old man did not spare now as he excessively desired in his mind to ransom his beloved son.

Dramatically, symbolically, in the manner of the Trojans, Schliemann filled a double cup with wine, poured a libation from one spout to the gods and goddesses of Troy and drank from the other spout. He passed the double cup to Sophia, who did the same.

The treasure included two diadems, one of which contained 2,168 chain links, rings, leafs, and charms; and the other 16,353 separate pieces—all of pure gold. Schliemann lifted the larger of the two and placed it on the head of the dark-haired, twenty-year-old Greek beauty. He draped about her throat a necklace containing 4,090 individual pieces of hand-wrought gold. "Helen," he whispered with a catch in his voice. "Helen of Troy."

In addition to the jewelry, the cache consisted of a gold bottle, gold bars, and a wide-ranging group of earrings, finger rings, buttons, bracelets, and pendants—again, all of pure gold. There were also items of silver and electrum, and a copper shield and cauldron, bronze plates and weapons.

What was their collection worth? Schliemann later placed a value of $200,000 on it; coincidentally, the approximate cost of his Trojan outlay, about $3 million in today's eroded dollar mart. But, obviously, the true value of these objects transcended the marketplace. Their value was inestimable, their beauty infinite. The collection was unique. "Not one of the earrings has any resemblance in form to Hellenic, Roman, Egyptian, or Assyrian earrings," an astonished Schliemann recorded in his journal.

Looking back later on the exact location where the treasure was uncovered, Schliemann made a stunning discovery. He wrote:

> I now perceive that the cutting which I made in April 1870 was *exactly* at the proper point, and that if I had only continued it, I should in a few weeks have uncovered the most remarkable buildings of Troy, namely, the Palace of King Priam, the Scaean Gate, the Great Surrounding Wall, and the Great Tower of Priam. And, of course, Priam's Treasure. But by prematurely abandoning this cut, I had to make colossal excavations from east to west and from north to south through the entire hill in order to find [them].

Schliemann naturally identified the find as Priam's Treasure. But was the original owner Priam? Was this his treasure? His Troy? No one, to this day, has answered these questions.

In a practical vein, how did these primitive people manufacture such jewelry? Schliemann invited Carlo Giuliano, then the most celebrated goldsmith in London, to examine the collection. Giuliano concluded that the leaves of both diadems were cut with a bronze punch from thin gold plate. Giuliano reported:

> To make the very thin wire, the Trojans could have used only ingots of very pure gold, which they forced through the holes of the draw-plate, and which they could gradually and easily

reduce to an extreme fineness. Alloyed gold could not have been used to make such very thin wire.

To fashion tiny gold stars and similar charms, the Trojan goldsmith took a piece of gold, put it on hot charcoals, and melted it with a blowpipe, thus making a globular grain. Then, he perforated it with a round punch, placed it on a mandril, and cut out the grooves with another oblong punch. But before doing so, he heated it square.

Even Giuliano expressed wonder:

> How the primitive goldsmith could do all this fine work, and in particular, how he could accomplish the minute granular work on the earrings, where grains of gold infinitely minute were to be soldered into the microscopic grooves—how he could do all this without the aid of a lens—is an enigma. But it was done, and with a powerful lens we can easily distinguish the soldering, even on the smallest rings.

And where did the gold come from? The Troad borders on Phrygia, where according to legend—or is it a legend?—King Midas reigned, and it touches on the Valley of Pacolus, which was famous in the classical period for its auriferous sands. According to Strabo, the Roman historian, gold mines also existed in the Troad. "Above the territory of the Abydians in the Troad lies Astyra, a ruined city, now belonging to Abydos," Strabo wrote, "but formerly the city was independent and had gold mines, which are now poor and exhausted."

Schliemann, the wily gunrunner, now came to the fore. In a manner which remains a secret to this day, he and Sophia smuggled the treasure out of Turkey, across the Aegean and into Greece. In Athens, as an extra precautionary maneuver, they divided the treasure into small parcels and scattered it among the legion of Egnostromenos'. Sophia's brothers and sisters, aunts and uncles, and endless array of cousins hid the packages in their vineyards and stables and under floor boards. Despite the voluminous amount of material Schliemann left to posterity, he provided no clues to his smuggling operation any more than he divulged the intimate nature of his business operations during the Crimean War and the American Civil War. A compulsive note taker—present-day tape would have been his delight—he somehow was able to overcome the otherwise irresistible inclination to reduce his every waking moment to paper.

There is circumstantial evidence that his close friends, the Calverts, with their access to diplomatic bags, played a role in helping remove the treasure from the Troad. But this is conjecture and must so be labeled. In any event, just as Schliemann covertly undertook to dig at Hissarlik in 1870 without a *firman,* he and Sophia covertly abandoned the site three years later. They had found their Troy, and they could prove it, or so they thought.

As for the exact date on which the treasure was unearthed, the point, although moot and of modest historical consequence, has long puzzled observers. It continues to remain an area of speculation in any reconstruction of the discovery of Troy. "We discontinued the excavations on June 17, 1873," Schliemann said in 1880, seven years later. This indicated that he either suspended the dig on the day the treasure was found or that it was found earlier and that he continued to ransack the hill for several days in the hope of finding more gold. Four years later, however, in 1884, he cloaked the find in deeper mystery. "The great treasure [was] found by me at the end of May 1873," he said. If his objective was to confound the Turks and Greeks of his day, he succeeded admirably.

In the last entry in his field journal for the year, dated June 17, 1873, two days after his deadline, Schliemann wrote:

> I value truth above everything, and I rejoice that my three years' excavations have laid open Homeric Troy . . . and that I have proved *The Iliad* to be based on real facts.
>
> I venture to hope that the civilized world . . . will accept with delight and enthusiasm the certainty that Ilium did really exist, that a large portion of it has now been brought to light, and that Homer, even though he exaggerates, nevertheless sings of events that actually happened.

It was a vain hope.

As for the treasure itself, he announced that "I shall never make a traffick of it. My large collections of Trojan antiquities have a value which cannot be calculated," he continued. "But they shall never be sold." And he kept his word. He gave them away. Yet he is still maligned as the money-mad merchant who lusted for gold.

# XIV

The Critics

*Like a wild boar upon the mountain when
he stands at bay in the forest glades
and routs the hounds and lusty
youths that have attacked
him.*

The Iliad, BOOK XVII

NEWS OF SCHLIEMANN'S announcement he had found the lost city of Troy and the fabled treasure of Priam jolted the Western world. His claim was greeted with bewilderment, skepticism, and envy.

During the excavations at Hissarlik, Schliemann did little to discourage reports on the progress of his grand enterprise. On the contrary, the inveterate letter writer and publicist plied the press with information. By contemporary standards, the letters were news handouts. He also made himself accessible to correspondents posted to Athens. A colorful figure, in the parlance of the newspaperman's trade, he made good copy. The spectacular, sometimes sensational, coverage of his finds, especially Priam's Treasure, did for archaeology what the legendary Babe Ruth and his sixty home runs did for baseball. For the first time, the science of archaeology captured the public's imagination.

Most scholars, however, were dubious about his claims. Many were not only doubtful but downright hostile. The upstart had upstaged them. He had no scholarly credentials, no union card, other than a doctorate from the obscure University of Rostock which, the cynics felt, may have bent a little in awarding the degree since Schliemann was a native, nouveau riche Mecklenburger, and a potential contributor to the alumni fund. Imagine, Schliemann had never even obtained a baccalaureate, and he dropped out of the only institution of higher learning he ever attended, the Sorbonne. Worse, Schliemann was hardly above the class of a street vendor, albeit a wealthy one. In class-conscious Europe, gentlemen were born, not made. Many of his critics, however, probably would not have hesitated to accept his tainted money if he had set up a Schliemann Foundation which, of course, he did not. Schliemann, the self-educated taskmaster, did not believe in grants-in-aid. Clearly, there existed a subterranean psychological abyss between Schliemann and the scholars which would never be wholly bridged. Yet, incongruously, this egocentric and strong-willed individual, often aggressive and startling in dealings with others to compensate for his inferiority complex, struggled—like his native Germany of that era—for recognition, for respect, for acclaim. As a businessman, Schliemann would never be completely accepted by the high society of his era, the pace set by the aristocracy almost everywhere except in France. Science, which ignited the Industrial Revolution, and capitalism, which thrust commoners to center stage, however, provided Schliemann with an entrée into places which otherwise would be barred to him. In the end he was accepted —with reluctance, like the suspected member of the Mafia who is admitted to the exclusive country club. But Schliemann was not accepted for almost twenty years and by then, as a result of his endeavors and vision, he had reduced his sacred Troy to but one star—of the first magnitude, to be sure—within the constellation of the Bronze Age of the Aegean world.

Irrepressibly, Schliemann rushed into print with his claims in 1874, within a year of unearthing Priam's Treasure. In Leipzig, F. A. Brockhaus published his *Trojanische Alterthumer,* an octavo volume, accompanied by a large quarto "Atlas" of 217 photographic plates, containing maps, plans, and views of the Plain of Troy and illustrated by 4,000 drawings selected from among the principal objects he had brought to light. He no sooner had obtained the page proofs than he prepared French and English editions. The English edition was published simultaneously by John Murray in London and Scribner, Welford and Armstrong in New York. To this day, *Troy and Its Remains,* "a narrative of researches and discoveries made on the site of Ilium, and in the Trojan Plain," retains the spontaneity, impetuosity, and freshness of his field journals.

If *Ithaca, the Peloponnesus and Troy* created a stir in 1869, *Troy and Its Remains* unleashed a storm five years later. To paraphrase Homer, as a great wave that comes thundering at the mouth of some heaven-born river, and the rocks that jut into the sea ring with the roar of the breakers that beat and buffet them—even with such a roar did Schliemann's critics come on.

Some critics dismissed his claim to Troy as nonsense. Engaging in *a priori* argument, a British professor observed that since Troy never existed how could Schliemann find it? Locating Troy, he implied, was tantamount to announcing the discovery of Jack's beanstalk. Schliemann gave vent to a classical riposte. "If I have excavated for three years at Hissarlik without discovering anything," Schliemann wrote in *The Academy,* a leading scholarly journal, "I would have to accept this observation as perfectly just but since my labors have been crowned with success . . . the learned professor's remark is unjust as it is unfounded."

Others accused him of bringing down Homer's epic poetry from "the heights of pure imagination." In point of fact, Schliemann's discovery gave Homer a dazzling new dimension and raised his poetry to even greater heights.

Many of his critics contended that since Troy had disappeared centuries before Homer's birth—Homer was born around 800 B.C. and Troy was believed to have disappeared at least 400 years earlier—how could the poet describe a city he had never seen; a blind poet at that? Indeed, was that why he was called the "blind" poet in antiquity? Rushing to Homer's defense, Schliemann characterized Homer as an "echo" of the past who set to poetry the story of the Trojan War as it was handed down for generations among the peoples of the Aegean.

The critics, Schliemann heatedly argued, forgot that Homer was a poet and not an historian and that "nothing is more natural than that he should exaggerate everything with poetic license"—as did his protégé, Schliemann, who was neither an historian nor a poet.

Justifiably, the scholars came down hard on Schliemann's instant labeling of his discoveries—Priam's Treasure, in particular—although he had not found a single, solitary inscription among the ruins to identify his find. "I cannot, of course, prove that the name of this king, the owner of this treasure, was really Priam," Schliemann crackled, "but I give him this name because he is so called by Homer and in all the traditions." When Schliemann retreated, the critics pressed the attack. In desperation, Schliemann bellowed: "As soon as it is proved that Homer and the tradition were wrong, and that Troy's last king was called 'Smith,' I shall at once call him so."

His editor, Philip Smith, laughed, and on Christmas Eve, 1874, while Smith's children trimmed the tree, he came to Schliemann's defense by observing that those who believed Troy to be a myth and Priam a shadow "need not grudge Schliemann the satisfaction of applying a *nominis umbra* to his find." There may be doubt about the name of Priam since Schliemann found no inscription at the dig, Smith wrote, "but the name of Troy can no longer be withheld from the splendid ruins."

But these were relatively mild criticisms compared to the demolition experts who accused him of faking his finds. The director of the Athens University Library, for example, snidely remarked to the press that perhaps Schliemann discovered his treasures "not at Hissarlik but at the second-hand dealers." This line of assault, however, was quickly abandoned when Charles Newton of the British Museum traveled to Athens for the sole purpose of examining Schliemann's collection and returned to London to attest publicly to its authenticity.

Still others, notably Professor E. Brentano of Frankfurt, complained that Schliemann's ruins at Hissarlik were "comparatively modern," certainly no earlier than the Greek classical period. This talk of pre-Hellenic and prehistoric civilization at Troy was absurd, he said, and he denounced

Schliemann's theories as "brittle and rotten." Brentano's argument lost its edge when, in a fit of insanity, he committed suicide. But this did not deter Professor R. C. Jebb of Scotland, who picked up the theme and suggested that some of Schliemann's principal finds belonged to the Roman era. Better still, Professor Rudolf Stephani of St. Petersburg was even more strongly convinced that Schliemann's Troy was probably no older than A.D. 400 or 500 and that "the Trojan gold ornaments and utensils were brought from the south of Russia by bands of Goths and Scythians." Schliemann was momentarily nonplussed. "I must say that this is the most fantastic of all fantastic theories," he sputtered.

Among the other fantastic assaults on his credibility were attacks on his person. In Europe, it was widely whispered that Schliemann had been carried away by ambition and was "ruining himself by his archaeological explorations to the prejudice of his children [in Russia and Greece] who will be penniless after his death." So strong was this rumor that in 1880, two years before Sophia gave birth to their second and last child, Agamemnon, Schliemann declared he "found it necessary" to make a public accounting of his estate to put an end to such scurrilous attacks. "Although on account of my present scientific pursuits I am bound to keep aloof from all sorts of speculation," Schliemann stentoriously intoned, he still earned $50,000 annually in rents on properties in Paris in addition to "a small interest on my capital." Typically secretive in matters of genuine privacy, he omitted disclosing the amount of his capital. By circulating such stories, the critics focused attention on his marital affairs, the existence of two Schliemann families, one in Greece and the other in Russia, at a time when divorce was considered immoral. The innuendos also drew notice to his activities in the marketplace—Schliemann the speculator, the smuggler, the treasure seeker whose only ambition was the acquisition of gold.

Schliemann's psyche was bruised by these unrelenting encounters and he took pains to answer every critic, although he feigned disinterest in what others said about him. For example, in *Troy and Its Remains,* he devoted eight pages to answering one of his critics and then, exhausted, terminated the rebuttal by gratuitously informing his readers in his usual offensive manner that "it will be easily understood, being engaged with my superhuman works, I have not a moment to spare and therefore I cannot waste my precious time with idle talk." His lack of "a moment to spare" notwithstanding, from Athens he almost simultaneously wrote a friend at the British Museum to "kindly send me articles which you may see against me in order that I may be able to defend myself."

Schliemann, feeling isolated and beleaguered from being under constant fire, was gratified when a group of scholars flew to his defense. He referred to this doughty band as "my honored and learned friends"; in a sense, these were, like his mixed private army of Bulgars, Albanians, and Turks, members of "Schliemann's Irregulars." They stood up to the Establishment, and they included some of the most prominent scholars of the period, among them Professors Max Muller and A. H. Sayce of Oxford, Rudolf Virchow of Berlin, Emile Bournouf of Paris, and J. P. Mahaffey of Dublin. They drew up the wagons.

Muller, writing from Oxford, comforted him. "I am delighted to hear of your success—you fully deserve it," Muller penned. "Never mind the attacks of the press. . . . They are soon forgotten, even if they are read. . . ."

And Virchow publicly declared:

> I recognize the duty of bringing my testimony [to bear] against the host of doubters, who, with good or ill intentions, have never tired of carping alike at the trustworthiness and significance of his discoveries. Who would have undertaken such great works, continued through so many years—have spent such large means out of his fortune—have dug through layers of debris heaped one on the other in a series that seemed almost endless, down to the deep-lying virgin soil—except a man who was penetrated [c.q.] with an assured, nay, an enthusiastic conviction? The Burnt City would still have lain to this day hidden in the earth, had not imagination guided the spade.

Similarly aroused, Sayce, philologist and authority on the Assyrians and Babylonians, seized on Schliemann's mercantile background to beat his critics on the head with it. He chided:

Why is it that Dr. Schliemann's example has not been followed by some of the rich men of whom England is full? Why
cannot they spare for science a little of the wealth that is now
lavished upon the breeding of horses or the maintenance of a
dog-kennel?... Surely England must contain one or two, at least,
who would be willing to help in recovering the earlier history
of our civilization.

But the criticism continued, and on through the remainder
of his life. At times, the critics were reduced to criticizing themselves. When Schliemann brought out *Troy and Its Remains,*
the book was ignored or dismissed as making claims which
lacked authority. In his second and fuller treatment of the excavations at Hissarlik, *Ilios: The City and Country of the Trojans,* published six years later, Schliemann solicited scholarly
papers from the academic community and published their
views in the appendix. This fueled new criticism. Schliemann
was now accused of "presenting to us in his work a number of
dissertations written by his collaborators and other scholars
who support his theories." He was damned if he did and
damned if he didn't.

These attacks gave the supreme egotist a martyr's complex.
In a letter to a friend, in 1874, Schliemann wrote, "It is the fate
of all discoverers to be envied, ill-threatened, pursued and li-
beled and all this will only cease at my death." He was wrong.
After his death, into the middle of the twentieth century and
beyond, Schliemann was still portrayed as an adventurer, profit
maker, treasure hunter, a man who was driven in his quest for
Troy by the belief that he would find gold, although—as his
actions bear witness—he had turned his back on gold in California, abandoned his immensely profitable mercantile enterprise in Russia, and later gave away his Trojan collection.

The attacks notwithstanding, the self-taught grocer's apprentice gained entry into the most dazzling circles of the nineteenth century. The Beautiful People of his time held as many
opposing views about him as did the scholarly community. The
Dutch Queen, Sophia, was enchanted by his discoveries and
welcomed him to Rijswijk; the Greek monarch, Constantine,
shunned him as a squatter. The Iron Chancellor was too busy
unifying Germany and seeking to dominate Europe to pay him

more than passing notice and that more out of his own interest in *The Iliad* as a military treatise, and, perhaps, with a view to inducing Schliemann, through flattery, to donate his Trojan gold to Berlin. Britain's Prime Minister, William Gladstone, however, the Homeric scholar, put aside the affairs of the largest empire in history since Genghis Khan and entered into a lively correspondence with him, and dined and wined him at 10 Downing Street, in Whitehall.

In this fashion, Schliemann, through his increasingly intimate contacts with a handful of scholars and celebrities, achieved something which, in the recesses of his mind, may have lain beyond Troy—a desire to be accepted as a peer by the Establishment. His lower-class origin, his broken home life, the adversities of his youth, his role in the marketplace, all notwithstanding, Troy lifted him above his class. He proved that gentlemen were not only born but made. Doors which were closed in his childhood, the farmhouse of the prosperous Meincke family, the estate of the Duke of Mecklenburg-Schwerin, now stood open. Was it society, then, which molded him? Not necessarily. Paul, his brother, reared in the same environment, viewed the world through a different prism. He subscribed to the injunction in Ecclesiastes that vanity of vanities, all *is* vanity; in Homer's words, "Man is the vainest of all creatures that have their being upon the earth." Unlike Heinrich, though the issue of the same womb, Paul was contented with the pastoral setting into which he was born.

Why was Heinrich Schliemann possessed by Troy? Was it Troy for Troy's sake? Or was it because, shrewdly, he sensed that it could set him apart from other men and win him the respect which would otherwise be denied him? All of us die, each makes his own grave.

Whatever the motivation, the doors opened, and Schliemann's relationship with Gladstone is an illuminating illustration.

During Christmas, 1873, following his discovery of Priam's —Smith's—Treasure, Schliemann instructed his publisher to send Gladstone a copy of the new book. Schliemann had long been attracted to Gladstone who, before entering politics, was a recognized Greek scholar whose three-volume *Homer and the Homeric Age* Schliemann consumed when it was published in 1858. In that series, Gladstone suggested that the Trojan war was not so much an East-West struggle as a civil war.

Gladstone held the premiership four times (he played musical chairs with Disraeli). Like Schliemann, Gladstone was combative, intense, industrious and a devotee of Homer, whom Gladstone called "one of my four great teachers." If Schliemann, brilliantly successful as he was, felt stifled in commerce, Gladstone exhibited similar symptoms in politics. Schliemann's letter was dispatched by packet from Athens on December 28 and arrived in London on January 8, exceptionally good time. Gladstone replied the next day. He no sooner began reading Schliemann's book, "with admiration and extraordinary interest," he said, than "one of my daughters snatched it away." Gladstone promptly put the greengrocer's clerk at ease by remarking that given the hardship of his youth, "I still the more admire your success." He expressed the hope that Schliemann would visit London in the new year (which Schliemann did) so "that I may be favored with some opportunity of making your acquaintance."

Gladstone's reply made Schliemann's day, and their subsequent correspondence reflected an increasingly close intellectual association as Gladstone emerged as one of Schliemann's most powerful allies in the struggle for scholarly and popular opinion. In 1877, at Schliemann's request, Gladstone wrote the preface to his book on excavations at Mycenae. The title page of *Mycenae: Discoveries at Mycenae and Tiryns* is quaint. The author is identified as "Dr. Henry Schliemann, citizen of the United States of America"; the author of the preface is identified as "the Right Hon. W. E. Gladstone, M.P."

In the foreword, Gladstone frankly confessed that his own "first impression" of Schliemann's excavations was that of "a strangely bewildered admiration combined with a preponderance of skepticism." But, he continued, there is, in ancient poetry, a destiny stronger than the will of the gods and "to me, Dr. Schliemann is the vicegerent and organ of that destiny."

In pursuit of recognition and respect by association, Schliemann developed into a notorious name-dropper, both conversationally and in his writing, a habit which put off many of his associates. For example, discussing the pithoi he found at Troy, he wrote:

> Certainly the large jars of the second city are rudely made: where they are broken, we see an enormous mass of pieces of silicious stone, or mica, many of them a quarter of an inch thick; but nevertheless, as his Highness Prince Otto Bismarck, the Chancellor of the German Empire, ingeniously remarked to me, in July, 1879, at Kissingen, the manufacture of these large jars proves already a high degree of civilization, for to make them is just as difficult as to bake them, and they can, consequently, only have been manufactured by a people who had an experience of centuries in the potter's art.

And when so Gilbert and Sullivan a character as the Emperor of Brazil visited his excavation, Schliemann dedicated his volume on Mycenae as follows: "His Majesty Dom Pedro II, Emperor of Brazil, with the profound respect of the Author."

The reports of his discoveries, the ensuing controversy, and the publication of *Troy and Its Remains* with its details on the treasure trove, enraged the Turks. The Constantinople press accused him of "shamefully" violating the *firman* granted by the Sultan. The permit expressly stated that he agreed to share his find with the Turkish government on a half-and-half basis. In the delicate political climate of the day, the Turks persuaded their erstwhile enemies, the Greeks, to permit the Turkish authorities to search the Schliemann home in Athens. A squad of Turkish "plumbers" descended on the house, determined to recover the gold and plug future leaks. They, of course, found nothing.

Schliemann was furious. "I have the most perfect right to that treasure," he exploded. Under the terms of the *firman*, Schliemann pointed out, he was granted the "right to carry away my half out of Turkey." But, he added, in 1872, by ministerial decree, he was forbidden to export any part of his share of the discoveries, although authorized to sell it in Turkey, "The Turkish government," Schliemann charged, "by this new decree, broke our written contract in the fullest sense of the word.

"I was released from every obligation," he declared, "and I no longer troubled myself in the slightest."

For the next two years, through 1875, Schliemann fought a running legal battle with the Turks and a running debate with his critics. In the midst of the uproar, he planned new excavations, worked on the galleys and proofs of the various editions of his book, carried on his multifaceted correspondence—writing his bankers one day, his relatives at Ankershagen the next —and pouring over stock market quotations like a horseplayer analyzing a tip sheet in front of a betting window.

The Greeks not only sided with the Turks in the court wrangle, but the Athenian academicians were contemptuous of "this German smuggler of American nationality," as one Greek critic called him. This reaction from his beloved Greeks stung him. If nowhere else, he expected to receive the accolades of the Greeks. Indeed, he planned to build a museum in Athens to house his treasure chest. Yet the same old, ugly tales circulated in the coffee houses—he was a divorcé, a speculator, a war profiteer, a smuggler, and, with finality, a gold seeker.

But however much the Greeks mistrusted and denounced him, Schliemann held the trumps—the treasure. In anger, he decided not to give his Trojan collection to Greece. The Athenians considered him little more than a criminal and speculator. He would not disappoint them. Schliemann thereupon put up his treasures for sale.

He wrote the British Museum that "I have decided to break forever with Greece," and offered them his collection (they thought the price, $400,000, excessive). He offered the collection outright to the Louvre, but for some inexplicable reason, the Parisian authorities did not respond to the offer; doubtlessly, his letter is still lying there, entwined in red tape. He offered the treasures to Italy, and to a member of the Russian nobility (at the cut-rate price of $250,000). Interestingly, he never considered the United States as a depository. America for him, within a cultural context, was a desert, exemplified by Barnum's museum at New York and the dearth of Greek studies in Indianapolis; as for California, the less said the better.

Craftily, like Odysseus, Schliemann made no secret of his plans to dispose of the collection either as a giveaway or for money. His behavior gave the lie to his pledge that he would never traffic in his collections of Trojan antiquities. Whatever his underlying plan, and when it came to understanding the marketplace, the merchant prince was in a class by himself, his irascible behavior had a stunning impact on both the Greeks and the Turks. They saw the treasure forever slip from their hands. To what extent the Greek judiciary was independent is debatable. The court dismissed the Turkish claim to half the treasure and ordered an out-of-court settlement. From the Athenian standpoint, as long as Schliemann retained possession of the collection, Greece might yet stand to be the beneficiary. For their part, the Turks also suddenly proved conciliatory. Modestly, they accepted what Schliemann described as "an amiable arrangement." Amiable, indeed. The Turks agreed to drop further legal activity in return for a $5,000 settlement, which hardly covered their court expenses. Schliemann, with a view to obtaining a new *firman* so that he could resume his work at Troy, proved even more amenable. Figuratively, he slipped the rubber band off his bankroll and presented the Turks with four times that amount. As an additional peace offering, he also shipped the Imperial Museum at Constantinople seven large vases and four sacks of stone implements from the Neolithic Age at Hissarlik. Oddly enough, he thus became the first of the museum's benefactors. Although all *firmans* in the past had been issued on the condition that half of the discovered antiquities be turned over to the museum, until then, the Constantinople authorities had never received any articles from anyone. The reason was not hard to see. The museum was not open to the public and, it was said, the armed Turks at the front gate frequently refused admittance even to its director.

With the lawsuit behind him and displaying his talent for public relations, Schliemann launched a campaign to win over Greek public opinion just as he had placated the ire of the Turks. His ulterior motive: He wanted a permit to excavate in Greece, too.

When the Venetians occupied Athens in the fifteenth century, they erected an eighty-foot tower from the slabs of marble of the Acropolis as a memorial to their presence. It was unnecessary, their presence would never be forgotten. During the bombardment of Turkish-occupied Athens, the Venetians hit the Parthenon where the Turks stored their gunpowder and blew it up. In Venice, perhaps, the tower would blend into the background of canals, churches, and ornate palaces. In Athens, it was an eyesore, and it blocked an unobstructed view of the Acropolis. The Greeks grumbled about its presence for centuries but, typically, they did nothing about it, except grumble the more. To the great delight of the Athenians, Schliemann announced that at his own expense he would demolish the structure. The press applauded his civic virtue; so did the government. The demolition job cost Schliemann $2,325. While the Greeks were overjoyed by the tower's removal, its destruction brought grief to the thousands of owls that inhabited it. Based on his own experience, Schliemann dryly remarked, "It is impossible to please everyone."

Eager to resume his excavation, Schliemann found that, his public relations compaigns notwithstanding, he could not obtain a *firman* from the Turks or a permit to dig in Greece. Both governments continued to mistrust him. They suspected that his real interest, as Safvet Pascha implied, in 1869, when Schliemann first applied for a *firman,* was the discovery of treasure. "The Turks appear to think that Hissarlik is a vast gold mine," he complained. He promised the Turks that he would excavate Troy "for the exclusive benefit of the Turkish government." But burned once, the Turks were reluctant to be burned twice. They hinted that perhaps if he donated part of Priam's treasure to the Imperial Museum, they would relent. Schliemann refused to discuss the proposition.

No less obstructive were the Greeks. Schliemann sought permission to dig at Mycenae and Ithaca (where he had rummaged around in 1868 during his first visit to Greece). But the Greeks were reluctant to grant him permission. Like the Turks, however, they still had an eye on the treasure, which Schliemann would retain for another decade before deciding on whom to bestow it. When he made his choice, he gave it away free.

During these lengthy and humiliating negotiations, Schliemann considered abandoning the Aegean altogether and excavating in Italy where he had been assured the cooperation of the Roman authorities. If, according to the popular view,

Schliemann's objective was treasure for treasure's sake, he should have crossed the Adriatic. But Schliemann was hypnotized by Homer. Of this, there can be little doubt. He was bound to the Aegean world as securely as Odysseus to the mast as his vessel slipped by the enchanted isle of the Sirens.

Schliemann's desire to get on with further excavations puts his character in sharper focus. Given the discovery of Troy, why did he continue to drive himself? Why didn't he "rest on his laurels"? He was fifty-two, complained occasionally of intense earaches, possessed a youthful and spirited wife, and was the father of a new baby. Society lionized him—well, in London and Amsterdam certainly—and, given his financial resources, his town house in Paris, the controversy which swirled endlessly around him, in time, the Continental smart set would sit at his table. But he was not a dilettante. The life of the idle rich appalled him as sinful and wasteful, although he wanted their recognition and respect.

Unwittingly, perhaps, his discoveries at Troy transformed him into an archaeologist. His interest in the world of the past acquired irreversible momentum. He proved that *The Iliad,* the story of the Trojan War, was not complete fantasy. Now he burned with desire to vindicate Homer's *Odyssey,* the story of the postwar period, the return of Odysseus to Ithaca, and the return of Agamemnon, "the King of Men" and the conqueror of Troy, to Mycenae. Schliemann had restored Priam to life; now he planned to resurrect his adversary, Agamemnon.

Agamemnon was hardly greeted as the conquering hero. On his return to Mycenae, at a victory banquet, he was slain by his wife, Clytemnestra, and her lover, Aegisthus, his cousin. The story is as enduring as that of the Wooden Horse. Consigned to Hades, the dead king gave, in *The Odyssey,* this account of his murder:

> Aegisthus and my wicked wife were the death of me between them. He asked me to his house, feasted me, and then butchered me most miserably as though I were a fat beast in a slaughter house, while all around me my comrades were slain like sheep or pigs, for the wedding breakfast, or picnic, or gorgeous banquet of some great nobleman. . . . You never saw anything so

truly pitiable as the way in which we fell in that cloister, with the mixing bowl and the loaded tables lying all about, and the ground reeking with our blood. I heard Priam's daughter Cassandra scream as Clytemnestra killed her close beside me. I lay dying upon the earth with the sword in my body, and raised my hands to kill the slut of a murderess, but she slipped away from me; she would not even close my lips nor my eyes when I was dying, for there is nothing in this world so cruel and shameless as a woman when she has fallen into such guilt as hers was. Fancy murdering your own husband. And I thought I was going to be welcomed home by my children and my servants. . . .

Agamemnon's gravesite was pinpointed in antiquity in the *Description of Greece,* written two centuries before the birth of Christ by Pausanias, the Greek geographer and traveler, of whom it is said, "without him, the ruins of Greece would for the most part be a labyrinth without a clue, a riddle without an answer." According to tradition, Pausanias reported, the bodies of Atreus, who founded the Mycenaean dynasty, and that of his son Agamemnon, who led the Achaean confederation against Troy, were buried within the walls of Mycenae. Clytemnestra and Aegisthus were buried outside the walls because "they were thought unworthy of burial within it, where Agamemnon lies and those who were killed together with him."

This is a classic case of misinterpretation. Mycenae had two separate and distinct sets of walls, one encircling the Acropolis, and the other girdling the town outside its battlements; this was especially known to the scholars of the age. To Schliemann and, one would suspect, to any other reasonable observer, the royal tombs should lie within the walls of the Acropolis and the graves of the murderers outside the selfsame walls, the more so since the entrance was guarded by two sculptured lions, as royal a symbol in the West then as now.

But just as most scholars put Troy at Bounarbashi and not Hissarlik in Schliemann's day, they also interpreted Pausanias' report as meaning that the slain were buried within and the slayers outside the city walls. Even so, the story of Agamemnon and Clytemnestra was as mythical as Troy and the Trojan War itself. As a consequence, nobody took the trouble to excavate the site. Schliemann, like Columbus, achieved his fame by default.

In 1868, during his initial visit to Ithaca, the Peloponessus, and Troy, Schliemann briefly inspected the Mycenaean Acropolis and concluded, obnoxiously as usual, that everyone was out of step excepting himself. The sepulcher at Mycenae, the royal tomb of King Agamemnon, he declared, must be looked for within the roughly 555-foot circumference of the Acropolis beyond the Lion Gate, and not in the lower city. This theory was published the following year side by side with his controversial views on Hissarlik. "As this interpretation of mine was in opposition to that of all other scholars," Schliemann said, "it was at the time refused a hearing."

Having uncovered Priam's Pergamus, he was determined to unearth Agamemnon's tomb. He recognized what most of his critics failed to understand: If *The Iliad* was not wholly a figment of Homer's imagination then, perforce, neither was *The Odyssey.*

Impatient, restless, in the midst of the Turkish law suit, in 1874, Schliemann slipped off to Mycenae to inspect the site of his next dig. But the demands of the lawsuit required him to be present in Athens and "circumstances," as he put it, forced him to temporarily abandon the new enterprise.

At the close of 1875, the Athenian authorities relented. But they saddled his permit with conditions. He could only dig at Mycenae; an inspector from the Greek Archaeological Society, especially appointed by the government, must be on hand at the dig; he could excavate at the site only one area at a time; and all his discoveries, if any, were to become the property of the Greek government. No simple-minded treasure hunter would accept such terms. Schliemann leaped at the opportunity.

With Sophia clinging to his arm, Heinrich Schliemann descended on Mycenae like a whirlwind. His critics enjoyed the spectacle. An unsigned piece in the London *Times* was vicious. An anonymous scholar taunted:

> Schliemann continues to deny the world of intellectuals who have devoted their *entire* lives to the world of the past. But, let him proceed and prove himself to be but the butt of our amusement. Graves will never be found within the citadel walls unless the destroyer of Troy seeds graves during the night.

# XV

⊓⊔⊔⊔⊔⊔⊔⊓

⊓⊔⊔⊔⊔⊔⊔⊔⊓

# The Mycenaean Campaign

*The strong city of Mycenae . . . rich in gold*
*. . . sent a hundred ships under the*
*command of King Agamemnon*
*. . . the greatest king.*

The Iliad, BOOK II

UNLIKE TROY, whose location, if not existence, was disputed, both the location and existence of Mycenae were known since antiquity. Mycenae was not so much buried as neglected. It played no role in the Greek classical age although, according to Homer, when Agamemnon led his forces against Troy, Mycenae was a hub of the Aegean world.

Astride the Plain of Argos, situated for defensive reasons in a recess between two mountain peaks, the Mycenaean Acropolis occupied a rocky height shaped like an irregular triangle and sloped toward the west. In addition to its natural defenses, the Acropolis was surrounded by Cyclopean walls between thirteen and thirty-five feet thick. Notwithstanding their antiquity, the Mycenaean ruins were in a better state of preservation than those of any of the other Homeric cities about which Pausanias wrote. In Schliemann's day, the circuit walls stood as forbiddingly as when they were built at the dawn of Western civilization. The main entrance to the citadel was through the Lions' Gate, situated in the northwest corner of the defensive rampart. The opening was almost ten feet wide and eleven feet

175

high. Over the gate's lintel, on a triangular slab, hovered two lions in high relief. What lay beyond that entranceway? For thousands of years and into the nineteenth century, nobody had ever troubled to find out.

Schliemann and Sophia arrived at Mycenae on August 7, 1876, traveling along the same road which Pausanias described in his "Fodor" of Greece. They established headquarters at Argos, one of the birthplaces of Homer, situated about six miles from the ruins of the rock citadel. Word of the Schliemanns' arrival in town spread rapidly, and he encountered little difficulty organizing a work brigade.

Since the trench concept worked at Troy, he adopted, and adapted, it to Mycenae. Schliemann sent a dozen men to the Lions' Gate to open up a forty-foot passageway into the Acropolis proper while he put forty-three men to work inside the Acropolis to dig a trench 113 feet long and 113 feet wide at a distance of forty feet from the Gate.

After two "idle" years in Athens, Schliemann was back in his element, the dig. "I know that, after Troy, I could not possibly render a greater service to science than by excavating at Mycenae," he pompously proclaimed. He should have also acknowledged an ulterior motive: to further strengthen Homer's case. *The Iliad,* he proved, was based on fact; so must *The Odyssey.*

For the next two months, "with wonderful results," he wrote, Schliemann pressed ahead with the excavation in the oppressive heat of late summer. Describing the work as "very hard," owing to the huge blocks of stone which impeded his path, he, nevertheless, recovered from the earth thousands of potsherds, the cultural dactylographs of prehistoric civilization, and more than 200 terra-cotta idols in the form of a cow, the symbol of Hera, sister and wife of Zeus, goddess of women, the queen of the gods and the queen of heaven. Schliemann thus promptly established that the cow was to Mycenae what the owl was to Troy—the tutelary deity of the fortress. He also unearthed small figurines of horses, lions, rams, and an elephant, "which seems to prove that the Greeks knew this animal many centuries before the classical period." The excavation appeared so promising that Schliemann expanded his work gang to 125 men and five horse carts.

As usual, the merchant prince kept tight rein on the wage scale. His day laborers earned about two and a half drachmas daily (about three cents); the foremen, double that figure. Carts he rented at eight drachmas (less than ten cents) per day. To his delight, the Greek workers were stronger and more industrious than the Turkish and Levantine Greek laborers at Hissarlik.

During the campaign, Schliemann spent a large part of the time rowing with M. Stamatakis, who superintended the excavation as the representative of the Greek government. Although Schliemann detested him and often demeaned him by calling him a "government clerk," Stamatakis was an archaeologist in his own right and held the rank of royal commissioner.

Schliemann paid the price for his impatience at Troy. His reputation as the "destroyer of Troy" was widespread, and Athens formally instructed Stamatakis to restrain Schliemann. Repeatedly, as a result, Schliemann complained that "I have been obliged to stop the work for a time" as he sought permission from Stamatakis to demolish a wall or some other obstruction in the path of his twin trenches.

These incessant battles between Schliemann and Stamatakis gave Sophia the opportunity to come into her own. She issued orders to the foremen, took measurements, and recorded notes. Stamatakis' sensibilities were offended by the presence of a woman, a Greek woman no less, at a camp composed solely of men. Fastidious and prudish in social matters, the Greek middle and upper classes of the period were no less Victorian than Victoria's England.

In the lower city of Mycenae, beneath the circuit walls of the Acropolis, the most remarkable structures were several mausoleums shaped like beehives. They were between twenty-five and fifty feet in height and diameter. These odd-shaped structures, which Schliemann described as a "great chamber which resembles a dome or a vast beehive," were locally called ovens because of their shape. They were also known as treasuries since, according to tradition, like the Egyptians who buried treasure with their rulers, the kings of Mycenae, during the "beehive dynasty," reputedly did likewise. The largest of these ovens was assigned to Atreus, the father of Agamemnon. Since the existence of the treasuries was known in antiquity, they had been plundered and replundered throughout the centuries. A few hundred yards from the Lions' Gate, however, an unnamed beehive, in ruins, protruded from the soil, its dome in a collapsed state and its entranceway or *dromos* covered by earth and debris.

Schliemann handed Sophia a spade and pickax and put her in charge of excavating it. She was on her own.

Attired in a flowing skirt and a long-sleeved jacket with high collar and two rows of buttons, her radiant black hair tucked under a black derby, she organized a crew of thirty men and five horse carts, and successfully recovered from the debris a large fragment of a frieze of blue marble—ornamented with a double row of herringbones—several copper knife blades, bronze spear points, and an idol depicting Hera, the goddess of women. Sophia was in the vanguard of the woman's liberation movement in archaeology. Displaying anything but male chauvinism, Schliemann proudly christened the beehive, "Mrs. Schliemann's Treasury."

But she never completed the excavation. Stamatakis, resentful of her growing authority at the site, refused to grant her permission to remove the foundations of a house of the Greek classical period which partially covered the treasury's dromos. Schliemann was furious; he and Stamatakis almost came to blows.

"In the treasury the difficulties were far greater than I had anticipated, particularly from the delegate of the Greek government," Schliemann later wrote. He consoled Sophia. "Treasure may be hidden in the larger border stones and debris which [we] have been forced to leave behind, but I scarcely believe it," he said. The potsherds she unearthed from the dromos, he pointed out, were of a different period from the fragments of pottery she discovered beneath the chamber or tholos of the dome. Therefore, he concluded, the oven had probably been plundered in antiquity.

Stamatakis won the battle of the treasury but lost the war at Mycenae. Flushed with victory, he sought to have Sophia permanently excluded from the site.

Through Sophia, Stamatakis realized, Schliemann established instant rapport with the workers at the expense of his authority as the government's overseer at the dig. In effect, he was reduced to the role of a petty bureaucrat. Within the terms of reference he received from Athens, Stamatakis envisioned Schliemann working under him or at least in partnership. Following the incident at Mrs. Schliemann's treasury, Stamatakis urged the authorities at Athens to bar Sophia from the dig. With reason, he argued that keeping an eye on one Schliemann was sufficiently difficult—he complained, for example, that Schliemann rose before daybreak and retired after midnight and that he, Stamatakis, was on the verge of exhaustion as his shadow, which was probably true. But keeping an eye on two Schliemanns at one and the same time was an impossibility.

In a rage, Schliemann threatened to close the dig. The government resolved the confrontation by permitting Sophia to remain at Mycenae, but Athens dispatched a detail of guards to assist Stamatakis in policing her as well as her husband's activities.

As a team, Heinrich and Sophia directed the excavation from sunrise until sunset. As in the Troad, the Muses challenged them. "We suffer severely from the scorching sun and incessant tempest, which blows the dust into the eyes and inflames them," Schliemann wrote. But the romance of archaeology held them firmly. "In spite of the annoyances, nothing more interesting can be imagined than the excavation of a prehistoric city of immortal glory, where nearly every object, even to the fragments of pottery, reveals a new page of history."

From a study of archaeology, one may draw the impression that in antiquity people left a deliberate trail of potsherds in their wake. Hardly. The potsherds of yesterday were nothing more than the beer cans and Cokè bottles which litter contemporary construction sites and cemeteries. Even today, gravediggers take refreshment on the site in the heat of summer and are apt to cover their litter with a spadeful of earth. In antiquity, of course, the pottery, in the shape of jars and drinking vessels, contained wine or water.

By September 9, 1876, Schliemann expressed satisfaction that Homer was correct in characterizing Mycenae as "rich in gold." Schliemann had found no gold but, he explained, "the real wealth of the city is certainly confirmed by the costly style of its architecture." Once again, Schliemann gave the lie to those who simplistically defamed him as a man who solely lusted for gold.

As the work proceeded, Schliemann and his workers brought to light, at a depth of about ten feet, in the center of the Acropolis, a second Cyclopean wall which ran parallel with the great circuit wall of the rock citadel and enclosed a relatively small area, less than 100 square feet. Within this inner circle, he discovered, four feet further down, the ashes of burned animal matter and bones and two parallel lines of upright slabs. In relief, the slabs depicted scenes of men riding chariots in battle and on the hunt. Unlike Homer's chariot of the gods, however, which had eight spoke wheels, the Mycenaean vehicles had four spokes. "These sculptured slabs mark the site of tombs," Schliemann recorded with unerring accuracy in his notes. With Sophia at his side, he ordered the men to dig deeper beneath the first slab. And faster. With each spadeful of earth, their heartbeats quickened.

More ashes were uncovered. "I at first thought they were from human bodies," he wrote. Among the ashes was a gold button on which was engraved a circle and within it a triangle. He turned it over in the palm of his hand. Pure gold. Several more shovelfuls of earth and he possessed eleven more buttons, all fashioned from gold. The pace of the dig and his pulse accelerated still further.

Then, at a depth of ten and a half feet, a cloudburst halted the excavation. The soft earth in the shaft turned to mud and was unworkable. It would take days for the pit to dry out. In his impulsive manner, an offshoot of his restlessness and impatience, he abandoned the shaft and turned his attention to the second stela. He sensed that he was on the track of an important discovery.

At a depth of twenty-five feet from the surface of the Acropolis, Schliemann cried out, "Sophia! Sophia!"

When she joined him at the bottom of the shaft she exclaimed, "My God!"

He had found three bodies "smothered"—Schliemann's word—in gold. Each body was draped with five gold diadems, two of the bodies were each adorned with gold laurel leaves.

The sepulcher, cut out of rock, also contained "many curious objects," including cow-shaped idols, fragments of colored glass, small knives of obsidian, the fragments of a gold-plated silver vase, a bronze knife. The bones and skulls had been preserved but they had suffered so much from moisture that when he reached out and touched them, they dissolved as if in a dream. Judging by the earrings, bracelets, and the other jewelry, the bodies were those of women. In the grave, Schliemann found a child's face mask made of gold. Apparently, the infant's body had crumbled into dust.

After they recovered their presence of mind, the first question that sprang from their lips was, "Who were they?" Schliemann blanched. He was emotionally drained. Cassandra, he recalled, had borne twins and, according to Greek tradition, the infants were slaughtered by Aegisthus together with their mother in the aftermath of that fateful banquet for Agamemnon.

Returning to the surface in a frenzy, he ordered the work gangs to dig up the whole area beneath the other grave markers. Schliemann behaved like a man possessed. In his impatience, he and two workmen were almost killed.

In the course of the excavation, the workers unloosened a large boulder which protruded into one of the grave shafts, somewhat like a plateau. Schliemann noticed that a crack in the rock had widened and that two men were working below it. Once again the man of action surged to the fore. "I literally dragged the two men from their position, when all at once the rock fell with a thundering crash, and we were all three knocked down by its splinters," he recorded. Bruised and badly shaken, they escaped serious injury.

At twenty-nine feet into the third shaft, Schliemann discovered three more bodies. He could barely control his emotions. "The bodies were literally laden with jewels," he wrote. They were covered with gold plates—701 in all—some bearing the motifs of leaves, others of insects, cuttlefish and serpents. Schliemann's imagination ran riot. "I suppose all these golden discs are miniature copies of shields," he wrote. When he found three squares of gold, each no larger than a cube of sugar and each engraved in intaglio with exquisite vignettes of a lion

hunt and two warriors in combat, Schliemann instantly iden-
tified the scenes: Hercules killing the Nemean lion, and
Achilles and Hector in mortal combat beneath the walls of
Troy.

On the brow of one body was a crown of gold, "one of the
most precious objects that I collected at Mycenae," he later
said. The crown was slightly more than two feet in length and
was fashioned from pure gold. Bracelets, rings, and idols—also
of gold—littered the gravesite. One body, astonishingly, was
covered with an elaborate cross of gold. A gold cross in devout
Greece? "If I had found it alone," the pastor's son said, "I should
not have claimed for it very remote antiquity, but the conditions under which it lay in the sepulcher make it impossible to
suppose that the object found there was of a different age."

The fourth grave shaft contained five bodies, "literally
smothered in jewels," the trembling Schliemann repeated as
he ran out of descriptive words.

The faces of four were covered with large masks of gold in
rude repoussé work. One mask displayed an oval, youthful face
with a high forehead. Another, a round face with full cheeks,
small forehead, and small mouth. The third, the portrait of a
man advanced in years, with wrinkles at the corners of his
mouth. The fourth mask was that of a lion. The symbol of a
king?

But the discovery of the masks upset him, an indication
that he was more interested in Homer than gold. "Neither in
Homer nor in any of the later classics do we find any allusion
to the custom of burying the dead with masks representing
their portrait," he said, "or with any masks at all."

On two bodies, he found large cameo rings depicting a hunt
and a battle. In the hunt, a man with raised bow is aiming at
a leaping stag while his companion holds the reins of a stallion-
drawn chariot. The battle scene shows four warriors bearing
shields and spears, engaged in combat. Each of the vignettes
was less than two inches in length, but the scenes were brilliantly rendered. How did the sculptor execute the design without even a magnifying glass? Schliemann was mystified (so are
contemporary archaeologists). "When I brought to light these
wonderful signets, I involuntarily exclaimed: Only a poet who

had objects of art like these continually before his eyes could compose those divine poems," Schliemann said. His critics notwithstanding, Gladstone's eminent explorer had enriched Homer.

From the bodies of the fourth sepulcher, Schliemann, with Sophia at his side, recovered breastplates of gold, *kraters*, and a two-handled goblet which weighed four pounds Troy,* copper tripods and cauldrons, bronze swords and lances. The tomb was strewn with bits and pieces of pottery, some fragments wheel-made, others handmade, some black and others green with black spiral bands, and still others dark red or light yellow with black ornamentation.

The fifth sepulcher contained only one body. Around the skull, which was too fragile to be saved, was a gold diadem, a collection of weapons, and a richly ornamented cup of gold.

By now, it was December; the weather had improved, and the mud in the first shaft had dried. After digging seventeen feet further into the first shaft, Schliemann uncovered a tomb twenty-one feet in length cut into bottom rock. It contained three bodies, the corpse in the middle, the most important of the trio, rifled. This, Schliemann conjectured, explained the earlier discovery of the dozen gold buttons. He said:

> Most likely, someone sank a shaft to examine the tomb, struck the body in question, plundered it recklessly, and for fear of being detected, carried off his booty in such a hurry that he only thought of saving the large massive gold ornaments, such as the mask, breast-cover, the diadems and the bronze swords and, in remounting to the surface, dropped many of the smaller objects, such as the twelve gold buttons which I found at intervals in digging down.

Both the plunderer of the Heroic Age and—from the standpoint of the dead—the plunderer of the Victorian Age—had selected the identical spot to sink their first shaft.

---

*Not to be confused with Homer's Troy. In England and the United States, precious metals and jewels are weighed by the Troy system—so named from Troyes in France. By this method, 3.086 grains equals 1 carat, and 5,760 grains equals 1 pound. Under the common Avoirdupois system, Schliemann's cup weighed slightly more than 3 pounds 4 ounces.

The two other bodies in the first shaft, undisturbed, were sheathed in gold.

Despite critical biographers, Schliemann again demonstrated that his primary interest was not in gold but in Homer. "Perhaps more important and interesting than all the jewels found in this tomb was a small quadrangular wooden box, of which I picked up two sides, on each of which are carved in relief a lion and a dog," Schliemann wrote later. The wood was moist and soft like a sponge, but Schliemann dried it in the sun. "Small as these sculptures are," he said, "they are nevertheless of capital interest to science because they prove to us that the art of carving in wood flourished in the mythic Heroic Age." Then he quoted a reference to carved, wooden boxes in Homer.

In the first shaft grave, Schliemann and Sophia also found large quantities of bivalves—among them, several unopened oysters—and a similarly large number of boars' teeth. Apparently, the dead were provided with provisions for the journey to Hades.

In the course of opening the graves, whenever the workers struck a bed of pebbles and a mass of white clay, they returned to the surface of the Acropolis. Heinrich and Sophia then took personal charge of the excavation. "On our knees in the mud," Sophia later reminisced, "my husband and I had to cut out one by one the precious finds." And as she remembered those glorious days of her youth, she added, "Our enthusiasm was so great that we often thought we had breakfasted and dined where we had not got anything at all for the whole day."

All told, they had found the bodies of fifteen adults and two or three children. The manner of burial indicated a primitive effort at preservation of the remains. The white clay, for example, was apparently used to seal off moisture. Interestingly, in 1972, archaeologists in China uncovered a well-preserved body of a woman—dead more than two millennia—whose body was encased with an airtight series of six coffins, buried at sixty feet and sealed off by a layer of white clay three feet deep—to keep out moisture.

Each of the bodies Schliemann and Sophia touched crumbled on exposure to the air, and only a few bones could be saved. But there was an exception to the rule. The exception, to Schliemann's shock, was mummified.

All its flesh had been wonderfully preserved under its ponder-
ous golden mask. There was no vestige of hair, but both eyes
were perfectly visible, also the mouth, which, owing to the enormous weight that had pressed upon it, was wide open, and
showed thirty-two beautiful teeth . . . [But] the nose was entirely
gone.

Even with the gold breastplate covering the chest, so little
of the breast had been preserved that the inner side of the spine
was visible in many places. In its squeezed and mutilated state,
the body measured less than two and a half feet from the top
of the head to the loins, but the large thigh bones left no doubt
about the man's real size and pathologists later judged that he
had died at about the age of 35.

Schliemann was determined to preserve the body and, as a
precautionary gambit, he sent for a local artist "to get at least
an oil-painting made," he said, "for I was afraid that the body
would crumble to pieces."

To his great joy, a druggist in Argos hardened the body by
pouring on it a mixture of alcohol and gum-sandarac. A small
trench was then cut around the body and a horizontal incision
made so that the body could be lifted out and placed on a plank.
A carpenter then built a box around it. Schliemann said:

> With the miserable instruments alone available here it was
> no easy task to detach the large slab horizontally from the rock,
> but it was still much more difficult to bring it in the wooden box
> from the depths of the sepulcher, to the surface. But, the capital
> interest which this body of the remote Heroic Age has for
> science, and the buoyant hope of preserving it, made all the
> labor appear light.

In its makeshift coffin, the body was transported on men's
shoulders for more than a mile to the village of Charvati and
then shipped to Athens for study.

Schliemann never estimated the value of his Mycenaean
treasure, which was turned over to the Greek government for
public exhibition at Athens and is on display to this very day.
But the market value was clearly a thousandfold that of his
Trojan collection. Indeed, the wealth he unearthed at Mycenae
has been exceeded only once in archaeology, by Howard Car-

ter's recovery intact, in 1922, of the tomb of the Pharaoh Tutankhamen.

It is difficult to appreciate the thoughts which tumbled through Schliemann's mind with his latest discoveries. Carl Schuchhardt, the director of the Kestner Museum in Hanover, an intimate associate who published the results of Schliemann's excavations in 1891, provided a hint. "If the Trojan treasures seemed a remarkable reward for his labor," he wrote, "no wonder his delight knew no bounds when, from the kings' graves in the fortress of Mycenae, he dug up such masses of gold as even he, the millionaire, had perhaps never before seen upon one spot." Schuchhardt added with a tone of disbelief: "Nearly all the ornaments worn by the dead, diadems, masks, breastplates, bracelets, earrings, were worked in solid gold."

Schliemann, despite his arrogance, egotism, and pomposity in public, was humble in private. He never believed in the reality of his good fortune. Enveloped in an Homeric haze, a haze which thickened as his life lengthened, Schliemann was endowed with the ability to put out his hand, touch history, and live it.

Reports of Schliemann's latest discoveries excited the Western world. The director general of antiquities at Athens, Professor Panagiotes Eustratiades, dispatched three government officials and a professor of archaeology to Mycenae—as Schliemann diplomatically phrased it—"to assist me in guarding the treasure." More likely, they were sent to ensure that he did not steal it for such was his reputation among the Greeks.

The news that a tolerably well-preserved body of a man of the fabled Heroic Age had been found, covered, no less, with ornaments of pure gold, "spread like wildfire," Schliemann recalled, and thousands of people came from the surrounding towns and villages of Argos, Nauplia, and Charvati "to see the wonders." Athens rushed a detachment of troops to the site to protect it from gold hunters and souvenir collectors.

Schliemann wrote:

For the first time since its capture by the Argives in 468 B.C., and so for the first time during 2,344 years, the Acropolis of

Mycenae has a garrison, whose watchfires seen by night throughout the whole Plain of Argos carry back to mind the watch kept for Agamemnon's return from Troy, and the signal which warned Clytemnestra and her paramour of his approach.

But this time the object of the occupation by soldiery is of a more peaceful character, for it is merely intended to inspire awe among the country-people, and to prevent them from making clandestine excavations in the tombs, or approaching them while we are working in them.

Seared earlier by the critics for naming the gold of Hissarlik "Priam's Treasure," Schliemann adopted the attitude of damn-the-critics-full-speed-ahead.

"I do not for a moment hesitate to proclaim," he declared impetuously, "that I have found here the sepulchers [of] . . . the 'king of men,' Agamemnon, his charioteer Eurymedon, Cassandra, and their companions."

The critics jeered when he set out to find Agamemnon's Mycenae. Now he taunted them. "Here in the Acropolis of Mycenae the tombs are no myth," he said. "They are a tangible reality."

Didn't everything fit? Pausanias, for example, had written more than 2,000 years earlier:

Among the ruins of Mycenae are the subterranean buildings of Atreus and his children, in which they preserved their treasures. There lies his tomb and the tombs of Agamemnon's fellow warriors who on their homecoming from Troy were slain at the banquet of Aegisthus. There, too, lies the tomb of Agamemnon and that of Eurymedon, his charioteer. Teledamus and Pelops were interred in the same tomb. Electra lies there, too.

Schliemann pitted his discoveries against Pausanias' description.

The identity of the mode of burial, the perfect similarity of all the tombs, their very close proximity, the impossibility of admitting that three or even five royal personages of immeasurable wealth, who had died a natural death at long intervals of time, should have been huddled together in the same tomb, and, finally, the great resemblance of all the ornaments, which show exactly the same style of art and the same epoch—all these facts are so many proofs that all the twelve men, three women and perhaps two or three children had been murdered simultaneously and [buried] at the same time.

But once again, his discoveries solved nothing; on the contrary, as at Troy, his excavations raised new questions.

How could Schliemann be so sure that this was the burial ground of Agamemnon and his followers? As at Troy, Schliemann found no inscriptions, no evidence of writing. Very well, suppose the king's name at Mycenae was not Agamemnon, but Smith. Even so, this did not explain what services he and his companions had rendered to have received the signal honor of burial in an acropolis—unless it was the conquest of Troy. Until and since then, no other example of an acropolis serving as a place of burial has been uncovered in the Aegean world. Albeit, the small building of the Caryatides in the Acropolis of Athens is popularly known as the Sepulcher of Cercrops, the first ruler of Athens. But Cercrops was a sun god; thus the story of his burial in the Acropolis is a myth as even Schliemann, the destroyer of myths, once observed.

Putting aside questions of identification—after all, it has been said before, what is in a name—how does one explain the artistry and techniques of the Mycenaean goldsmiths? By illustration, were the masks of the dead made in their lifetime or after death? Probably after death is a fair assumption. But this reasoning raises a more profound question. How could the masks have been made so quickly? In Mycenae, as in most hot climates, the dead are usually buried within twenty-four hours unless, of course, they are embalmed, which is admittedly known in Homer; for example, silver-footed Thetis "dropped ambrosia and red nectar into the wounds of Patroclus, that his body might suffer no change."

But the overriding conclusion crushed Schliemann. In Homer, both in *The Iliad* and *The Odyssey,* the dead are cremated and their ashes placed in urns; the only exception is the case of Sarpedon, an offspring of the gods and companion of Achilles and Patroclus who is slain by Hector and is carried from the battlefield by Sleep and Death to be returned and *buried* in his native land on the western side of the Aegean, that is, the Greek mainland.*

If the Trojans cremated their dead, why did the Mycenaeans bury their dead—better still, attempt mummification—sheath their bodies in gold, line their tombs with food, treasure, and other funerary goods? Such a death style is not found in Homer. It speaks more of the Nile than the Aegean. To the present, there is no explanation for what Schliemann found. Indeed, since his discovery almost a century ago, nothing comparable has been found anywhere with the compass of the prehistoric, preclassical, pre-Hellenic world. Schliemann, of course, was perplexed. It seemed that his Agamemnon lived in an age different from that of Priam. How could this be? In his pursuit of truth, Schliemann trapped himself. Inwardly, he recognized the inconsistencies inherent in Homer.

He conceded:

> The want of ornamentation on the Trojan jewels, the handmade uncolored pottery with impressed or engraved ornamentation, and finally, the want of iron and glass, convinced me that the ruins of Troy belong to such a remote antiquity, as to proceed by ages the ruins of Mycenae.

Schliemann appreciated the consequences of this conclusion. It left him wide open to his critics. Wrestling with the problem, he produced an ingenious solution. He said weakly:

> I believe that Homer had only known the siege and destruction of Troy from an ancient tradition commemorated by preceding poets, and that, for favors received, he introduced his contemporaries as actors in his great tragedy. But I never doubted that a king of Mycenae, by name Agamemnon, his charioteer Eurymedon, a Princess Cassandra, and their followers had been treacherously murdered either by Aegisthus at a banquet "like an ox at the manger," as Homer says, or in the bath by Clytemnestra as the later tragic poets [Aeschylus and Euripides] represent.

---

*This, incidentally, is the same Sarpedon who caused a sensation in 1973 when the Metropolitan Museum of Art in New York City paid $1 million for a *krater* signed by Euphronius, an Athenian potter and vase painter who lived 2,500 years ago, on which he depicted the scene from Homer.

Loyalist that he was, however weak his defense, Schliemann felt compelled to support Homer. Perhaps his faith in Homer was misguided. Yet he could never forget that it was Homer who had led him to Troy and Mycenae.

Like Columbus, Schliemann did not simply discover a new continent but a new world. As his friend Virchow commented, "Here begins an entirely new science"—the science of archaeology.

After the five shaft graves were combed out, the impatient Schliemann hurried back to Athens with new plans in mind. A year later, Stamatakis, his rival, continuing the excavation, uncovered a sixth shaft within the grave circle. Two skeletons were recovered, both in a far better state of preservation than anything Schliemann had found. But their faces bore no gold masks and their bodies no gold breastplates. Alone, Schliemann found gold at Mycenae.

# XVI

⎍⎍⎍⎍⎍⎍⎍⎍

⎍⎍⎍⎍⎍⎍⎍⎍

# Exploring New Worlds

*He offered many burnt sacrifices ... for he
had succeeded far beyond his
expectations.*

The Odyssey, BOOK III

ON HIS RETURN to Athens, Schliemann was the center of a renewed storm. The critics were unrelenting. Their attacks were sharper than ever, reflecting "envy, jealousy and hatred," Schliemann surmised in a letter to Muller at Oxford. Once again, the self-educated country bumpkin of lower-class origin had upstaged many of the authorities of his day.

As in the case of Troy, several scholars contended that Schliemann's finds were from a relatively modern age. Professor Ernest Curtius of Berlin thought that one of the gold masks resembled a Byzantine head of Christ. *The Times* of London expressed a conviction that the grave circle belonged to Celtics or Gallians who invaded Greece in 300 B.C. and that the treasures had been looted from Greek temples and museums. The gored Schliemann roared:

> But it is a historical fact confirmed by Pausanias, and well-known by every English child, but marvelous to say, unknown to *The Times*' editor, that the Celts or Gallians went from Thermopylae through Aetolia, which they ravaged, straight to Delphi, where they were defeated and from which they fled never to return.

Some of the attacks should have provided Schliemann with comic relief. In 1878, for example, the Hellenic Archaeological Society, which became the custodian of the Mycenean Acropolis, constructed a retaining wall out of old blocks to buttress the excavated area. Later, a London architect, accompanied by a group of academicians, descended on Mycenae for an inspection, spied the wall, and proclaimed that the Acropolis was of modern construction. Schliemann agreed. "In fact," he chided them, "that part of the enclosure was built 1,878 years after Christ."

His constructive critics, however, felt that the sepulchers could not possibly contain the bodies of Agamemnon, Eurymedon, Cassandra, and their followers for the reason that they were killed by their enemies, who had usurped their power and would not have buried them with treasure. Did the Indonesians bury Sukarno with treasure? Did the Chileans bury Allende with honors? And what ever became of Lin Piao's remains?

Before the testimony of Homer, Schliemann contended, this objection falls to the ground. In Homer, even he who killed his enemy buried him in full armor, with all his weapons. For example, Andromache told Hector how Achilles had slain her father and "yet stripped he not Eition of his arms, through the restraint of religious awe, but burnt him with all his panoply heaped high his tomb." The Mycenaean dead were not cremated, yet he hurried on.

"It would therefore appear," Schliemann said, "that in burying the fifteen royal personages with immense treasure, the murderers merely acted according to an ancient custom, and consequently only fulfilled a sacred duty." For that matter, it may simply have been politics. Richard mourned Clarence. Rommel was accorded a state funeral by Hitler.

Even the contrasting style of burial between the Troy of *The Iliad* and the Mycenae of *The Odyssey* provided Schliemann with an out. The murderers at Mycenae, he argued, were at full liberty regarding the mode of burial and sought as ignominious a method as possible, dumping them "like impure animals into miserable holes." Obviously, Schliemann was taking as much liberty on defense as his critics on offense.

As in the aftermath at Troy, Muller again came to the aid of his beleaguered friend, providing a dash of encouragement, the nourishment so sorely needed to sustain Schliemann's consuming ego. "However widely opinions may differ on the date and purport of the antiquities which you have brought to light," Muller wrote, "there can be but one opinion on the great service you have rendered to archaeology and I congratulate most sincerely on your success." Muller himself was not wholly in agreement with Schliemann's conclusions, although he was in the vanguard of Schliemann's defense. While Muller felt that Schliemann had, indeed, discovered a new world, something much more real than the mythology and poetical inventions of Homer, Muller did not consider the kernels of *The Iliad* and *The Odyssey* as history surrounded by legend—Schliemann's romantic view—but the other way around, as legends surrounded by historical and geographical realities.

As the controversy swirled, Schliemann was engaged in the publication of his work on Mycenae—in the parlance of the current trade, a coffee table edition, heavily illustrated and containing colored plates. "The publication of my work on Mycenae in English and German occupied the whole of 1877," he recalled in his memoirs. "The French edition kept me busy until the summer of 1878." Thus, again, as in the case of Troy, Schliemann was caught up in galleys and page proofs, rushing into print in an unscholarly way on his "really wonderful success . . . on my immense and marvelous treasures." His books, in one respect, are curiosity pieces. As some people are prone to think aloud, he wrote aloud. As a writer, he lacked discipline. As a result, the books are hastily organized, and in many instances, he corrects himself in print, striking out with one thesis, abandoning it in favor of another, and then returning to it at the end without logical sequence. "Contradictions," he called them. His editors probably had other words for his organization. Walter Leaf, the brilliant Homeric scholar, who helped Schuchhardt prepare a summary of Schliemann's discoveries in 1891, struggled with Schliemann's books. "The difficulty is yet more perplexing when an entire change of views takes place during the publication of a single volume," he said, and cited a classic example in the case of a later work, *Tiryns*.

"Many a student of *Tiryns* must have been for a time at sea
when he found an elaborate explanation of the citadel walls in
the text of the volume absolutely contradicted, without a word
of reference forward, in an equally elaborate appendix," Leaf
said. But Schliemann refused to permit his publishers to tam-
per with his manuscripts.

Schliemann's disconcerting literary organization notwithstanding, like his excavations, his books were "really wonderful successes." In London, the first edition of *Troy and Its Ruins*
sold out, and from New York his publisher wrote, "Your Mycenae has met with the most flattering reception." Graciously,
Schliemann wrote Gladstone the good news and concluded,
"For all of this I am entirely indebted to your wonderful preface."

In the midst of the controversies and the ebb and flow of the
page proofs, every delivery of mail to Athens contained re-
quests for advice on how to go about excavating a site or offers
to head new expeditions. In reply to a call for help from Baron
Boguschweski, an old Russian friend and scholar, Schliemann
wrote, "I strongly advise you to sink shafts . . . in those places
where you think the accumulation of rubbish to be gratifying."
And he patiently explained, "In digging down to the virgin soil,
you naturally pass through the strata of ruins of all the peoples
who have inhabited the premises in the course of the ages."

A British group wrote that they planned an archaeological
foray into Yucatan, the land of the Mayans, and offered him
direction of the expedition. Schliemann was flattered. "Indeed," he replied, "I am quite proud to see that my works at
Troy and Mycenae have given you such a high opinion of me
as an explorer." But he felt he must decline. Citing a crowded
calendar, he came to the heart of his decision. "I think," he said,
"I ought to remain in Homeric archaeology for the remainder
of my life." Then, in his offensive manner, he could not refrain
from a gratuitous jab. In selecting someone else for the Mexican adventure, he said, the sponsors should bear in mind that
"an explorer must be a self-taught man, excavation being an
art by itself which cannot be learned in colleges." An eye for an
eye.

Honors also poured in, especially from Britain. He was, for

example, accorded a D.C.L. (Doctor of Canon Law) by Oxford and made an honorary fellow of Queen's College. His election to the Society of London Antiquarians as an honorary member especially pleased him. In a letter of acceptance, he committed a Freudian slip. "Please confer to the president and to the members of the society my sincere thanks for this insignificant honor," he wrote. Obviously, he meant to write "this not insignificant honor." A short time later, in 1877, he and Sophia journeyed to London where she—not he—delivered a speech before the Royal Archaeological Institute. A report of the meeting described the company as "large and brilliant." Among those present were representatives of the royal family (the Duke of Argyle), the House of Lords (Lord Houghton), the House of Commons (including, of course, Gladstone); members of the literary community, including poet Robert Browning; celebrities, such as Rear Admiral Spratt, who as a lieutenant had befriended Schliemann; Baron Julius Reuter, whose news agency carried reports of Schliemann's discoveries around the world; John Murray, Schliemann's publisher; and members of that growing band of scholarly irregulars, for example, Professor Karl Blind.

In this setting of overstuffed Victorian chairs, crystal chandeliers, and gaslight lamps; in an age when women should be seen and not heard; and in a time when a lady's white glove never bore a smudge, Sophia, the twenty-six-year-old Athenian, now pregnant for the second time, spoke of her role in the Troad and the Peloponessus. "The part I have taken in the discoveries is but small, in Troy as well as in Mycenae," she said demurely in English. "I have only superintended thirty workmen."

From the audience, Schliemann glowed. He had helped her prepare the speech—part of it was pure Schliemannesque, for example, the insistence that every English schoolboy learn Greek—and he could not avoid the temptation of slipping the shaft to the Establishment to which he had now been finally admitted, at least in Britain. The meeting gave Sophia a standing ovation.

One note, albeit of minor character, marred the occasion. The Turkish Ambassador was prevented from being present by a "previous engagement." This was hardly surprising; for, Schliemann was again embroiled with the Turks: this time over the question of a new *firman*.

On his return to Athens from Mycenae, Schliemann had hurriedly sought to renew his *firman* but encountered difficulties. His discovery of treasure at Mycenae reawakened thoughts among the Turks of their Trojan loss. Why, the Turks reasoned, was Schliemann, the gold seeker, so set on returning to Hissarlik? Obviously, to find more gold. In private, Schliemann complained that the Turks still thought Hissarlik "a vast gold mine."

But Constantinople could not deny the *firman* for long. The rediscovery of Troy and Mycenae had aroused universal interest; in Constantinople, it was the ideal, non-political conversation piece at diplomatic receptions. Schliemann was aware of his newly acquired leverage on the Turks. To Gladstone's embarrassment, he wrote the British prime minister and asked him to put pressure on his ambassador to the court of the Sublime Porte to help him to get a new *firman*. Indeed, Gladstone was so embarrassed that he consented to do so in a postal card to Schliemann rather than a private letter which his political opponents could misconstrue as a case of influence-peddling.

Schliemann also wrote to Queen Sophia of Holland and sent her a dozen figurines from "my collection of Greek antiquities"—none from Troy, it should be observed—and confided in her that he was breaking Greek law which forbade the export of antiquities and that the shipment would be undertaken clandestinely. Having made her a co-conspirator, he reported that he had battled the Turks for two months with a view to obtaining a new *firman* and implied that a little pressure from the Dutch ambassador would help weaken Turkish resistence. No doubt, he would have written Emperor Dom Pedro but, alas, Brazil did not have an envoy at Constantinople.

In the end, the Turks buckled and granted him a new *firman*. Schliemann later attributed his success to "the aid of my honored friend Sir Austen Henry Layard, Ambassador of Her Britannic Majesty at Constantinople, who smoothed away all my difficulties with the Turkish government." The relationship between Schliemann and Layard, however, went beyond their tie to Gladstone. Like Schliemann, Layard was brusque and had a passion for archaeology. Unlike Schliemann, he was favored from birth by wealth and position. As a member of the British diplomatic service, at the age of 28, he uncovered Nineveh, the Assyrian capital of antiquity. When the British government refused to finance his plan to search for the lost city of Babylon, he gave up archaeology (although not his interest in it), entered politics, served briefly as Undersecretary of Foreign Affairs, and later returned to the diplomatic service. Schliemann had long admired Layard and, in 1880, he dedicated *Ilios,* his third book on Troy, as follows:

> The Right Honorable Sir Austen Henry Layard, G.C.B., D.C.L., The Pioneer in Recovering the Lost History of the Ancient Cities of Western Asia by Means of the Pickaxe and the Spade, in Acknowledgement of his Kind and Effective Aid to the Excavations on the Site of Troy, as Ambassador to the Sublime Porte, This Work is Respectfully and Gratefully Dedicated by the Author.

These were hectic years for Schliemann. In March 1878, he no sooner returned from London and received his new *firman* than Sophia gave birth to their second and last child. Foiled in naming their first child after Hector, the defender of Troy, Schliemann had settled for the name of Hector's wife, Andromache. This time, he assured Sophia, the baby would be a boy and he chose the name Agamemnon, the king of men, in honor of their triumph at Mycenae. It was a boy, and a good thing, too. Schliemann would have been hard pressed to follow the pattern and name a daughter after Clytemnestra.

As Schliemann prepared to return to Hissarlik and launch his fourth campaign, he suffered a period of deafness accompanied by severe pain in his eardrums. Schliemann was tiring. A clue is provided in a letter from Muller during Schliemann's visit to Oxford shortly before Christmas the year before, in 1877. "I feel certain from what I saw of you yesterday that you have been overworking yourself," Muller wrote. He advised Schliemann to take "a complete rest"—no visitors, no letters, no newspapers. "I hope," he added, "you will do so before you begin fresh work at Troy."

Schliemann rest? Muller must have known better.

# XVII

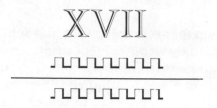

# Astride the Aegean

*All things are in the hands of heaven.*
The Iliad, BOOK XIX

FOR THE NEXT dozen years, between 1878 and 1890, in the autumn of his life, Schliemann excavated the length and breadth of the Aegean. In his restless, shotgun style, he put his spade and pickax to work on the crest of Mount Ida, in the environs of Ithaca, at Orchomenus and Tiryns, and, repeatedly, in the Troad. He developed plans to excavate Knossos on Crete.

With each dig, he unearthed another piece of the pre-Hellenic jigsaw puzzle. But the more he dug, the more he recognized that in one lifetime he could not put the pieces together to form a complete picture of the gravid epoch of Western civilization. Like all archaeologists, working in the earth among the ghostly remains of the worlds of the past, he was on intimate terms with sleep and death. "My days are counted," he wrote to an American admirer while declining an invitation to join the lecture circuit in the United States. "My minutes are precious."

During this terminal phase of his life, the Muses never abandoned him. Nor did he abandon them as he made unending pilgrimages to his beloved Troy, whose attraction for him never faded. At Hissarlik, he carried out new campaigns in 1878–1879, 1882, and in 1889. Each visit, he swore, would be the last. "I shall stop forever excavating Troy," he announced in 1879. Five years later he declared, "My work at Troy is now ended forever." And in 1890, the last year of his life, the familiar, slender figure, in a dust-streaked Bond Street suit, his head covered from the sun by a black bowler, could be seen rummaging through the fantasy of his childhood and maturity.

Schliemann's work at Troy never ended, of course, and after his death Sophia carried on his grand enterprise. But, as his notes indicated, the revisits to Priam's Pergamus over the years provided an emotional tuneup and even provided him with a sense of sexual gratification.

Exploring the summit of Mount Ida, which he reached mule-borne after a nine-hour journey over a narrow, circuitous trail, as "on a plate," he saw before him the whole of the Troad. "With special delight," he said, "my eye rested on the Plain of Troy." To him, the summit of Mount Ida resembled a gigantic throne. The blue hyacinths and violets recalled the nuptial couch of Zeus and Hera. He confessed:

> The beautiful passage of *The Iliad,* in which the nuptials of these two great deities are described, has always had a great interest for me. But here, on the very spot where the poet represents the event to have taken place, [my] interest is overpowering, and with delight I recited several times the divine verses describing the nuptials.

In Western literature, the passage is among the most touching of lovemaking scenes. ". . . for the present let us devote ourselves to love and to the enjoyment of one another," Zeus said to Hera. "Never yet have I been so overpowered by passion neither for goddess nor mortal woman as I am at this moment for yourself." With this, the son of Kronos caught up his wife in his embrace and, Homer recounted:

> . . . thereupon the earth sprouted them a cushion of young grass, with dew-bespangled lotus, crocus, and hyacinth, so soft and thick that it raised them well above the ground. Here they laid themselves down and overhead they were covered by a fair

cloud of gold, from which there fell glittering dew-drops. Thus, then, did the sire of all things repose peacefully on the crest of Ida, overcome at once by sleep and love, as he held his spouse in his arms.

Zeus, according to Homer, built an altar and sacred precinct on the summit of Mount Ida and Schliemann, who blended his poetic fantasies with scientific reality, set about to excavate it without success. "I have searched here in vain for traces," he lamented.

Invariably, Schliemann's biographers click off his life like a television set following his discovery of the shaft graves at Mycenae. In their view, his life peaked on the Peloponnesus because the gold seeker or fortune hunter failed to find more gold. This is unjust. It is also untrue. Schliemann unearthed more gold. But more important in understanding his accomplishments, as a later generation of archaeologists recognized, his post-Mycenaean excavations widened the horizons of the preclassical Bronze Age of the Aegean which was unknown before he touched his spade to the earth. Inestimably, the work of the last dozen years of his life enriched the literature and science of archaeology beyond the weight of all the gold he ever found. Loudly, the record speaks for itself.

In 1878, Schliemann returned to Troy accompanied by two scholarly collaborators, "my honored friends," he called them —Virchow, his closest companion, and Emile Burnouf, a Parisian and director of the French School at Athens. Virchow studied the flora, fauna, and geological characteristics of the Trojan Plain with a view to determining the factual accuracy of Homer. Bournouf, an engineer and painter, drafted plans and maps of Troy and made sketches of Schliemann's principal finds. "Both assisted me in my researches to the utmost of their ability," Schliemann later remarked. Actually, they instilled a sense of discipline in him and, under their guidance, he refined his methods. Indirectly, too, his scholarly critics exercised a healthy influence on him, although he would have been the last to admit it. Schliemann, for example, abandoned his steam-roller technique. Without credit to his opponents, he adopted their arguments as his own. "It being especially important to

preserve the houses of the Burnt City," Schliemann now asserted, "I gradually excavated the ruins of the three upper cities horizontally, *layer by layer,* until I reached the easily recog-
nizable calcined debris of the third or Burnt City" [italics
added]. Then, he boasted, he excavated "house by house [and] in
this manner I was able to excavate all the houses of the third
city without injuring their walls."

But while he diluted his methodology, his providential
ability at finding treasure remained undiluted.

Six years earlier, of course, he had unearthed Priam's
Treasure, but after his departure from Hissarlik, the ruins of
Troy remained as ignored and isolated as they were before he
brought them to light. In point of fact, from the time of
Schliemann's first glimpse of Hissarlik in 1868 until his death
more than twenty years later, he alone ransacked the ruins
while the debate about the authenticity of his discoveries continued forcefully. Few of his critics visited Hissarlik; no univer-
sities or governments mounted campaigns of their own.* And
yet, throughout history recorded and unrecorded, Homer and
Troy were a center of interest and curiosity in the Western
world. As late as 1932, when the University of Cincinnati campaign was launched, its director, Carl W. Blegen, presently the
dean of American archaeologists, felt constrained to explain
the reasons for the expedition thusly: "Troy had remained
more or less neglected." Why, given the whirl of controversy
around Troy, did it suffer neglect? There is a contemporary
parallel which may explain this phenomenon. Troy's neglect
after Schliemann's discovery was no less astonishing than
man's landing on the moon in 1969 and, shortly thereafter, the
abandonment of manned space flights, although, since Creation, man has dreamed of touching the stars. Centuries from
now, historians will find it hard to explain that, after the conquest of space, mankind was distracted by more pressing problems at home—and space exploration was so costly . . . almost
the price of a good war. To the generation of the distant future,

---

*Among archaeologists, there is a gentleman's agreement that the last
previous excavator of a site has a prior claim to the right of digging at the site;
by the same token, the last excavator may transfer his right, in the interests of
science, to another party.

these will seem rather weak arguments for abandoning, however temporarily, the greatest adventure of man.

Schliemann's core interest on his return to Troy was the
third or Burned City which he had designated as Homer's Troy.
For two reasons, from an archaeological point of view, he was
anxious to resume the excavation. He still searched for a scrap
of writing to prove conclusively, once and for all, that he had
found the Troy of his youth. In the light of his discoveries at
Mycenae, he now also searched for evidence which would link
the Burned City and the shaft graves—Priam and Agamemnon,
*The Iliad* and *The Odyssey.*

On October 21, 1878, as Schliemann cleared the debris from
the third stratum of Troy, he was joined by seven officers from
*H.M.S. Monarch.* The British sloop-of-war, on a mission of
charting the coast, hove to in the cove where Agamemnon's
invasion fleet had moored thirty centuries earlier. Out of curiosity, the officers journeyed the three miles to Hissarlik and
introduced themselves to Schliemann. Visitors at the remote
spot always delighted him, and he gave the liberty party a
warm welcome, plied them with Trojan wine, and invited them
to join him as he continued to excavate the Burnt City that
afternoon.

On this occasion, in their presence, he unearthed a vase
filled with white and blue powder. As he emptied the contents,
a treasure of jewels tumbled out, including twenty gold earrings, four gold charms, a large quantity of gold beads and wire,
several gold buttons and a bracelet of electrum. Schliemann
dubbed the collection, "The Little Treasure." There is no record
of how the officers of *Monarch* reacted; surely some of them
must have felt the discovery a put on.

Shortly thereafter, Schliemann found two smaller treasures, both contained in broken terra-cotta vases "with a good
deal of the same white powder which I noticed in the other
treasure." The new treasure troves contained several gold
chains or links, probably for a necklace or diadem, a gold bar,
and assorted objects of gold. From his description of these finds,
it appears he uncovered the shop of a goldsmith or gold merchant. But this was not all. Three feet from this double discovery, he found still another treasure. It included a silver dagger,

bronze battle-axes, and two gold bracelets, each weighing the equivalent of eighteen gold sovereigns, or 4.6 oz.

The following year, 1879, Schliemann returned to Troy. "Up to the middle of March I suffered cruelly from the north wind, which was so icy cold that it was impossible to read or write in my wooden barracks, and it was only possible to keep oneself warm by active exercise in the trenches," he wrote. As for "active exercise," despite the cold, and perhaps because of it, he did not abandon his customary early morning sea dip. "To avoid taking cold," he said, "I went, as I had always done, very early every morning on horseback to the Hellespont to take my sea bath, but I always returned to Hissarlik before sunrise and before work commenced." Two of Schliemann's armed body-guards always accompanied him on these excursions. The rides, before daybreak, over a poor trail, were not without incident. One morning, in the dark, he rode so close to the edge of a bridge that the horse slipped and both man and horse fell onto the bank of the stream. "The horse having fallen upon me," he later said, "I could not extricate myself from beneath it, and my gendarmes having gone ahead, could not hear my cries." He lay in this position for some minutes until his men, in search of him, retraced their path. "Since that accident," Schliemann wrote, "I always alight before passing a Turkish bridge, and I lead my horse over by the bridle."

The new year marked the discovery of two more hoards of precious metal at Troy. One cache contained several gold discs which reminded Schliemann of those he found in the grave circle at Mycenae. Three inches in diameter, they bore representations of flowers, all in repoussé work. "It is difficult to explain how the Trojans produced such patterns," Schliemann said. The assumption today is that a smith laid the gold plate on a block of lead and hammered the ornamentation into it.

The second cache was recovered in the company of Virchow and Bournouf—neither one of whom ever found any treasure at Troy. This time, their Houdini unearthed two heavy gold bracelets, several gold earrings, and a winged bird—also fabricated from pure gold—in flight. Most remarkable of all, Schliemann brought to light a bronze dagger whose handle was ornamented with a couchant cow. Hera? Schliemann, mellowing, growing more cautious, reserved comment.

In accordance with his new *firman*, Schliemann turned two-thirds of the treasures over to the Imperial Museum at Constantinople and retained one-third for his private collection in Athens. In a memoir, he wrote:

> I had terminated the exploration of Hissarlik in June, 1879. The publication of my work *Ilios,* which was brought out simultaneously in English by Messrs. Harper Brothers at New York and Mr. John Murray at London, and in Germany by Mr. M. A. Brockhaus at Leipzig, kept me occupied during a year and a half. As soon as I had finished these I proceeded to execute the plan I had found for a long time past of exploring Orchomenus.

In Homer, only three cities bear the epithet "rich in gold," Troy, Mycenae, and Orchomenus. The treasure he brought to the surface in the first two cities proved that they deserved the Homeric epithet. Why not the third? Once again, as at Troy and Mycenae, Schliemann triumphed, in part, by default. Nobody had ever thought of excavating Orchomenus.

He and Sophia arrived at the Boetian city in November 1880. The air was unusually crisp. The Muses continued to serve as his outriders; within a month he uncovered a large, oven-shaped tholos similar in style to the Treasury of Atreus and the Treasury of Mrs. Schliemann. But, just as his character displayed a subtle change when he declined to identify the handle of the Trojan dagger as that of Hera, at Orchomenus he again displayed new-found scholarly reserve. In antiquity, the citadel was the seat of the Minyae dynasty and, in a rapturous letter to Gladstone, Schliemann told how he and Sophia had discovered the beehive at Orchomenus. However, he contented himself by describing the ruins as the "so-called Treasury of Minyas." Four years earlier, an impulsive Schliemann would have shouted to the world that the beehive "beyond doubt" was the Treasury of Minyas.

Buried between twenty-three and thirty-five feet of debris, the mausoleum consisted of large blocks of black marble. Many of the stones of tholos or vaulted ceiling, bore evidence that bronze plates decorated the interior walls. Not one was left. The tomb had been plundered in antiquity. But in the eastern wall of the tomb, Schliemann discovered an ornamented door which led to a small chamber whose untouched ceiling consisted of blocks of marble, one and one-half feet thick, entirely covered with bas-reliefs. The mosaic consisted of exquisitely sculpted spirals and rosettes. The design was breathtaking, and he and Sophia stood motionless as they gazed on the ceiling in wonderment.

Apparently, the dead were buried in the small chamber, and the small door was opened only to admit a corpse. In the adjoining large chamber, the rites of the dead probably were performed. In the absence of writing, at least thus far, the nature of these rites remains unknown.

Excavating the floor of the small chamber, he and Sophia found "superimposed layers of ashes and other material twelve feet deep, perhaps the result of sacrificial fires," he said. The "so-called" Treasury of Minyas also yielded blue, green, yellow, and black pottery "such as I found at Mycenae," he continued. More important, the smaller chamber was similar in design to the grave shafts at Mycenae. The room was sunk straight into rock, lined with rubble walls and closed with stone slabs. The treasury marked a transition from the shaft graves to the beehive tombs. The link between Mycenae and Orchomenus was manifest. Once again, Schliemann had lent credibility to Homer. Like an oil stain, Schliemann's Aegean world—unheard of in his day—spread to encompass an ever-larger area.

In the material sense, Schliemann found no gold at Orchomenus. Nevertheless, he was excited by the discovery of the new beehive and labeled his campaign there "my very successful excavation." But although he refined his methods of excavation, his attention span remained short. At Mycenae, he had rushed off after unearthing the five shaft graves, missing the sixth. At Orchomenus, he also quickly moved on. More than a half century later, as modern archaeologists retraced his footprints at Orchomenus, the German team of Furtwangler and Bulle unearthed at Orchomenus three cities, one superimposed upon the other, as in Troy, stretching from the late New Stone Age through the Bronze Age. Schliemann, however, was content to leave his calling card.

In the wake of his discoveries at Orchomenus, as after

Mycenae, Schliemann felt an irresistible urge to return to Troy.
To Schliemann, Troy still possessed the key to the puzzle of the
preclassical age. But the key continued to elude him. For although he repeatedly proclaimed that the third, or Burned City,
was Homer's Troy, he had yet to uncover tangible evidence.
Suppose it lay at another stratum?

Before returning to Priam's Pergamus, he spent most of the
following year bringing out *Orchomenus,* which Brockhaus
published in Germany. Forgoing English and French editions
of this new volume, in 1882, he launched another major Trojan
campaign. This time, he was accompanied by Wilhelm Dorpfeld, the man who would continue Schliemann's work after his
death. Dorpfeld served as the human link from Schliemann to
Blegen, from the founder of the science of archaelogy to the
present-day generation of archaeologists.

Dorpfeld was one of Germany's bright young architects.
Schliemann had met him briefly at Berlin the year before and
was immediately impressed. Dorpfeld had vision and imagination in equal amounts to his technical knowledge and ability.
In archaeology, Dorpfeld was everything that Schliemann was
not. Whereas Schliemann preferred to excavate with dynamite
caps, Dorpfeld preferred bottlecaps. Whereas Schliemann flit-
ted impatiently from site to site like a hare, Dorpfeld plodded
methodically along at the pace of a tortoise. In one essential
they were alike, however. They were devoted to Homer—and to
Troy.

The pair no sooner reopened the old barracks on March 1,
1882, and settled down to work than Schliemann again ran
afoul of officialdom. His quarrels with Stamatakis were
preliminaries compared to the main event which he fought
with Beder Eddin, the official inspector assigned by Constantinople to Hissarlik to maintain an eye on Schliemann's activities. "I have carried on archaeological excavations in Turkey
for a number of years," Schliemann fumed, "but it has never
been my ill-fortune to have such a monster of a delegate as
Beder Eddin." The arrogant and self-conceited Schliemann denounced the Turk as "arrogant and self-conceited." Poured
from a similar mold, their strong personalities grated on one
another. Just as Stamatakis had sought to undercut

Schliemann by attacking Sophia, Beder Eddin turned on Dorpfeld.

Dorpfeld planned to take measurements of the site and
draft a definitive plan for each of the successive cities at Hissarlik. When Dorpfeld unpacked his instruments—a Gunter's
chain, telescope, range finder—Eddin at once telegraphed the
military governor of the Dardanelles of his suspicion that
Schliemann and Dorpfeld "were merely using the excavations
at Troy as a pretext for taking plans of the fortress of Koum
Kaleh." The military governor promptly relayed the intelligence to the grand master of artillery at Constantinople. In
turn, the grand master barred Dorpfeld from using his instruments and, indeed, warned him against drawing up any plans
at all.

When Schliemann and Dorpfeld, climbing around the
ruins, conferred together and took notes, Eddin again denounced them to the military governor. Clandestinely, he complained, they took measurements and made plans. Accordingly,
Constantinople issued new orders: Dorpfeld was prohibited
from taking notes at Troy under threat of being shipped "in
chains to Constantinople." Aroused, the sixty-year-old
Schliemann descended on the German Embassy for assistance.
Koum Kaleh, five miles from Hissarlik, he said, was "a miserable fortress . . . and altogether invisible from Troy."

The embassy took his case to the Turkish Foreign Office
and, for five months, the new campaign at Troy marked time.
Schliemann, in a rage, denounced Eddin as "an unmitigated
plague in archaeological pursuits." As a last resort,
Schliemann appealed for help to the German Chancellor,
Prince Otto von Bismarck. The Turks retreated and permitted
Schliemann to draw up plans provided only that they were
limited to Hissarlik. However, no measurements were permitted above ground. Since the horizon is to the surveyor what
ruins are to an archaeologist, the revised *firman*, Schliemann
howled, was "useless." Finally, the newly appointed German
ambassador addressed himself directly to the Sublime Porte.
The Turkish ruler recognized the idiocy of the situation and
issued an *irade,* or imperial decree, which permitted
Schliemann and Dorpfeld to carry on their campaign as

planned. Schliemann's exploitation of the Germans reflected his marketplace shrewdness. Within a generation, during World War I, Germany and Turkey were allies. Indeed, the Turks and Germans combined their forces, shattering Churchill's grand design for seizing the Troad and the Hellespont and launching a drive against the Central Powers from their rear. During that bloody battle—known in history as the Gallipoli Campaign—new fortifications were built within the view of Homer's Troy. In the intervening years, man's nature and Troy's strategic location had remained substantially unchanged.

Much to his dismay, as a result of his work at Troy in 1881–1882, Schliemann was compelled to retreat publicly from previous claims. Dorpfeld proved to him that "I had not rightly distinguished and separated the ruins of the two following settlements, namely, the second and third." Dorpfeld convinced him that the burned bricks of the third layer included bricks of the second city which the new Trojan inhabitants had reused. "The Burned City proper is, therefore, not the third but the second city," a chagrined Schliemann wrote in *Troja*, his last major work on Troy. If Dorpfeld was right, however, then Schliemann had been correct in originally assigning Priam's Pergamus to the second city when he and Sophia had initially excavated Troy more than a decade earlier.

With aplomb, Schliemann now shifted his loyalties from the third to the second city, whose inhabitants he now hailed as "remarkable." These were the true Trojans. The second city, he declared, possessed "wonderful" engineers and architects, and he spoke highly of Trojan civilization. All hail to the second city, the city of Priam's Palace, the Scaean Gate, the Great Tower! Of course, neither he nor Dorpfeld found any inscription in the second stratum, or for that matter in any other strata, which conclusively proved that the ruins of the second layer marked the Troy of the heroic Homeric Age.

In the course of their new campaign, Dorpfeld also proved to Schliemann that there were nine, not seven, cities superimposed upon each other in the hill of Hissarlik. If anything, Schliemann was probably now more confused and more anxious than ever to unearth tangible evidence attesting to which stratum was noble Troy.

Dorpfeld, to Schliemann's satisfaction, uncovered a scrap of architectural intelligence which strengthened the case that Hissarlik embodied Homer's Troy. It also lent credence to what Walter Leaf of Cambridge later called an "uncanny rite" associated with the fall of Troy.

Dorpfeld detected in the sixth stratum a well lying almost beneath the ruins of the temple Schliemann had discovered a decade earlier and ascribed to the Greek classical period. The well's only access was by an underground passage leading outside the circuit walls. Schliemann and Dorpfeld wrestled interminably with this puzzle until a Berlin classicist, Professor A. Bruckner, offered the solution.

During the sacking of Troy, a Locrian warrior found Cassandra, Priam's most beautiful daughter, clinging to the gold and ivory statue of Ilian Athena, Troy's patron deity. He dragged her off, violating the honor of the young girl and the goddess. Thus, according to Greek tradition, the wrath of the gods descended on Locris. After the fall of Troy, the city-state on the Greek mainland was racked by famine and pestilence. The Locrians were advised by an oracle that they would have no relief until they propitiated Athena, and this could only be accomplished by sending each year for 1,000 years two maidens to her Trojan sanctuary. Thereafter, to appease the goddess, the Locrians—a matriarchal society, no less—selected two maidens annually and deposited them at night along the coastline of the Troad. The two girls had to gain access to the temple of Ilian Athena without being detected by the Trojan sentries. If detected, the descendants of the original Trojans slew them on the spot, mutilated their bodies, and threw them into the sea. Those who succeeded in reaching Troy undetected found their way into the temple through a secret passage in the circuit wall. Within the temple, their lives were guaranteed. They were clothed in the single garment of the slave, their heads shaven. Barefoot, they spent the remainder of their days in service to the goddess doing menial tasks, such as washing down the sanctuary, sweeping, and so forth. "There can be no doubt that this strange custom was actually carried out," Leaf unequivocally stated. The evidence further suggests that this custom lasted until about 300 B.C. when the goddess was appeased. This would have placed the fall of Troy at around 1300

B.C.; modern archaeologists date the fall of Troy at 1260 B.C.

The secret passage discovered by Dorpfeld and Schliemann not only led through the defensive walls but to a well located in the epicenter of the temple of Ilian Athena, thereby lending credence to their discovery and to the strange tale. Nor is this the only story in which a secret passage to the temple plays a part. Tradition also tells of how Odysseus, aided by Diomedes, gained access to the sanctuary "through a narrow culvert not unmired" and made off with the statue of the goddess just as Paris had stolen Helen from Menelaus, the immediate cause of the Trojan War.

In 1876, while awaiting the outcome of the Turkish lawsuit, Schliemann and Sophia had briefly visited Tiryns, Mycenae's sister city and the legendary birthplace of Heracles, renowned for his strength and particularly the Twelve Labors—slaying a lion barehanded, obtaining the three golden apples from the Garden of the Hesperides, and so forth. According to tradition, his thirteenth labor was the most difficult. The King of Thespia —situated in the district of Boetia where Schliemann unearthed the palace at Orchomenus—desired that his fifty daughters should each bear a child by Heracles. In his thirteenth feat of strength, in one night he made love to forty-nine of the maidens. The fiftieth refused his offer and died a virgin. (The daughters gave birth to 51 sons, the Thespians, including two sets of twins.)

In the course of their visit to Tiryns, Schliemann found a Cyclopean circuit wall which was upwards of fifty feet thick and "in a pretty good state of preservation," he said. If he removed 36,000 cubic meters of debris, he felt, he could bring the Acropolis of Tiryns to sunlight. But he was so intent on shifting his operations from Troy to Mycenae, from *The Iliad* to *The Odyssey,* that he put off serious work at Tiryns with the casual remark, "I hope to accomplish this work some day."

That "some day" was in 1884.

"I am now able to realize my long-deferred hope of exploring Tiryns," he wrote that year. Once again, Schliemann turned to Dorpfeld for assistance, and their collaboration at Troy two years earlier had proved so mutually satisfactory that Dorpfeld readily agreed. Schliemann envisaged a massive campaign and shipped from Athens to Tiryns, over difficult roads, forty English wheelbarrows, three windlasses, fifty shovels, fifty pickaxes, twenty-five hoes, and other equipment. As usual, he undertook the campaign completely at his own expense. Through 1884 and into 1885, the work of excavating Tiryns moved forward.

Belying his sixty-two years, Schliemann led as vigorous a life at Tiryns—located one mile from the sea—as at Troy almost twenty years earlier. "My habit was to rise at 3:45 A.M., swallow four grains of quinine as a preservative against fever, and then take a sea bath," he later recalled. A boatman, whom he paid about two and a half cents, waited at the quay each morning at 4:00 A.M. and then rowed Schliemann into the open sea where he swam for five or ten minutes. "I was obliged to climb into the boat again by the oar," Schliemann explained, "but long practice had made this somewhat difficult operation easy and safe." After his dip, the Spartan drank a cup of black coffee without sugar at the Agamemnon, a coffeehouse which opened at that hour. Schliemann then climbed aboard a one-horse shay and set out for the excavation site, punctiliously arriving just before sunrise.

Dorpfeld, a normal human being, joined him at 8:00 A.M. each day, and they breakfasted together among the ruins. Their fare was sumptuous—fresh bread, sheep cheese, oranges, rezinato, a local white or red wine, and Chicago corned beef which the house of Schroder supplied to their former office boy. At noon, Schliemann and Dorpfeld broke off their work for an hour's nap. "One never rests as well as when thoroughly tired with hard work," he said in *Tiryns,* his sixth book on archaeology, which John Murray published two years later in London. "We never enjoy more refreshing sleep than during this midday hour in the Acropolis of Tiryns." After the day's work, he and Dorpfeld dined nightly at the Hotel des Etrangers, in nearby Nauplia, and discussed the day's events. Dinner usually consisted of soup, spiked with a dash of Leibig's Extract of Meat —also a gift from his former employers—cheese, oranges, and a bottle of rezinato. Although fish and fresh vegetables were plentiful, Schliemann sighed, the Greek chef "so ill-cooked them with quantities of olive oil that to our taste they were almost useless." Travelers in Greece to this very day are apt to whisper similarly.

The excavations began on March 17. For the first time, Schliemann had to forgo "the pleasure of employing my old servant Nicholas Zaphyros Giannakis," the majordomo of all his campaigns since 1870. The year before, in 1883, Nicholas had drowned while swimming in the Scamander within the shadow of the walls of Troy which he had helped to unearth.

Schliemann's work force consisted of seventy laborers, mostly Albanians but including fifteen of the best Greek workers who had labored with him eight years earlier at Mycenae. Good work, Schliemann always felt, should be rewarded. The winter was mild, and when he and Dorpfeld arrived at Tiryns "the trees were already clothed in the richest green and the field decked with flowers," Schliemann wrote.

As at Orchomenus, Schliemann's excavation at Tiryns, while hardly as spectacular as his discoveries at Troy and Mycenae—at least as far as the popular press was concerned— produced, in his own opinion and those of succeeding generations of archaeologists, "wonderful results." He employed that phrase in a letter to Gladstone on June 16, 1884. "In my architect Dr. Dorpfeld's opinion and in my own," he said, "I discovered the palace of the mythical kings of Tiryns." The news of the find spread rapidly in scholarly circles and a member of the British Museum enthusiastically wrote him, "I am amazed at your luck."

Like Mycenae, Tiryns was situated on the edge of the Argolian Plain. But Mycenae was hidden nine miles inland and built into the rocky spurs which rise from the plain. A rock citadel, Mycenae dominated the trade routes linking the Gulf of Corinth with the Gulf of Argos. By contrast, Tiryns was, like Troy, built near the sea. The Acropolis of Tiryns afforded a view of the sheltered bay which provided sea access to the Cyclades, the offshore islands of the Greek mainland; to the Troad across the Aegean east-by-north; and to Crete east-by-south. As at Mycenae, Schliemann uncovered an elaborate defense system at Tiryns. To gain access to the fortress palace, around which nestled the huts of farmers, fishermen, and craftsmen, invaders were compelled to fight their way through three gates arranged as a labyrinth.

At Tiryns, Schliemann and Dorpfeld laid bare the circuit walls of the Acropolis, its watchtowers, galleries, chambers, and inner squares. The major accomplishment was excavating the royal palace although no graves were found, neither of the shaft nor beehive design.

Schliemann's triumph at Tiryns was the discovery of magnificent wall paintings in the rooms of the palace, executed as frescoes, that is, painted on wet, freshly spread lime plaster. The floors of the palace were divided into squares and each square was painted with a different decoration. Tiryns' artists employed only four colors—white, yellow, red, and blue. Green, orange, and purple were conspicuously absent although they must have known these colors. Moreover, the colors were of uniform intensity. No gradations of tone were employed. Schliemann and Dorpfeld were stunned by the beauty of the brilliantly executed paintings which attested to the richness of civilization in the preclassical, pre-Hellenic age. Once again, Schliemann vindicated Homer. Among the wall paintings, the *chef d'oeuvre,* as Schuchhardt later called it, depicted a charging bull with a man on his back executing a somersault, a hint of the great Minoan civilization which Sir Arthur Evans would unearth on Crete at the turn of the century.

As usual, Schliemann rushed into print with his discovery. In 1885, *Tiryns* was published simultaneously at London and New York. As in his other works, he name-dropped liberally in an apparent bid to win acclaim and respect by association—a pathetic effort which revealed his social and intellectual insecurity, pathetic because the celebrities he mentioned are remembered in posterity not in their own right but only because during their lifetime they brushed Schliemann. "My excavation in Tiryns," he wrote, "had the high honor, in April 1884, of a visit from his Royal Highness, The Crown Prince of Saxe-Meiningen, so distinguished by his love of science and learning." Lord and Lady Pembroke also dropped in at Tiryns, probably for a spot of tea. Even Arnold Brockhaus, the son of his Leipzig publisher, drew a mention when he visited the dig. The book's dedication is a touching attempt at academic prestige by association. *Tiryns* is not simply dedicated to James

Fergusson, the London architect and historian who was among his earliest defenders, but to "James Fergusson, Esq., C.I.E., D.C.L., LLD. F.R.S., R.F., I.B.A., M.R.A.S., Hon. Mem. R.S.L. & c."

The physical, emotional, and mental strain on Schliemann was taking its toll. With the publication of *Tiryns,* Schliemann professed for the first time a "desire to withdraw from archaeology" and "to pass the rest of my life quietly. I feel," the aging warrior said, "I cannot stand any longer this tremendous work."

Also he was haunted by the fear of failure, the obverse side of unprecedented success. He wrote:

> Whenever I put the spade into the ground, I always discovered new worlds for archaeology—at Troy, Mycenae, Orchomenus, Tiryns—each of them have brought to light wonders. But fortune is a capricious woman; perhaps she would now turn me her back; perhaps I should henceforward only find fiascos.

# XVIII

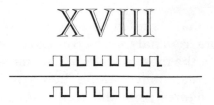

# Sleep and Death

*His eyes were closed in death, his soul left
his body . . . mourning its sad fate,
and bidding farewell to the
youth and vigor of its
manhood.*

The Iliad, BOOK XVI

SCHLIEMANN'S TRIUMPHS and failures in the field aside, the last dozen years of his life glistened as the gold he found at Troy. The merchant archaeologist won the recognition and respect long denied him. For a man who spent the better part of his life to prove that the legends of Homer were based on fact, he experienced the sensation of becoming a legend himself, like the hosts of the Heroic Age who crowded his dreams and waking moments.

Introspective in nature despite his bluster in public, as he aged, he gradually withdrew from the real world and entered the Homeric world. At home, he spoke to Sophia and the children, Andromache and Agamemnon, only in classical Greek. He named his servants after figures from *The Iliad*—the governess was called Danae and the nurse Polyxena. He designed and built his own Pergamus in the heart of the most fashionable district in Athens. It was as imposing and as uncomfortable as a museum which, in a way, it was.

Situated along the Rue de L'Universite, *Iliou Melathron*, palace or abode of Ilios or Troy, was the Athens' Crystal Palace

*215*

in its day. Schliemann stinted on nothing in its construction, importing marble from Italy, china from Dresden, iron railings from England. In the mosaic floors of the mansion, the motifs of Trojan *kraters* dominated. Along the walls ran friezes with landscapes and figures from the Heroic Age and quotations from Homer (in classical Greek, of course). In the ancient Greek tradition, the rooms were sparsely furnished and the furniture austere. Like a Priam or Agamemnon thirty centuries before him, Schliemann superintended the construction of his private acropolis and conferred almost daily on the site with his architects, artists and artisans, bricklayers, stone cutters, carpenters.

In 1880 *Iliou Melathron* was formally christened at a ball on the scale of the fete he arranged in Sophia's honor at Place St. Michel that Parisian winter eleven years earlier. The guests were drawn from every stratum of Athenian society, from royalty to the foremen who worked with him in the Troad, at Mycenae and Tiryns. Typically, perhaps, he clashed with Greek officialdom on the eve of the ball. The roof of the mansion was graced with the sculpted figures of the gods and goddesses of the Homeric era in their naked, classical beauty. The municipal authorities protested their indecent exposure, a bare-breasted, white rock Aphrodite, goddess of love, for example. Schliemann, always ready to do battle with bureaucrats, ascended to the roof of the mansion and draped street clothes on the figures. He even tied a bonnet on Aphrodite's head. The spectacle drew crowds of amused spectators and blocked traffic around the building. Ridiculed, the officials retreated.

Carl Schuchhardt, who collaborated with Schliemann in writing a summary of his discoveries, *Schliemann's Excavations: An Archaeological and Historical Study,* published simultaneously in Leipzig, London, and New York in 1891, recalled a visit to *Iliou Melathron*, as the autumn of Schliemann's life deepened.

> The visitor was admitted by the porter Bellerophon and conducted by the footman Telamon to the master, who was generally found reading one of his Greek classics, and stopping at intervals to complain of the number of stock exchange lists

brought by the morning post from Paris, London and Berlin. These used to lie piled upon a chair by his side, and had an incongruous appearance among the other surroundings.

Schliemann was no longer engaged in business, "but the management of his great fortune," Schuchhardt explained, obliged him to watch the big boards.

As in the remote Troad, Schliemann was delighted to receive visitors. As indrawn as he was, he enjoyed a forum before which his ego could strut briefly. A gracious host, he quickly poured the visitor a glass of rezinato. He offered Greek sweetmeats. But he was restless and uncomfortable with small talk and promptly steered the conversation into serious channels, brushing his index finger across his graying moustache, his thin voice rising and falling to emphasize a point. As Virchow, Bournouf, Dorpfeld, and other intimates before him learned, a different Schliemann emerged when Sophia or the children bounded into the room. "It was only within this circle that the warmth and tenderness of [his] character came out," Schuchhardt said.

The relationship between Schliemann and Sophia deepened with the years. As he approached sixty-nine, Sophia, at thirty-eight, was in the full bloom of womanhood. Only one issue ever seriously divided them, the disposal of Priam's Treasure.

As he grew older, Schliemann became increasingly aware of the need to find a permanent home for the treasure. When they moved into *Iliou Melathron,* Schliemann wrote, "If I do not present [the treasure] in my lifetime, they shall at all events pass, in virtue of my last will, to the museum of the nation I love and esteem most."

His last will and testament was recorded in Marion County, Indiana, on January 10, 1889. The German-born Schliemann wrote the will in French and Greek and filed it in his land of legal adoption. In the will, Schliemann did not forget the past. How could any archeologist do so? He left Catherine 100,000 Swiss francs "in cash and in gold" and to Serge and Nadehsda, the surviving two of their three children (Natalya died in 1870 during a bitter St. Petersburg winter), three houses in Paris and a house and other property in Indianapolis. He acquired the title deed to the latter after settling in Greece and according to Eli Lilly, the Indiana historian, "probably to support Dr. Schliemann's American citizenship." To Andromache and Agamemnon, he willed:

> all the residue of my personal and real estate which shall be found belonging to me at the time of my death, except, however, the house known under the name of Iliou Melathron . . . said house and garden as well as the furniture, library and antiques which are therewith with the exception of my Trojan antique set, I give to my wife Sophia.

The "exception" tells the story. From the outset, Schliemann entertained no thought of selling his collection for profit. He intended to give it away to the "museum of the nation I love and esteem most." But which nation? That was his problem. He owed so much to so many: Holland, which sheltered him in the depths of his poverty; America, which gave him the protection of her citizenship; Greece, where he found Sophia and made his home; Russia, where he amassed his fortune; Turkey, which possessed the greatest treasure of all, Troy; England, which extended him recognition and respect from the beginning.

How about Germany, the land of his birth? Schliemann viewed Germany with mixed emotions. Germany had turned him out, had refused him an opportunity. The most virulent attacks on him came from German lecterns and pens. He himself had turned his back on the Fatherland and refused to visit it, except perfunctorily, usually in transit from one place to another.

Sophia, of course, strongly felt that the proper home for Priam's Treasure was Greece, whose sons and daughters sang of Troy as long as men could remember. But Greek officialdom ruffled Schliemann, treated him like a carpetbagger. In any event, the Greeks already possessed the richest treasure he or any other archaeologist had ever unearthed, the gold of Mycenae.

For years, Schliemann struggled with the problem. Then,

suddenly, the solution presented itself. He and Virchow rested together at a lunch break during the Trojan campaign of 1879, the summer before *Iliou Melathron* was built. Schliemann talked about the treasure and the problem of disposal. Virchow was his closest friend and by talking to him, Schliemann talked to himself. Suddenly, in the midst of his monologue, Virchow gathered up a sprig of blackthorn, which flowers in Germany as well as Greece, and handed it to Schliemann. "A nosegay," he said softly, "from Ankershagen." As Virchow later told the story, "That broke the ice."

But Schliemann exacted a price, a balm for his consuming ego, his vanity: German, nay Prussian, recognition and respect. In return for the treasure, he wanted a *Pour le Mérite,* the highest award of the German Empire, election to the Berlin Academy, and the exhibition of the treasure in a "Heinrich Schliemann" wing of the Berlin museum. Virchow acted as go-between with Bismarck, a consummate politician, who was prepared to do anything, well, almost anything, to get possession of the treasure in the light of the growing German folklore that the Trojans were Aryans and that the Germans were their descendants. In truth, the Germans looked on Troy in much the same way as the Romans before them. Within a Western context, for a martial people, Troy epitomized Ares, the god of war, son of Zeus and Hera, illicit lover of Aphrodite, who sired Fear, Panic, and Rout, the god symbolized by the dog and the vulture.

Schliemann's desire to find a museum in Berlin to house his collection was hardly a problem and the question was quickly settled. But the *Pour le Mérite* presented problems. Governed somewhat on the Rotary principle, it was awarded only when a member of the order died and even then, the honor could only be extended to someone in the same field of endeavor—music, medicine, and so forth. As for the Berlin Academy, Virchow suggested that Schliemann was waving a flag in front of a bull. Schliemann laughed and conceded that he had suggested the Academy out of curiosity. But he did not laugh when he demanded that the Fatherland accord him official recognition. Bismarck provided a solution within his power. Schliemann would be made an honorary citizen of Berlin, an honor bestowed only twice before in the history of the

German capital—on Moltke and Bismarck himself.
Schliemann accepted. Thus, the pastor's son, the grocer's apprentice, the self-made millionaire merchant from the lower
classes was placed on an equal footing with the Prussian ruling
class.

The negotiations were concluded early in 1881 and on
January 24 of that year, the Kaiser, in an edict, decreed that the
collection:

> shall be consigned to the charge of the Prussian government,
> and afterwards preserved in the Ethnological museum at Ber-
> lin, now in the course of construction, in as many special rooms
> as necessary for exhibiting it to advantage; and that the rooms
> shall be set apart for this purpose and shall always bear the
> donor's name.

The following July 7, the Crown Prince, Wilhelm, escorted
Schliemann and Sophia to a grand banquet at Berlin in his
honor. At the dinner, Sophia brushed away a tear. Was it a tear
of joy for Heinrich? Or was it a tear of sadness over the fate of
her ancestors' heritage in the northland of the barbaric Hun?

Ankershagen was elated over the success of its most famous son. Almost all the elders of the village recalled an anec-
dote involving young Heinrich, the dreamer and curiosity
seeker. His father's notorious behavior, his mother's broken
life, his rejection by the villagers, all was forgotten and/or for-
given as Ankershagen glowed in his glory.

As Schliemann's fame spread through his native Germany,
he returned to Ankershagen in 1883, accompanied by Sophia
and the children. Like the ghosts from the past trooping up
from Hades, the faces of his youth, now lined with age, appeared before his door—Neidhoeffer, who recited verses from
Homer as he did in a drunken stupor forty-six years earlier;
Anders, who gave him his first lesson in Latin; Frau Uckstaedt,
who now operated the Furstenberg grocery store; and others.
Some had passed on—Hopping Peter, for one. With Sophia,
Agamemnon now five, and twelve-year-old Andromache,
Schliemann guided his family through the main streets and
side streets of his childhood and reexplored the mysteries of

Ankershagen—the ruined castle with its secret walls and buried treasure, Henning von Holstein's sepulcher from which his left foot had still not reappeared, and the garden in the back of his father's house which was haunted by a maiden who rose at midnight holding a silver bowl.

And what about Minna, the Minna with whom he had exchanged vows of eternal love?

In 1880, as *Ilios,* which contained his autobiographical sketch, went to press, Schliemann had qualms about his personal revelations. Minna was a married woman, the wife of a farmer in Friedland. Suddenly, Schliemann realized that the reference to their puppy-love affair might embarrass her. But he lacked the courage to write her directly, one of the few times he displayed cowardice. Instead, he employed the diplomatic skill of the merchant prince. He sent Minna's older sister, Louise, now Frau Frolich, a cameo from Troy and in an accompanying letter, in his overbearing manner, he disclosed that "in my great new work in English, about Troy, I also made you immortal." Then, in a moderate and less obnoxious tone, he explained that "in a rather cumbersome manner . . . I talk about my childhood." There is no copy of her reply, but it was apparently warm and satisfactory because the following Christmas, with *Ilios* in print, Schliemann summoned up the courage to send a copy directly to Minna, his first contact with her in almost four decades. "Should you find that I have exaggerated our friendship of fifty years," he wrote, "please do not take it amiss, but solely ascribe it to my attachment to you."

In this roundabout fashion, he prepared for his return to his native village, and in that summer of 1883, he invited the childless Minna and her husband to visit them at Ankershagen. When her horse carriage drew up before the pastor's old house, Heinrich rushed out and graciously assisted her to the ground. A plump woman of sixty-one, typical of those found in German villages to this day, Schliemann planted a symbolic kiss on each cheek and escorted her and Herr Richers inside to meet Sophia.

Apparently the meeting went off like an old class reunion. At Christmas that year, he sent her a gift from his Trojan collection and she replied haltingly in a thank-you note:

Dear Heinrich . . . you have given me holiday joy and I thank you warmly . . . but I do not know how to reciprocate. Next year, if God wills, I hope to visit the Schliemann Museum in Berlin. I was greatly interested in seeing you all, especially to have met your wife and those darling children. . . . Friendliest regards and wishes from your old friend, Minna.

Schliemann never revisited Ankershagen; nor did he ever see Minna again. His curiosity was sated. Germany was no longer his homeland, Minna no longer his love. Homer had led him from Ankershagen to a new world and in that new world he had found Troy and Sophia.

On their return to Greece from Germany, honors continued to flood his mail. He was elected an honorary fellow of Queen's College, Oxford, and Queen Victoria bestowed on him the Gold Medal for Merit. Schliemann was the first American, the English press observed, to be accorded this honor. In Athens, his writing also took up more and more time. The German and American editions of *Ilios* were exhausted within two years and, at the insistence of his French publisher, he worked on a new, French edition. He also completed German and French editions of *Tiryns.*

But the years of toil took their toll. "I have overworked myself," Schliemann acknowledged in a letter to his Dublin friend, Professor Mahaffy, "and I continue to overwork myself." But he could not stop working. As he wrote in 1871, when he chafed at the delay in receiving a new *firman* to excavate Troy, "Inactivity . . . literally kills me *morally* and *physically.*" He underlined both words.

After 1884, his health was in noticeable decline. The earaches returned with greater intensity, his periods of deafness multiplied and lengthened. From Egypt, which he was anxious to revisit (and did with Dorpfeld, briefly, in 1888), Professor Sayce, one of the original Schliemann irregulars, wrote, "You must not think of excavating until you are quite well again." An archaeologist, Sayce observed, is obliged to undergo hardship in the field and when the excavation is completed, however unfruitful it may be, he has to write an account of it. "So you must nurse your health first," Sayce concluded in his 1884 letter, "and then when you are well again begin to think about fresh conquests."

Three years later, in 1887, Sayce again implored that he slow down. "Your letter has filled me with grief," he said. "I am extremely sorry to hear that you and Mrs. Schliemann are so far from well. Your health is of paramount importance, and everything else ought to be sacrificed to it."

Yet he plotted new voyages into the unknown Bronze Age of the Aegean world.

Intuitively, Schliemann felt that perhaps Knossos, on Crete, held the key to the preclassical, pre-Hellenic period. How did the Bronze Age come into being? How did it fade? Who inhabited it? What religion did these people practice? How was their society organized? To what extent was this embryo Western civilization influenced by the older and more sophisticated civilizations of Africa and Asia? Perhaps, Schliemann felt, he could find a trace of writing on Crete. How could so rich a Bronze Age culture flourish without writing? How, for example, were records kept? They must have kept records in one form or other. Of course, the writing may have been confined to perishable materials which failed to withstand the passage of time.

Whatever the case, Schliemann focused on Knossos. His friends were divided. Sayce, returning by ship from Egypt in May 1885, wrote that, when his vessel slipped by Crete, snow lay so deep on the island that it was close to the shoreline and that the island was so large (3,186 square miles) that nobody could uncover a prehistoric civilization there unless by "accident." By accident? Schliemann had uncovered a whole world by accident. Sayce's argument was unimpressive; in truth, he may have sought to dissuade Schliemann in view of his deteriorating health. Muller, however, encouraged Schliemann's flights of fancy about Knossos, the mythical capital of King Minos, father of Ariadne, who, with a ball of thread, led her lover, Theseus, out of the labyrinth where Minos had confined him to be devoured by the Minotaur. "Crete is a perfect rookery of nations," Muller wrote, "and there, if anywhere, you ought to find the first attempts at *writing,* as adapted to Western wants." (Italics added.)

Indeed, two years earlier, in 1883, Schliemann applied to the Turks for a *firman* to excavate at Knossos; and a year after Muller's letter arrived, he visited the island, hastily inspected it, made an intuitive judgment, and dug an experimental trench where some ruins showed above the ground. But, as usual, Schliemann engaged in a violent quarrel with the owners of the land. By now, his fame had spread and he was known as the millionaire treasure hunter. Schliemann intended to purchase the site but the landowners asked an exorbitant price. In anger, Schliemann broke off negotiations. Shrewdly, or so he thought, he planned to hold his hand until the price was right. The wrangle at the marketplace level cost him a discovery which rivaled Troy and Mycenae, the discovery of the fabulous preclassical Minoan civilization which Evans unearthed on the very same spot. Beyond the value of gold, Evans made the most precious find of all, Minoan script.

During these last dozen years, the critics kept up their barrages on both sides of the Atlantic. "Schliemann's luck has run out," *The New York Times* reported on his discovery of Tiryns, "He has found no more gold, nor things of any value." And the correspondent of *The Times* of London joined a group of British and American scholars on a tour of Mycenae and Tiryns and announced "revolutionary conclusions." In sum, he reported, Schliemann was a fake. An April 24, 1886 story in *The Times* reported:

> Our party came unanimously to the conclusion that both of these constructions—that of the tomb at Mycenae and the palace at Tiryns—are the remains of some obscure barbarous tribe which reoccupied the ruins of the older cities and established a temporary rule there during the decay of Greece.

Three days later, another dispatch charged that Schliemann's finds were "wretched barbaric work of no archaeological character." It concluded that the ruins of Mycenae were Celtic in origin and those of Tiryns, Byzantine. In support of these accusations, the report drew on the Greek academic community. "I am in excellent Athenian archaeological company in my opinion that the 'prehistoric palace' of Tiryns," the anonymous correspondent wrote, "is one of the most extraordinary hallucinations of an unscientific enthusiast which literature can record." In short, Schliemann was the Clifford Irving of the day.

These criticisms shook Schliemann, especially the articles in *The Times* of London.

*"The Times,"* he wrote Muller, "which has been my excellent friend for a long number of years, now all at once becomes my enemy . . . and treats me . . . like a stupid enthusiast." Rhetorically, he asked:

> What are my sins? . . . I have excavated for many years under monstrous hardships and with an expense of upwards of 40,000 pounds [$200,000] in the pestilential plain of Troy . . . and brought to light from beneath mountains of ruins, a burned city. . . . I have found the royal tombs of Mycenae with their treasure. . . . I have excavated the treasure and *tholos* with wonderful ceiling in Orchomenus. . . . I have excavated the prehistoric palace of the kings of Tiryns, a discovery which is considered by all archaeologists even more important than . . . Mycenae or Troy.

Muller consoled him. "I hate the unfairness of newspapers, it is such cowardly unfairness," he wrote. "However, it generally produces the opposite effect."

As the Oxford scholar perceived, the incessant attacks on both shores of the Atlantic attracted new defenders to Schliemann's camp, among them, significantly, Arthur J. Evans, who was destined to become the most powerful voice in archaeology after the turn of the century. A former foreign correspondent of the *Manchester Guardian,* the then thirty-five-year-old Evans (who was later knighted) served as curator of Oxford's Ashmolean Museum. Sarcastically, he wrote *The Times* that it was the newspaper's fault "if Dr. Schliemann is not by this time finally demolished."

He said in a May 8 letter which *The Times* published:

> I am not writing to you to plead [Schliemann's] case. . . . As one who has also examined the results of Dr. Schliemann's excavations on the spot, whatever may be "the hallucinations of an unscientific enthusiast," the conclusions drawn by the explorer of Troy and Mycenae are responsible and modest beside some of those of your correspondent.

Warming up, Evans accused *The Times* of "preposterous perversities," and then exclaimed: "Rude barbarians, indeed!

. . . [Mycenae's rulers] did not choose to associate with their interment a single weapon, coin or ornament or as much as a fragment of a vase belonging to the Hellenic Age in which they lived, or to any epoch of historical Greece." Those buried in the grave circle, he impishly theorized, were probably archaeologists who selected only objects of antiquity to be buried with them. "We have before us, in fact, a race of Celtic Schliemanns," he mocked the paper.

This was the same Evans alluded to earlier, who picked up the spade and pickax as they fell from Schliemann's hands and implemented Schliemann's plan to excavate Knossos. In the 1900s, he not only discovered the Bronze Age civilization of Crete, which he named Minoan after the legendary monarch, but he also found the first evidence of writing in the preclassical age, Linear A and Linear B. A half century later, Michael Ventris, another amateur and "stupid enthusiast" like Schliemann, and John Chadwick, his associate, announced their decipherment of Linear B and suggested it was an archaic form of classical Greek, the missing link between the pre-Hellenic and Hellenic periods; the nature of Linear A is still debated. Like Schliemann, Evans financed his excavations from personal funds. Like Schliemann, he was badly bruised by the critics when he announced the discovery of the Palace of Minos. In the annals of archaeology, certainly the archaeology of the Aegean basin, Evans is the most celebrated figure after Schliemann.

Angered by *The Times'* attack, Schliemann sprang to the counterattack like a wounded lion. He demanded a hearing at London to defend himself. On July 2 of that year, accompanied by Dorpfeld, Schliemann journeyed to the center of the earth to confront his critics at a meeting of the Society of Antiquarians. Professor J. H. Middleton of Cambridge organized Schliemann's defense. The meeting was uproarious and took place on the same day as a crucial election in which Gladstone was returned to power by a slim margin; at stake in the election was Gladstone's policy of disengagement in Ireland. *The Times* report of the Schliemann debate captures the tension on its editorial page:

Never, perhaps, since a biological dispute at the French Institute excited Goethe more than a great political controversy in Germany at the time has been anything like a parallel to the keen discussion yesterday at the rooms of the Society of Antiquarians in the midst of the most critical election which England has witnessed during the present century. The combat was truly heroic.

*The Times* then went to the core criticism of Schliemann. "[He] is a little too apt to find Homer and the Homeric Age in everything that he discovers beneath the soil of Greece and the Troad," the commentary said, and it concluded: "He has not satisfied his critics."

What more could he do other than present the conclusions of Dorpfeld, one of Europe's outstanding architects, and personally review his treasures, none of which were of Greek, Celtic, or Byzantine design; indeed, they were of a style unknown before in history. Dismayed, Schliemann turned his back on London. He returned to Greece and never visited England again.

But the hassle with the press was of relatively minor import compared to the new criticism launched by the academic community. The attack was directed by Captain E. Botticher, whom Schliemann contemptuously referred to as "Herr Hauptmann Botticher of the Prussian artillery." Botticher, an historian, sustained his offensive for six years, between 1883 and 1890. It grew in intensity and attracted an ever-widening circle of scholars.

Botticher argued that Hissarlik was not the site of Troy. It was a crematorium, the site of a huge fire necropolis. The successive strata of the hill were not the result of habitation, but of continuous cremation. Priam's Palace and the other structures Schliemann discovered were buildings in which the bodies of the dead were stored, burned, and their bones preserved. This was also true of Tiryns.

Expanding on his theme through the years, Botticher accused Schliemann and Dorpfeld of faking their plans of Troy and, among other things, of purposely destroying evidence of the existence of the furnaces at Troy. This, he implied, explained Schliemann's destructive rampages at Hissarlik.

Schliemann's friends were appalled. They advised him to meet the attack with silence. But Schliemann's failure to answer these accusations "bred in him [Botticher] increasing self-confidence," as Schuchhardt later admitted. Schliemann wrote Botticher "letter upon letter" in the hope of getting him to recant in private. Exasperated, he invited Botticher to accompany him to Troy in the autumn of 1889 in the belief that the Prussian's theories would be laid to rest in the presence of the ruins itself, which Botticher had never seen. At first, Botticher resisted the invitation, but, in the end, he was forced to accept the offer or weaken his case. Thus was born the First International Conference at Troy.

The conclave, underwritten by Schliemann, was held among the ruins that November. Schliemann invited to Troy as arbiters, Professor Niemann of the Academy of Fine Arts at Vienna and Major Steffen, who drafted the plans at Mycenae. After a study of the ruins, in the company of Botticher, the arbiters testified to the "absolute authenticity" of the Schliemann-Dorpfeld plans of Troy. Botticher retreated, but only halfway. In mid-December, he returned to Germany, publicly withdrew his charge of *mala fides* and, on the basis of his firsthand inspection of the hill, even more forcefully reiterated his earlier position that Troy was a fire necropolis.

Almost exhausted by twenty years of cascading criticism, preoccupied with plans to excavate Knossos, troubled by recurring earaches and periods of deafness, Schliemann mustered his fading strength and played out the clock as though it was still the first quarter. He summoned the Second International Conference at Troy the following year, 1890.

Schliemann was determined to vindicate himself—and Homer. The conference was on a major scale. Fourteen prominent figures from the worlds of archaeology, the arts, and the press attended, among them such savants as Virchow; Professor C. Waldstein, the director of the American School of Classical Studies in Athens—who also represented the Smithsonian Institution; O. Hamdy Bey, director of the Imperial Museum at Constantinople; M. C. Babin of the French Academy of Arts and Letters; Dr. Kurt Humann, director of the Berlin Museum; Dr. von Duhn, Professor of Archaeology at Heidelberg; and Dr. W. Grempler of Breslau.

At the end of March, the German-American-French-Turkish conferees issued a formal report which cleared Schliemann and Dorpfeld. They unanimously declared that the Schliemann-Dorpfeld plans of Troy "correspond accurately to the existing remains" and they held that "we affirm that in no part of the ruins have we found any signs that point to the burning of corpses."

In the late spring and summer of that year, more than 100 other specialists descended on Hissarlik, largely at Schliemann's expense. All rejected the theory of the fire necropolis. Botticher's case collapsed.

But just as Schliemann, under the pressure of the critics, modified his excavatory methods at Troy, adopting their layer-by-layer approach in later campaigns, the Botticher affair influenced his thinking. During more than two decades in the Troad, he uncovered evidence neither of Trojan writing nor of a Trojan cemetery. Evidence of writing may have decayed in the moisture of the earth. But where did the inhabitants of Hissarlik, through the millennia, bury their dead? As a result of the second conference, Schliemann diverted his attention from Knossos and confided in Frank Calvert, his old and similarly aging friend, that he planned to launch still another Trojan campaign the following year—a major excavation whose objective would be to dig up the plain around the hill in search of the Trojan necropolis.

Schliemann never lived to put his plan in motion.

In the autumn of 1890, his earaches returned with renewed intensity. This time Virchow, the physician and pathologist, recommended an operation. In November, Schliemann embarked alone for a clinic at Halle, on the outskirts of Leipzig, the city of pitched roofs and publishing houses through which he had walked with his first manuscript of Troy a lifetime earlier. Sophia wanted to accompany him on the journey but he insisted that she remain in Athens to care for Andromache, now past nineteen, and their twelve-year-old son, Agamemnon. "I'll be back by Christmas," he promised.

At the clinic, the surgeons discovered that both his eardrums were inflamed and confirmed Virchow's opinion that they necessitated surgery. They told him that his ritual of bathing regularly in the sea contributed to his condition. Confined to his hospital bed, racked by pain, as winter closed in, the explorer was overcome by the realization that he was approaching the end of the road. He and Sophia entered into a rich and moving correspondence. "By Zeus," he wrote her, "I shall marry you again in the hereafter." And, with tenderness, in an effort to revive his fighting spirit, she reminded him of her favorite line from *The Iliad,* the phrase she often had thrown at him in the past whenever he grew depressed or discouraged by his great undertaking. "Let us go forward and either win glory for ourselves," she wrote, "or yield it to another."

In early December, the operation appeared partially successful; hearing returned to one ear and the pain abated. Schliemann's spirits soared. The surgeons insisted that he remain in bed, but Christmas drew near and the obstinate, demanding Schliemann was determined to return to *Iliou Melathron* and his family circle for the holiday which, in his mind, linked the past with the present. Ignoring their strictures, he left Halle. Schliemann planned to take a boat from Naples to Piraeus, the port of Athens. A relapse delayed him, and he collapsed in Naples on Christmas Day, seized with syncope—a brief loss of consciousness associated with transient cerebral anemia. After a visit to Professor Cozzalino, a brain surgeon, sixty-one years to the day that, as an eight-year-old child, sitting before a crackling Yule log, he had leafed through the pages of Jerrer's *Universal History* and embarked on his lifelong quest for Troy, Schliemann was borne off, like his companions of the Heroic Age, by Sleep and Death.

A few days later, Dorpfeld arrived in Naples and escorted Schliemann's body to Athens.

In death, Greece recognized her son. The King ordered a state funeral: the flag of Greece with its white cross and blue stripes, flew at half-mast as it did for her other illustrious foreign patron, Byron. He was buried in accordance with his wish, on the hill of Colonus, south of the Ilissos. At the funeral, Sophia, in a barely audible voice, clutching Andromache and Agamemnon in each hand, recited Helen's farewell to Hector from the twenty-fourth and last book of *The Iliad.* "Twenty years are come and gone, . . ." she mourned, ". . . my tears flow both for you and for my unhappy self."

In Homer's words, she wept as she spoke and the vast crowd that was gathered round her joined in her lament.

Back in *Iliou Melathron*, Sophia was disenheartened by the attacks on him even in death. *The New York Times,* in an obituary on December 28, 1890, accorded him the title of "discoverer of Troy . . . although it is by no means certain that he has a right to the title." By way of explanation, the newspaper observed, "The weight of judgment upon the part of those who criticized him was that the author had not produced sufficient proof to substantiate his claim of discovery."

In her sorrow, Sophia pledged herself to carry on his last campaign. On January 26, 1891, a month to the day after his death, Sophia announced that "I now consider it my sacred duty to carry on the excavations at Hissarlik, and to complete them as my husband intended." He died, she said, "before he had had the satisfaction of putting the finishing touch to the great work which had been the dream of his youth." She was determined to accomplish what he had failed to do—conclusively identify Troy and silence the critics once and for all.

Sophia provided the funds; Dorpfeld, the forces. Schliemann's last campaign was launched on schedule that spring and extended into 1894. The result was touched with irony.

Dorpfeld never discovered the Trojan necropolis which Schliemann hoped to uncover—nor has anyone else since, for that matter. But in the sixth stratum he found potsherds which resembled those Schliemann found at Mycenae. The pottery was clearly of double origin, partly original Mycenaean ware, and therefore imported, and partly locally made, much cruder but characteristic of Mycenaean shapes and decorations. The sixth city, therefore, belonged within the same time frame as the shaft graves at Mycenae. Dorpfeld also suddenly realized that the Mycenaean fortress in the sixth stratum was thoroughly and deliberately destroyed by razing, through a human agency. Although he found traces of fire, the Cyclopean walls so typical of the Mycenaean period—unlike the walls of the earlier cities—withstood the test of fire and therefore the work of destroying the citadel was carried out by smashing the walls of Troy "with axes and hammers." Unassailably, the archaeological evidence pointed to one conclusion: the sixth city was Homer's Troy, the Troy of the Trojan War, the Pergamus ruled by Priam when Agamemnon sallied forth from his Mycenaean rock citadel to lead the invasion of the Troad more than thirty centuries before.

In his impatience, in his restlessness, in his haste to reach virgin soil and unearth Troy, Schliemann had bypassed the sixth stratum and later ignored it. Schliemann had found Troy, the Troy of Homer and the Troy of his fantasy, but he never knew it.

# Author's Note

*And now, O Muses . . . tell me—for you are*
*in all places so that you see all*
*things, while we know nothing*
*but by report.*

The Iliad, BOOK II

THE STUDY OF Hieronymus Bosch, *The Economist* observed recently, is almost as nightmarish as his painting. So little is known about the man himself; so little about the development of his art for he left no diaries or letters to help. For the opposite reasons, the study of Heinrich Schliemann is almost as nightmarish. Schliemann left a relative "Hissarlik" of diaries, field journals, personal and business correspondence, ticket stubs and exercise books, layer on layer, in a multiplicity of languages—Greek, English, Russian, French, Arabic, Spanish, and, of course, German. Yet the impressive amount of written material is misleading. Schliemann was a man of action, an explorer, not a man of letters. His driving spirit and the magnitude of his accomplishments can be assessed only by retracing the trench he cleared in his lifetime, not in reading the papers which he filled. His actions overshadowed his words. Even so, unlike Bosch, a study of Schliemann may be enriched by conventional sources: published works, private papers, and the accounts of his contemporaries, friends and foes alike. The author has drawn on these traditional sources but, hopefully, not at the expense of obscuring Schliemann's actions.

Schliemann wrote seven books on his Aegean explorations. All, except two, appeared in English as well as German editions. The exceptions are: *Ithaka, der Peloponnes und Troja* (Leipzig, Giesecke & Derrient, 1869) *and Orchomenus: Bericht über meine Ausgrabungen* (Leipzig, F. A. Brockhaus, 1881). The other five are as follows: *Troy and Its Remains* (London, John Murray, 1875); *Mycenae: A Narrative of Researches and Discoveries* (New York, Scribner, Armstrong & Co., 1878); *Ilios: The City and Country of the Trojans* (New York, Harper & Brown, 1880); *Troja: Results of the Latest Researches,* (New York, Harper & Bros., 1884); and *Tiryns: the Prehistoric Palace of the*

233

*King of Tiryns* (New York, Charles Scribner's Sons, 1885).

Among them, *Troy and Its Remains* retains a spontaneity, enthusiasm, and innocence which is never recaptured in his later works. *Ilios* is enriched by the inclusion of "an autobiography of the author." *Troja* reflects his maturity and expertise; it was written with Dorpfeld at his side. *Tiryns* and *Orchomenus* are dull and pedantic, quite out of character with the man's active, volatile nature. They were designed to impress his scholarly critics (who were not impressed). An effort to pull together Schliemann's exploits, to distill his books, was undertaken in 1886 by Carl Schuchhardt, whose work was published after Schliemann's death as *Schliemann's Excavations: An Archaeological and Historical Study* (London, Macmillan, 1891). The volume contains, in the appendix, Schliemann's report on his excavation at Troy in the summer of 1890, his last dig.

The bulk of Schliemann's private papers are stored at the Gennadius Library of the American School of Classical Studies in Athens. Some of it is on microfilm, and large portions of it have been published in Germany, Greece, and the United States. In a three-volume tour de force, published twenty-two years apart, Ernst Meyer edited the most important surviving Schliemann letters in their original languages, in *Briefe von Heinrich Schliemann* (Berlin, Walter de Gruyter, 1936) and *Briefwechsel: Heinrich Schliemann* (Berlin, Verlag Geb. Mann, 1953 and 1958). During World War II, Shirley H. Weber, the former librarian of the Gennadius at Athens, edited Schliemann's English and Spanish language diaries for the period covering his sojourn in North and Central America. These papers appeared as *Schliemann's First Visit to America 1850–1851* (Cambridge, Mass., Harvard University Press, 1942). The Schliemann papers which relate to his residence in Indiana were edited and richly footnoted by Eli Lilly in *Schliemann in Indianapolis* (Indianapolis, Indiana Historical Society, 1961). The Lilly volume contains the text of Schliemann's last will and testament, filed in Marion County, Indiana, 1889. The author has drawn on the work of Meyer, Weber, and Lilly and owes these editors, and their publishers, a special debt of gratitude. The author also wishes to acknowledge the great assistance he has received from Frank Nagy, chief of the library reference section, and Mary Kohn, reference librarian, both of Western Connecticut State College; Marianne Wolfe, director of the Danbury (Connecticut) Public Library; and his typist, Isabel Bates.

In addition, Donald Zochert, of the *Chicago Daily News,* with the cooperation of Francis R. Walton, the present director of Athens' Gennadius Library, and George Weller, who covered the Mediterranean and Aegean area for many years for the *Chicago Daily News,* published *Heinrich Schliemann's Chicago Journal* in the Spring-Summer 1973 issue of *Chicago History,* a journal of the Chicago Historical Society. At the outset of my research, Mr. Walton graciously permitted me free access to Schliemann's papers.

Throughout, whenever I have quoted Homer, I have used Samuel Butler's translation, the edition which was published in 1952 by the Encyclopaedia Britannica's Great Books series by their arrangement with Jonathan Cape Ltd., London. For an annotated version, see *Chapman's Homer,* Vol. I: *The Iliad* and Vol II: *The Odyssey and the Lesser Homerica* edited by Allardyce Nicoll (Princeton University Press, 1967).

Among the biographies of Schliemann, one is of special significance, Emil Ludwig's *Schliemann: The Story of a Gold-seeker* (Boston, Little, Brown & Co., 1931). Ludwig is the only Schliemann biographer who ever met his subject,

1931). Ludwig is the only Schliemann biographer who ever met his subject, albeit, at an age he could barely remember (Ludwig was born nine years before Schliemann's death). The opening line of Ludwig's biography is a teaser as he never takes the reader into his confidence beyond the first sentence. "As a child," Ludwig wrote, "before I had even learned to read, I shook hands with him at my father's table." During World War I, as a foreign correspondent, Ludwig met Sophia at Iliou Melathron, "a tall beautiful woman of about sixty . . . all in black and wearing a string of pearls." In 1925, Sophia, who did not remarry and who died eight years later, offered Ludwig her husband's private papers, a staggering collection of 20,000 documents.

Ludwig recognized that Schliemann's written papers afforded extremely meager material despite their volume, since Schliemann was essentially a man of action. Either as a result of his father's influence or that of Schliemann's critics or, perhaps, because of the tenor of Schliemann's writings, Ludwig found Schliemann objectionable. As a consequence, in his biography, Ludwig tarred Schliemann as a gold-seeker, an epithet which has hardened over the past forty-odd years. With perhaps one exception, the biographies and biographical sketches of Schliemann during that period have been poured from the inexplicable Ludwig mold, inexplicable because multi-millionaire Schliemann's actions so clearly belie this characterization. Nevertheless, Schliemann is invariably portrayed as a treasure hunter, a man with a mania for gold. The notable exception to the general rule is Lynn and Garry Poole's *One Passion, Two Loves* (New York, Crowell, 1966), which focuses on Sophia and treats Schliemann's excavations as a secondary theme.

In preparing the biography of a man of action, no reasonable assessment of his life can be developed without a working knowledge of the interpretation placed on the subject by those who followed the track he pioneered. Among contemporary archaeologists and Homeric scholars, Schliemann is accorded recognition and respect, almost reverence.

"The decisive step from myth to history and from literature to archaeology was taken by Heinrich Schliemann," M. LeRoy of the Faculty of Letters, Caen, writes. And Leonard Palmer of Oxford describes Schliemann as "the amateur genius [who] sent scholars and archaeologists back to Homer as a guide." Lord William Taylour, who worked with Alan Wace at Mycenae and Blegen at Pylos, said of Schliemann recently, "He discovered a new world for archaeology." C. M. Bowra, the Homeric scholar, holds that "there can be no doubt that Schliemann found his Troy." The equally distinguished French academician, Victor Berard, observed that Schliemann's "ardor set up a precedent which rivals and disciples did not fail to follow." And the greatest living authority on the archaeology of Troy, Blegen, is effusive. Blegen said:

> With his unshakable faith in Homer, his boundless energy and enthusiasm, his organizing ability, his resolute determination, and his unfailing persistence—all backed by abundant financial resources, which he had acquired by his own efforts—with all these qualifications, Schliemann overcame innumerable obstacles and difficulties and achieved a brilliant success.

Indeed, as early as 1941, Ann Terry-White, in her popularization of archaeology, characterized Schliemann as "the most famous of all archaeologists."

Almost a generation later, Jacquetta Hawkes, archaeologist and wife of J. B. Priestley, described Schliemann in identical terms as "the most famous of all archaeologists." And the late Michael Ventris and John Chadwick, who broke the Linear B cipher at Mycenae, Knossos, and Pylos, paid Schliemann an honor more lasting than all the honors he received in his lifetime. They dedicated their classic, *Documents in Mycenaean Greek* (Cambridge, Cambridge University Press, 1956), to "The memory of Heinrich Schliemann, 1822–1890, Father of Mycenaean Archaeology."

"The first proof that a golden age of Mycenae had really existed," they wrote, "was due to the vision and persistence of one man, Heinrich Schliemann."

Since Schliemann's exploits , the most impressive campaign in the Troad was conducted in 1932–1938 by the University of Cincinnati Expedition. A dozen years in the making, the expedition's four-volume study, written by Blegen, John L. Caskey, Marion Rawson, and Jerome Sperling, *Troy* (Princeton, N.J., Princeton University Press, 1950), like the work of Ventris and Chadwick, stands as a tribute to the "eminent explorer."

Dorpfeld visited the American team at Hissarlik periodically until his death in 1940, and whenever he did so, Schliemann's spirit walked with him. The expedition declared in *Troy:*

His [Dorpfeld's] infectious enthusiasm, eager interest in all that pertained to Troy, and his unrivalled knowledge of the architectural remains brought to light in the past excavations—a knowledge freely shared with those who came into association with him—were always a source of stimulation and inspiration to the members of the expedition staff.

The expedition confirmed Dorpfeld's broad division of Troy into nine principal layers—Schliemann's "cities"—but, employing modern techniques, they went further. They differentiated some forty-six strata of habitation at Hissarlik: ten attributed to Troy I, seven to Troy II, four to Troy III, five to Troy IV, four to Troy V, eight to Troy VI, one to Troy VIIa, two to Troy VIIb, two (or more) to Troy VIII, and three (or more) to Troy IX.

The spirit of Schliemann was ever present at the dig. Once again, gold was found at Troy. In Schliemann's burned city (Troy IIg), the expedition unearthed 1,472 beads of gold and 500 other objects of metal (silver and copper), stone, ivory, bone, terra cotta, and unbaked clay. Once again "whorls" were recovered. "The manner in which these objects were used is not certainly known," the excavators reported in *Troy*, paraphrasing Schliemann's earlier statement. Once again, no necropolis was found. After seven years of digging, the expedition was unable to determine how the early Trojans "normally disposed of their dead." Once again, in the light of the discovery of Linear A and Linear B, the search for writing at Troy went forward diligently, without success. The questions aired and left unanswered in Schliemann's day—Who were the Trojans? What was their end, and how did it come about?—are still unanswered. Clearly, the archaeologists of the present and future are not yet done with Troy.

That Schliemann's Troy was the Troy of Homer and the Troy of his dreams is now rarely doubted. "The important fact is that there is no alternative site," the expedition concluded in its final volume. "If Troy ever existed [and how can it really be doubted?], it must have occupied the hill at Hissarlik." Many years later, in *Troy and the Trojans* (New York, Praeger, 1963), Blegen established a chronology for ancient Troy which is now widely accepted, as follows: Troy I (3000–2500 B.C.), Troy II (2500–2200 B.C.); Troy III (2200–2050 B.C.), Troy IV (2050–1900 B.C.), Troy V (1900–1800 B.C.), Troy VI (1800–1300 B.C.), Troy VIIa (1300–1260 B.C.), Troy VIIb1 (1260–1190 B.C.), Troy VIIb2 (1190–1100 B.C.), and Troy VIII (700 B.C.).

Blegen's chronology brings Troy down to Homer, but lest this chronology give the impression that Troy now stands neglected, it should be observed that, as in the days of Alexander and Julius Caesar, pilgrims continue to visit the place which sings of the earliest days of Western civilization.

Indeed, at this writing, the Turkish Department of Cultural Affairs is rushing to completion the construction of a 26.2-foot replica of a horse—in wood, of course—within sight of the "godly walls of Troy" unearthed by Schliemann slightly more than a century ago.

Since Schliemann's death, archaeologists have carefully picked their way through the cultural mother lode he exposed not only at Troy but in the Troad, at Mycenae, Tiryns, Orchomenus, and elsewhere. In 1935, at Alaca Hoyuk, in Central Turkey, archaeologists uncovered goldware comparable in style and fabrication to Schliemann's treasure; shortly thereafter, they found at Kum Tepe, in the Troad, the remains of a civilization earlier than that of Troy I. Similar finds since then have been made on Lemnos and Lesbos, the Troad's offshore islands. And at Orchomenus, a German expedition unearthed six Bronze Age cities, one atop the other. Yet these and other discoveries since Schliemann's day have failed to provide answers to the basic questions about Troy and the Trojans.

Clearly, all the pieces of the Aegean puzzle have yet to be unearthed.

Often, as in a jigsaw puzzle, the pieces not only do not fit but seem to bear no relevancy to the picture. The most aggravating illustration was J. Papdimitriou's discovery in 1953 of a new grave circle outside the circuit walls of the Mycenaean Acropolis. Papdimitriou christened it Grave Circle B to differentiate it from Schliemann's find, which he named Grave Circle A. This discovery appeared to confirm the tradition concerning Agamemnon and Clytemnestra, except for one fact: Grave Circle B, which included twenty-four tombs, mostly in the form of shaft graves, was proven, by Carbon 14 testing and other methods, to be older than Grave Circle A. Like a dream, in which the pieces are related and yet unrelated, this and other discoveries in recent years, as in Schliemann's day, have served to confound rather than to clarify the story of the Aegean's preclassical, pre-Hellenic civilization.

In time, the pieces will fall together. Only within the past year, for example, a strip of miniature wall paintings was discovered on the island of Thera —which some believe was the Atlantis of antiquity—which Spyriodon Marinatos, Greece's Inspector General of Archaeology, described enthusiastically as "the most important historical document we have so far from the Bronze Age." It linked the peoples of the Aegean and Africa (Libya) in the period when Troy IV flourished.

As the result of Schliemann's finds at Troy, the controversy over the Trojan War acquired a new dimension. Schliemann proved Troy existed. Very well, then, the next question was: Was the Trojan War fought, and if so, why?

Even more perplexing was the disappearance of Schliemann's Bronze Age.

It did not progress directly into the Iron Age of Periclean Greece but suddenly dissolved, like an image in a shadow play, and was followed by a Dark Age which enveloped the Aegean and lasted for centuries.

There are as many answers to these questions as there are Homeric scholars, or so it seems.

Denys I. Page (*History and the Homeric Iliad,* Berkeley, University of California, 1959) views the Trojan War as an epic struggle between Mycenae and Troy to fill the vacuum of the declining Hittite Empire in Asia Minor. Another celebrated student of Homer, Walter Leaf (*Troy: A Study in Homeric Geography,* London, Macmillan, 1912), contended that the war was strategic and economic in character. In his opinion, Troy controlled the Hellespont and therefore the sea and overland trade routes between East and West. C. M. Bowra (*Tradition and Design in The Iliad,* London, Oxford University Press, 1930) argued trade was unimportant, that in the Heroic Age "fighting was their business." T. W. Allen, who edited *The Homeric Catalogue of Ships* (London: Oxford University Press, 1921) and was co-editor with W. R. Halliday and E. E. Sikes of *Homeric Hymns* (London: Oxford University Press, 1936), attributed the Trojan War to geopolitics. "The reason for the Trojan War was to remove the last power which dominated the Asiatic coast and prevented settlement," Allen theorized.

The sudden collapse of the Aegean's Bronze Age civilization is usually attributed to the "Dorian invasion," although archaeological evidence is wanting and there is less agreement on the nature of the Dark Ages than even on Troy itself.

Immanuel Velikovsky, in his *Worlds in Collision* (New York, Macmillan, 1950) argued that *The Iliad* contains a cosmic plot, that the battles of the gods signify the conjuncture or near miss of the planets Venus and Mars in 1500 B.C. (Schliemann's sixth city) and 700 B.C. (about the time of Homer). This conjuncture had a catastrophic effect on the planet Earth—tornadoes, fires, dark skies, chaos, and destruction. The Trojan War and the cosmic conflict, Velikovsky contended, were synchronous and that this is "the real meaning" of *The Iliad.* Many scholars frown on Velikovsky's work, although the freshness and originality of his mind are not denied. In a similar wicket, however, is Rhys Carpenter, a professor of classical archaeology at Bryn Mawr, who is widely respected as one of the most foremost Homeric scholars of our time. Carpenter also sought to unravel the mystery of the Dark Ages by developing an equally original concept. The Bronze Age civilization of the Aegean which Schliemann unearthed, he held, collapsed not as a result of an invasion from the outside but because of an evacuation from the inside, a dispersal, a *diaspora* of the inhabitants of Mycenae, Orchomenus, Tiryns, and other places. This was brought about by a sudden, dramatic, climatological change, and concomitant famine. In his conception, the Dorian invasion is nothing less than what Greek tradition calls the *Return of the Heraklids,* the return to these cities of the descendants of the *diaspora.* With the return of the Heraklids, the forward thrust of Greek civilization resumed and gave rise to the Classic Age. Carpenter does not quote Homer, as a Schliemann would; yet, I believe, Odysseus makes a strong case for famine as a cause of war in the Heroic Age. "A man cannot hide away the cravings of a hungry belly; and this is an enemy which gives much trouble to all men," Odysseus said (*The Odyssey,* Book XVII). "It is because of this that ships are fitted out to sail the seas, and to make war upon other people."

Last year, a new theory was put forward. After ten years of excavation at

Mycenae, Professor George Mylonas of Washington University, St. Louis, announced before a meeting of the Academy of Athens that he has concluded that the destruction of Mycenean civilization was "a result of civil strife and not foreign invasion." The civil war "broke out after the end of the war with Troy", Mylonas conjectured, and was set in motion by "the murder of the royal family," a view which is in harmony with Homer and the classic tradition.

In his last work on Troy, *Troja,* Schliemann, exhausted by the controversies he had provoked, wrote, "How many tens of years a new controversy may rage around Troy, I leave to the critics: *that* is their work; *mine* is done." He wrote those prophetic words almost a century ago.

This background note would be imcomplete without a reference to the fate of the Schliemann treasure. In the waning months of World War II, Schliemann's pottery collection was stored in the cellar of Lebus Castle, along the Oder. The Trojan gold was secreted in a bunker in the eastern sector of Berlin; several minor objects were hidden in an abandoned salt mine west of Berlin. The Americans recovered the objects in the mine and, in accordance with an agreement among the Allies, turned it over to the Allied Art Treasure Commission. They have since been returned to Germany. Lebus Castle, together with its hoard of Trojan *kraters* and potsherds, was blown to bits as the Russians crossed the Oder and established a bridgehead on the west bank in February 1945. Two months later, the Red Army overran Berlin's eastern perimeter, including the bunker adjoining the Berlin Zoo where the Trojan gold was concealed. Instead of turning the treasure over to the Commission, the Russians transported it under armed guard to Moscow. On October 11, 1965, the Pooles reported that "we saw twenty-eight minor objects from the Schliemann Collection at the Staatliche Museum in East Berlin"—but no gold. Some experts, the Pooles said, entertained the hope that "important pieces from the Schliemann Collection will be recovered within the next few years." That assessment was made almost a decade ago. Since then, some other Trojan objects have turned up, including the altar which Schliemann unearthed at Troy in 1873. But the gold is still largely missing. In 1972, however, as a result of a cultural exchange agreement between the Soviet Union and the West, concluded within the framework of the East-West détente, renewed hope stirred in the West that the surviving objects from the seat of Western civilization would again come to light. Last year, this expectancy heightened when the Soviet Union exhibited forty-one major Western paintings (Cezannes, Van Goghs, Matisses) in America, the first exhibition of Western art to be lent to the United States by the Soviet Union. Thus, the opportunity is at hand for an even more dramatic gesture by the Kremlin, placing the fabled gold of Troy on open display. For the moment, ironically, Schliemann's Collection, or what is left of it, appears to have wound up principally in the country where he made his initial fortune. Confounding the issue, in early 1974, as this book went to press, the two Germanies got into a row over who rightfully owned what is left of prewar Germany's Trojan and other art, a dispute set in motion by East Germany when it demanded West Berlin hand over what it has as a prerequisite to a cultural agreement between the two Germanies.

In *Ilios,* Schliemann said, "I should feel the profoundest satisfaction, and should esteem it as the greatest reward my ambition could aspire to, if it were generally acknowledged that I have been instrumental toward the attainment of [the] great aim of my life."

Who can deny him this reward? Clearly, he attained the great aim of his life—the discovery of Troy, the noble Troy of Homer.

Schliemann's methods were crude, his scholarly background inadequate. His interpretations of what he discovered, more often than not, were wrong, sometimes grotesquely so. Yet his impact on the West was profound. He shook the scholarship of the day to its foundations. For smug Westerners who knew all the answers, he demonstrated indisputably, tangibly, that they not only did not possess all the answers but did not even know all the questions.

He did more than revolutionize Western conceptions and misconceptions about the past. He founded modern archaeology. The scholars of his era never recovered from the shock of his discoveries, nor have present-day scholars. Archaeology has revealed a seemingly endless array of worlds from the past, some of which were thought to have existed and others which were not dreamed of. So much for upstairs.

Downstairs, almost singlehandedly, Schliemann symbolized the romance and adventure of archaeology. He excited the imagination of the public. He provided archaeology with the popularity so necessary to influence governments and institutions, as well as individuals of private means, like Schliemann himself, to underwrite the financial burdens of exploring the past and enriching the present.

When Schliemann demolished the hill at Hissarlik as he set out to do, albeit subconsciously, on that cold Christmas morning at Ankershagen, he gave an impulse to research with the spade and pickax, to archaeology. Just as Darwin gave us an understanding of the origin of species, Schliemann provided an understanding of the origin of civilizations.

In both the figurative and literal sense, in Homer's phrase, Schliemann was a "shaker of the earth."

# Index

241